Growing Unusual Vegetables

To Tom, Hector and Alice Wheeler
Happy Days!

Thanks to many people for their help in putting this book together: foremost and especially to Nicola Davies for her patience and encouragement; Peter Andrews at eco-logic books for getting me involved in the first place; to Owen Smith for founding the horticultural Behemoth that is Future Foods, and for his expertise; Dr Jeremy Cherfas for keeping my shoelaces tied; and to Clive Boursnell who did a sterling job on the photographs. And a big thanks to my mother and father, without whom etc!

Growing Unusual Vegetables

Weird and Wonderful Edibles and How to Grow Them

Simon Hickmott

eco-logic books

First Published in 2003 by
eco-logic books

www.eco-logicbooks.com

Reprinted and updated 2009

ISBN 9781899233113

Typesetting by Isis Design www.isis-design.co.uk
Printed and bound in the UK by 4edge

Further copies of this book may be ordered from eco-logic books. They also
sell, by mail order, books and other media that promote practical solutions to
environmental problems. Visit their web site at www.eco-logicbooks.com for a
complete list.

The Small Print
Whilst every effort has been made to ensure the accuracy of the information in this book the publisher and author accept no
responsibility for any errors or omissions. Whilst we have attempted to identify the common uses for some types of plants
described in this book we make no claim whatsoever as to the medicinal properties and uses of the plants.

Contents

Contents

Introduction

I grew my first unusual vegetable when I was nine years old. I was on holiday with my family when I was tempted into buying an intriguing little kit. It contained a small transparent pot, a short length of red cord and a seed. The seed in my kit was a peanut, but I could have opted for a banana, or a giant bean. I was pleased with my choice.

When I got home I followed the instructions dutifully: I twined the funny piece of red cord into the bottom of the pot and put the seed on it. I placed it on a warm windowsill and kept it moist but not too wet and within days the seed sprouted. I potted it on into a big old clay pot that took up most of my bedroom windowsill.

Soon my peanut plant was starting to obscure the view and block out the light. I took it into school where there were lots of large windows, plenty of warmth and an interested caretaker to water it at weekends. It was not long before the yellow, pea-like flowers appeared, followed by the seed pods, which, just as I had been promised, poked their way into the compost.

A few weeks later my plant started to look sick and began to turn yellow. When it really looked like its number was up, with a trembling bottom lip I turned the plant out of its pot to see what tragedy had befallen it. There among the roots were six perfect little peanut shells, each holding two perfect little peanuts.

If I had known then what I know now about growing peanuts I don't think I would have even attempted it. All the textbooks agree: peanuts do not grow well outside the tropics.

In spite of my success I was never tempted to become a peanut farmer, but I was inspired to try out a few other unusual plants. I grew a banana, not from a kit but from a packet of seeds. Within two years it had completely outgrown our house and was banished to an unheated greenhouse, where it perished over the winter. I wasn't too sorry as I discovered it was not a proper banana at all, but an ornamental thing called an Ensete. It looks like a banana plant and does produce banana-like fruits, but not ones you can eat.

Following that I tried growing all sorts of ornamental gourds – warty ones, striped ones, bottle-shaped ones, some with fruits shaped like a club. I varnished them to enhance their colours and make them glossy. What I forgot to do was dry them out first, so inside their varnish prison they quickly went rotten.

My family was beginning to get fed up with the allotment being taken up with my unusual plants. They were amusing to me but they weren't putting any food on the table. So I tried growing unusual edibles: I could have my fun, and the family didn't need to starve. Not that they necessarily wanted to eat what I grew!

I grew vegetable spaghetti – a type of marrow with fibrous flesh. After boiling the marrow whole, the flesh can be pulled out in spaghetti-like strands. I mixed these with salad cream to make a fairly repulsive sort of coleslaw. I grew courgettes – nothing unusual about them now, but in the Seventies they were a novelty. We fried them until they were almost carbon, thinking they needed thorough cooking. I also made an attempt on the world record for the largest pumpkin. After we'd taken out one wedge to make a huge pumpkin pie the rest of it was left to perish.

So it wasn't that I exactly failed with all of these things, we just needed to try them out in different ways. If I hadn't persisted with my pursuit of all that is weird and wonderful in the world of the edible, my family would not have discovered some gems which we eat today: mizuna, globe artichokes, pak choi, red peppers, aubergines.

Red peppers? Aubergines? How times have changed! John Organ in his excellent guide 'Rare Vegetables' describes red peppers. At the time he was writing, in 1960, they were considered a novelty. Today they are an essential ingredient in many dishes, and surely everyone knows that a green pepper is simply an unripe red pepper. Aubergines were once classed as 'foreign muck', but they're a familiar sight in the shops now all year round.

Today's novelties are tomorrow's crops

You only need to visit a Saturday market or call into your local supermarket to see the diversity of vegetables that are available. They have probably all been imported or grown in heated glasshouses, but with a little skill many can be persuaded to grow in a temperate climate. And not just by the adventurous gardener: many of these unusual vegetables have the potential to become a commercial crop.

A few years ago no one would have dreamt of attempting to grow sweet potatoes outdoors in our climate, but with recent developments by plant breeders this is now becoming a real possibility. Likewise it is now possible to grow soya beans in the cool climates of Britain and the northern United States when previously it was a crop associated only with warmer regions. Other crops that have, until now, been regarded as strictly for growing in warm climates have been receiving similar attention from plant breeders.

From ornamental to staple

Throughout northern and southern temperate regions of the world, the potato is now one of the most important food crops. But the journey to popularity for the potato was not an easy one. Potatoes originate in the western highlands of South America, the Andes, where they have been grown as a staple food for thousands of years. The tubers were first brought to Europe by the Spanish, in about 1570, and they soon found their way to English gardens. James Garrett recorded them in a drawing between 1589 and 1593, and Gerard included them in his Herbal published in 1597.

At first the potato was grown as a botanical curiosity. The leaves are poisonous and if the tubers are exposed to light they become unpalatable, so it was considered an unlikely food crop. These early introductions produced their tubers late in the season, after the autumn equinox, which in most of northern Europe closely coincides with the first autumn frosts. Tubers of a useful size were therefore only really achieved in coastal areas, such as the west of Ireland, where autumn frosts are usually late and infrequent. There the potato thrived and gradually became accepted as a useful crop.

Forms began to arise that showed no sensitivity to day length, producing tubers in the summer. These led to a potato craze in the Manchester area, recorded in Miller's Garden Dictionary in 1768. Growers competed to breed the earliest varieties and be the first with tubers for market.

Very soon the potato became one of Europe's most important food sources. It did particularly well in the damp climate and acidic soils of Ireland, and the entire population came to depend upon it. When the disease blight finally found its way from South America in 1845 the result was disastrous. Now we have a better understanding of potato blight and are able to manage it to some extent, but potato crops world-wide still live under its shadow each year.

The history of the humble potato is a complex and fascinating story, and it begs the question what other plants have been rejected as inedible or unpromising? What would have happened if, say, peanuts had been brought over from North America in the 16th Century, instead of the potato? William Cobbett dismissed groundnuts as "this villainous root" and "root of wretchedness". At the moment it is less popular and less high yielding than the potato, but its potential is now being realised. It has recently been the subject of intensive breeding work, and as the potato did 500 years ago, it may well exceed our expectations.

It was not just potatoes and groundnuts that suffered heavy criticism and scepticism when they were first introduced. The tomato was thought to be poisonous, because of its close relationship to Deadly Nightshade. For many years it was grown purely as an ornamental. Runner beans, too, were slow to be accepted as edible, since all parts of the plant are poisonous except the pods and seeds. For many years they were grown purely for ornament, a purpose for which they are now enjoying a deserved revival.

Not only do 'unusual' vegetables become well known and 'fashionable'; it works the other way too. Popular crops can fall out of favour and become unknown. Tastes in vegetables come and go. Why doesn't anyone grow skirret any more? And what came along to supersede scurvy grass?

What makes a vegetable unusual?

The title of this book could equally have been Growing Rare Vegetables. 'Unusual' is a difficult thing to define – what is out of the ordinary to one person may be quite mundane to another. I am sure that most people flicking through this book will spot a few vegetables that they instantly recognise, perhaps one that they have grown themselves. But to other readers that same vegetable might be completely new. There are a few crops that I know will be familiar to all readers since they are important food crops (soya beans, for instance). What is unusual about them is that people seldom attempt to grow them, particularly if they are considered to require a very different climate. I hope this book encourages gardeners to try them, and that is why they are included.

Why some vegetables will always remain unusual

There are some vegetables that are destined to always remain unusual, mostly because they are slow to increase. Chinese Yam is a good example. It has been in cultivation for many years and is good to eat, but has a very low reproductive rate. Chinese yam does not readily set seed, but is propagated from bulbils (little tubers produced in small quantities on the stem) or from pieces of the parent tuber. The tuber takes three years to grow into a useful-sized root. Unless a bulk method is devised for propagating this plant it will never be grown as a commercial crop.

Some vegetables are difficult to propagate, even though they produce abundant seed. Skirret, for instance, can be tricky to germinate, and bulbous rooted chervil needs winter pre-treatment to get it to come up – something which commercial growers are unlikely to do, especially for a crop which, let's face it, few people are familiar with, let alone likely to buy.

Other vegetables never get to market because they do not travel well. This is the case for many greens, some of which readily wilt. By the time they get to a shop they would be distinctly unappetising. Good King Henry is available early in the year when few other fresh, vitamin-rich greens are available, but it wilts so quickly that it has not caught on as a commercial crop.

Others vegetables may remain rare because they have never been suited to commercial cropping. The cultivation of sea kale, for example, does not lend itself to mechanisation at all. It can only realistically be grown by hand.

All of these 'difficulties' that keep vegetables off our market stalls and supermarket shelves are of little consequence to the gardener. By growing your own you have the time for slow crops and can enjoy your produce freshly picked.

How I chose the vegetables for this book

I have chosen to include in this book vegetables that can be grown in a cool temperate climate with the kind of resources available to most home gardeners. This means that most, but not all, tropical crops are excluded. I have left out crops that require a warm glasshouse environment throughout their life, but included those that just need a sunny windowsill in their early days. So whereas the winged bean (Psophocarpus), or some of the calabash gourds of Africa are not mentioned here, which would require almost constant artificial heat for them to thrive, I have included the bitter gourd and yard long bean. They do require some heat to start them off, but can do well in an unheated greenhouse for their main growing period. After all, many of our crops are grown this way already – cucumbers, for example.

Aquatic plants are usually considered suitable only for cultivation in warm climates, with the exception of watercress. In many parts of the world, particularly in the tropics, a lot of crops are grown in water: rice is a prime example. There are many others that can be grown wet and it is a simple matter to set up the facilities for growing them. A whole new dimension awaits the adventurous vegetable gardener who sets up a pool exclusively devoted to edible plants, and I have included plenty to try.

I have left out, on the whole, vegetables that are unusual forms of existing crops. So, unusual marrows and squash, and funny coloured beetroot do not get a mention. Most of what is profiled in this book is those vegetables that are unusual species of plants rather than variations on a theme. There are a couple of exceptions: pea bean is a type of climbing French bean, and walking stick cabbage is a selection of common kale. These are so often misunderstood or mistaken for something else that I felt the need to explain what they are.

Finally the vexed question of 'when is a vegetable not a vegetable?' As far as this book is concerned, a vegetable is classed as a vegetable by the way it is grown. Any fruits included in this book are all grown from seed to fruit the same year, the same way a tomato or a melon is grown. Fruits that grow on trees or shrubs, such as apples and pears, are out of the scope of this book.

Diversity and the organic gardener

The value of maintaining diversity in the organic garden cannot be over-emphasised. Monoculture is a sure way of inviting calamity: if one individual gets infested with a particular pest, the chances are the rest of the crop will go down with it after not very long. Seed companies tend to provide us with the opportunity to grow a rather restricted range of vegetables, and many of them are prone to attack by various pests and diseases. Despite our best efforts with rotations and maintaining a diverse garden, we can find that a particular disease or pest persists in an area year upon year. Instead of giving up or resorting to chemical methods, the organic gardener can make use of the wider range of vegetables that are available and switch to an alternative crop that is not affected by the problem.

For example, potatoes are susceptible to blight, which can be controlled in most seasons by cunning husbandry methods: planting early varieties and harvesting them before the blight attacks, or cutting off the foliage when blight becomes a problem. Some years, though, blight is relentless and can come at an unexpected moment. The little known but similar oca does not become infected with blight and is a viable alternative. The tubers are similar in flavour and texture to potatoes and it occupies the same place in the garden, requiring the same site and soil. Admittedly the tubers are generally smaller than potatoes, but if it were afforded the same amount of time and effort that has been given to developing the modern potato, then it would surely become as popular.

Culinary advice (and lack thereof)

I have tried to give culinary advice where I feel I am being honest in doing so, but I must confess that I have not been able to taste everything in the book. Most of the entries deserve culinary experimentation: their potential in the kitchen has yet to be realised. Knowing something about how they taste, or what common vegetable they taste or feel like, is a good starting point for experimentation. In some cases I have given vernacular uses, which are again a good basis for exploration in the kitchen.

It is interesting to note that some popular recipes have evolved over the years because of the difficulty in obtaining the main ingredient. The Spanish tomato-based dipping sauce that we know as salsa was originally made with tomatillos. It is presumably now made with tomatoes only because of the difficulties experienced in obtaining the authentic ingredient.

Cultivating Unusual Vegetables

There is seldom anything unusual about the way unusual vegetables are grown. On the whole, unusual vegetables are grown following standard techniques. If there is anything odd about their cultivation I have included it in the entry in the encyclopaedia. As a rule you will not go far wrong if you follow the guidance given for growing vegetables that are similar.

Most of the plants I have described are grown from seed, but some are grown from pieces of root or from cuttings. I have included a brief overview of seed sowing techniques here, but more detail about raising plants and general plant husbandry can be found in any good guide to growing vegetables, for example Mandy Pullen's book 'Valuable Vegetables'. Propagation techniques for hardy and tender perennials are specific, and where relevant they are described in detail in the encyclopaedia.

Seed sowing

Sowing Outdoors

Most hardy crops can be grown from seed sown direct into the ground. However, they will not germinate if conditions are poor. To germinate, seeds need water, warmth and good aeration. If the weather in the spring is miserable, delay sowing your seeds. You can get ahead of the weather using black polythene, cloches or horticultural fleece to help warm the soil. The polythene must be removed before sowing, but the others can be left in place after sowing to protect the seedlings.

Seeds can be sown in drills, or furrows. Mark the row with a line of string and run a hoe or stick along to mark the trench. Drill depth, as a general guide, should be about twice the size of the seeds. Large seeds, being easy to handle, can be sown at the correct spacing – this is known as space sowing. Smaller seeds should be scattered quite thinly along the line if possible at more-or-less the final spacing. If germination is expected to be poor, sow two or three seeds in a cluster at the correct final spacing, thinning them to one after germination. This is known as station sowing. Draw the soil over the seeds to fill the drill after sowing.

If you cultivate your vegetables in beds, growing them in blocks, you can simply scatter seed over the soil surface and rake it in. This is broadcast sowing. However, keeping the seedlings free of weeds can be difficult if they cannot be easily distinguished from weed seedlings, and hoeing is very difficult amongst the plants.

Sowing Indoors

Crops that are sensitive to cold need to be raised under glass or on the windowsill before planting out after the last frost has passed. Hardy plants can also be raised this way if conditions are not suitable for sowing outdoors, or for a head start. A propagator is not essential, but it is extremely useful for providing a constant temperature. A windowsill is fine, as long as it does not get cold at night. It is essential that seedlings are given as much light and air as possible as soon as they have germinated if they are to make sturdy plants. There is a tendency for seedlings to grow towards the light and become leggy, which can be prevented using a home made reflector box. A reflector box is simply a cardboard box lined with foil. The foil lining reflects light in all directions, ensuring the seedlings grow straight.

To grow enough plants for an average size garden from small seed, I recommend sowing the seed in a small pot. Using dwarf or half pots saves on growing medium. Fill the pot with the seed-sowing medium, level off the surface and tap the pot a couple of times to settle the compost. Firm and level the surface with the bottom of another pot. Scatter the seeds as evenly as possible over the surface of the compost. If you only want a few seedlings, only sow a few seeds, plus a couple of extra for luck.

If the seedlings need to be covered, sieve a little growing medium over them. After the seeds have germinated, they need to be 'pricked out': moved to individual containers with fresh growing medium. Be careful when transferring seedlings that the root suffers the minimum of damage, and do not handle the stems, which bruise easily – hold the plants by the leaves. Any particularly weak and feeble-looking seedlings should be discarded.

To raise more than just a few plants from small seed, sow them in modules or cells. This minimises the disturbance to the roots when planting out. Fill the cells with seed-sowing medium and tap the compost down. Firm the surface with the base of another cell tray, or with the firming tool provided with some modules. Sow a seed – for very tiny seeds it will have to be a pinch – in each cell. If more than one seed is sown they should be thinned after they have germinated. Sieve growing medium over the seeds to cover them. Cell-grown plants are ready to be planted out when the roots have filled the cells. They should be watered before transplanting.

Plants with large seed, such as any of the cucumber family or beans, can be started off individually in small pots. Over-fill each pot with seed-sowing medium but do not firm it or tap it down. Sow two seeds to each pot: plunge the seeds into the middle of the pot, firming the compost at the same time. A couple of sharp taps settles the seeds and the compost. After they have germinated, remove the weaker of the two seedlings.

When sowing tiny seed, such as those of rampion, it is very difficult to distribute the seeds evenly, and to see where they have been sown. Mixing the seed with very fine dry sand helps considerably, but do not use builder's sand.

Pests and diseases

In the encyclopaedia entries I have rarely mentioned pests or diseases. This is mostly because the plants described are not related to other common garden crops, and so they tend not to suffer from the usual pests and diseases. Which is not to say they will not attract aphids or red spider mite or any of the other ailments that affect all plants. However they are unlikely to be troubled by pests or diseases that are specific to a certain group of plants. Flea beetles, for instance, only affect Brassicas and their near relatives.

If a vegetable has a particular susceptibility to a pest or disease I have included it in the description. For example, crops such as ulluco that are propagated vegetatively can be devastated by viruses, which can accumulate in the plant tissue. On the other hand, if a crop has a particular resistance, as celtuce has to lettuce root aphid, I have mentioned that in the description.

Crop rotation

Continually growing one crop in the same patch of ground for years is asking for soil borne pests and diseases to accumulate and cause problems. Rotating crops around the vegetable plot each year is a sure way of keeping pests and diseases under control.

A rotation is also beneficial in terms of soil management and nutrient availability. Leafy crops take lots of nitrogen from the soil, whereas root crops tend to demand potash. Legumes replenish the nitrogen in the soil, and Brassicas usually follow to take advantage of this. Most roots do not appreciate fresh manure, so this is applied after they have cropped, before the leafy crops are planted.

Although many of our unusual vegetables are not related to commonly grown garden crops, they can fit in to a standard rotation. In the encyclopaedia I have included the rotation category in each entry. In the first instance this is based on pests and diseases that are likely to trouble them, according to their relationship to existing crops thus:

Category	Is susceptible to...
Brassicas	club root, flea beetle, root gall, root fly.
Legumes	no susceptibility, but fixes nitrogen.
Umbelliferous	violet root rot, black rot, root fly.
Solanaceous	blight, wireworm, viruses.
Onion family	downy mildew, onion fly, rust, white root rot.
Other	Does not fit into any particular category.
Permanent Bed	Perennial crops grown in the same place each year so do not fit into any rotation

As I said earlier, most of the unusual vegetables are not affected by the same pests and diseases as commonly grown garden crops, so this scheme can only take us so far. After disease susceptibilities I have used growing conditions to categorise plants. For example, vigorous members of the cucumber family (Cucurbitaceae) are in the rotation category 'Brassicas'. They are not related to the brassicas and do not share their pests and diseases, but they do require similar soil conditions.

However, most of the unusual vegetables covered in the encyclopaedia fall into the category 'Other.' Onions are an interesting case for excluding from the rotation. The usual (and very ancient) practice has been to grow onions continually on the same site. Only when disease becomes evident is the crop moved to fresh land.

Finding Your Way Around the Encyclopaedia

Latin Name

Under each heading is listed the Latin name. Not everyone is in the habit of using Latin names – they can seem awkward and pedantic – but because they are universally accurate they are included to remove any confusion. Many plants can be known under several different common names, but they can have only one Latin name.

Latin or botanical names are split into two parts, and sometimes have a third part attached:

Portulaca   **oleracea**   **(var. sativa)**
Genus   **species**   **(variety / subspecies)**

Some abbreviations used are:

- **spp.**   Short for species. Where a vegetable might consist of several species it is abbreviated thus. eg. Barbarea spp.
- **subsp.**   Subspecies. eg. Vigna unguicularis subsp. sesquipedalis.
- **var.**   Variety. A variety is different from a subspecies in that it has arisen in cultivation rather than in nature. eg. Skirret, Sium sisarum var. sisarum is distinct from its wild counterpart, S. sisarum subsp. lancifolium.
- **x**   A silent 'x', this stands for hybrid, for example Huckleberry, Solanum x burbankii.

- Following the conventions of the botanical classification system, once a genus name has been mentioned, further references to it are abbreviated to a single letter, as in the Sium example above. In the plural, the first letter of the genus name is doubled, eg. Land Cress BB. praecox, vernus & vulgaris.

- Sometimes a Latin name is changed by the botanical community, and to avoid confusion with the old one (which is often still widely in use by the gardening community) is given in brackets, eg. Polymnia [Smallanthus] sonchifolia.

Family Name

Plants are grouped by common characteristics into families, the name designated with the ending – aceae (pronounced ay-see). There are changes made to these family names from time to time, eg. Compositae is now Asteraceae, and Cruciferae is now correctly Brassicaceae. Although some of the family names used in this section are strictly "old fashioned" family names (with a simple -ae ending), these out-dated designations are still used as these are more familiar to gardeners.

Plant Category

The way a plant grows determines how it is to be grown and the place it occupies in the garden. A hardy perennial, for instance, occupies the same piece of ground year after year and needs no protection through winter; a half-hardy annual lives for just one year and is sensitive to frost, so needs to be raised under glass and planted out, and so on. The terms used are largely self-explanatory and follow the conventions used in other gardening literature, but are explained in the Glossary.

Hardiness Zones

The hardiness of garden plants is very subjective and is dependent upon many factors: soil drainage, maturity of the plant, wind speed and direction, rainfall and so on. While it is hard to be specific about hardiness and pronouncements on a species' suitability for growing in a particular area cannot be accurately given, as a starting point each is categorised according to hardiness zones. While this system may not be familiar to British gardeners, it is widely used in the United States and on continental Europe to give guidance as to what is or is not suitable to grow in a particular climate. The table given below is meant as guidance only, to inform the choice of planting and not as a guarantee that a particular plant will thrive in a given area unprotected. The use of protected cropping — even if it is by the use of cloches, fleece or a polytunnel — greatly extends the range of climates in which plants can be grown.

Zone	Minimum Temperatures Plants Can Withstand
ZONE 11	+5° C and above
ZONE 10	+ 5 TO 0° C
ZONE 9	0 TO −5° C
ZONE 8	−5 TO 10° C
ZONE 7	−10 TO −15° C
ZONE 6	−15 TO −20° C
ZONE 5	−20°C and below

Height

The heights given are the useful heights of the plant. Some leafy crops may grow much taller than stated if they are given the chance to flower and seed. For example, the height given for Land Cress is 20cm, but if it is allowed to flower it can run up to 1m and beyond, at which point it becomes bitter and unpalatable. Measurements throughout the book are given in metric.

Rotation

Crop rotation categories according to the conventions discussed in Crop rotation.

Greens

Plants whose leaves are good to eat, either cooked or eaten raw. Many are excellent weather-resistant alternatives to spinach: bayam, kangkong and orache, or New Zealand spinach which positively enjoys dry weather.

There are many salad plants which are completely winter hardy, far more so than lettuce and without the complications of winter chicory. And some are ancient crops — scurvy grass, buckshorn plantain and dandelion.

From Japan, there is the fragrant shungiku, to add variety to salads, and mitsuba, the Japanese parsley. Watercress is a familiar vegetable, but did you know it can be easily grown in the garden?

Abyssinian Cabbage

Latin Name – Brassica carinata
Family – Cruciferae
Type – Half Hardy Annual
Hardiness – Zone 7
Height – 120cm
Rotation – Treat as Brassicas

Often thought to be an Oriental green, this cabbage relative originates in Africa. It is particularly versatile, quick growing and tasty too.

Origin & History

This cabbage relative is perhaps one of the most recent edible plant introductions. It was discovered in Ethiopia in 1957, growing in plots around villages as an important staple for the villagers. Transplanted elsewhere, it has proved to be very versatile but slow to compete with more traditional members of the cabbage family. It has been extensively trialled in Texas, specifically the variety Tex-Sel, a name under which this vegetable is often known: texsel greens. It succeeded very well but has never caught on as a commercial crop there. In Canada it has been trialled as an oil seed crop.

It grows well throughout the US, and in Britain. In the Gardeners' World Vegetable Book (1981), Geoff Hamilton describes how "A recent expedition to Ethiopia brought back this entirely new vegetable to British gardeners." He found that it fared extremely well in British gardens, despite its tropical origins, far exceeding his expectations. "You may well think that a plant from such a hot part of the world would not do so well in our climate," he enthused, "but at Barnsdale [Geoff's garden] it really flourished."

Uses

As a cut-and-come-again green it is superb, maturing very quickly from sowings made successively. It cooks well, and has the flavour of spring cabbage; slightly tangy and delicious. Leaves can be picked from mature plants, and are good to eat even from plants which have been allowed to flower. The developing flower heads can be picked and eaten like broccoli.

Cultivation

Abyssinian cabbage is really very easy to grow, either grown at close spacing and picked young as cut-and-come-again, or left to grow full size. It does not heart like other cabbages, and quickly runs to seed from early sowings in response to lengthening days. It is not winter hardy but grows well even from an early sowing, and responds well to warm weather: it will put on remarkable growth grown in a polytunnel, for a rapid supply of fresh greens between other crops. It enjoys a well-cultivated soil and plenty of organic matter, and liberal watering.

Sowing – I like to make the first sowings in late February, direct into the ground in an unheated greenhouse. Take out drills spaced 15cm apart and sow thinly, cover the seeds 1cm deep. Sowings can

continue under glass into August. From mid April onwards seed can be sown outside.

Aftercare – Germination is fairly slow early in the year but progress becomes very rapid with lengthening days. The plants can be left to grow larger but it is better to keep successionally sowing for the youngest, most succulent leaves. Keep them free of weeds and water the plants regularly to ensure a good quality harvest.

Harvesting – The first leaves can be cut after eight weeks.

Varieties

Tex-Sel is the variety developed by Texas A&M University. It grows particularly well in the Texan climate, not becoming pungent in hot weather.

Tex Hex

Abyssinian cabbage can be found in catalogues in the Oriental Greens section where it is frequently incorrectly listed as Texsel Greens. While it might now be grown in China, it does not originate in the Orient.

Basella

Latin Name – Basella alba & Basella alba var. rubra
Family – Basellaceae
Type – Tender Perennial
Hardiness – Zone 10
Height – Climbing to 2m
Rotation – Treat as Brassicas

This tropical climber has edible fleshy leaves, eaten in any way you
might eat spinach. An exotic-looking, and useful, feature in a glasshouse
or conservatory.

Origin & History

Native to China and South East Asia, as well
as India and Sri Lanka. There are two forms
of this twining climber: the plain green form
is usually known as Malabar Spinach and is
the one most commonly grown for its
leaves; Ceylon Spinach is the red form, var.
rubra, which shows red in its stems and
leaves, and has red flowers.

Uses

Malabar Spinach is used as a spinach-like
green, eaten raw or lightly steamed. The
leaves have a pleasantly mucilaginous
texture. Ceylon Spinach's fleshy flowers
contain a red dye, used for a food dye or as a
rouge. Its leaves are also edible. In the tropics
both these climbers are commonly grown in
urban areas, framing doorways and windows
of houses to provide leaves which can be
picked when needed.

Cultivation

Although Basella is a tropical perennial, it
can be grown in temperate regions if treated
as an annual. It gives its best growth when
temperatures are 16°C or above which
means that, in areas where summers are
generally cool, best results are achieved
growing it in a greenhouse or conservatory.
Where conditions are good, it grows
vigorously and responds to deep, rich
cultivations, lots of water and humidity. It
can be propagated from seed or from
cuttings. When growing from seed, you'll

find that some red plants (Ceylon Spinach) will appear among the green ones, and maybe a few individuals with characteristics between the two. This is quite normal and is a good way of obtaining plants of both sorts.

Sow the seed in seed-sowing medium under glass or on a windowsill. A propagator is ideal, where temperatures can be maintained at a constant 20°C. The seeds are quite large and can be sown two to a 9cm pot, 1cm deep, and the weaker of the two seedlings removed after emerging. Although it is sensible to assume that a tropical plant such as this will require a long growing season, it is better to sow seeds quite late in the spring – mid May onwards – rather than struggle to maintain the right temperature and light levels from an earlier spring sowing.

Aftercare – Germination is rapid and development quick, too, as long as the temperature remains high. Admit lots of light but keep the humidity high if possible. The plants at first form large (and very beautiful) basal leaves before thinking about climbing, which they will start to do after mid-summer in temperate regions. Pot the plants on as they develop, eventually into a large tub, or plant them outside after the last frost in warm summer areas. Being climbing, they need to be provided with canes,

trellis or string for support. I have known some plants show no inclination to climb and have instead formed a very dense rosette of basal leaves.

Overwintering plants in temperate regions is not really a possibility unless under heated glass. They tend not to thrive over winter indoors as most houses cannot provide enough light. However, if you are maintaining them as a perennial, they can be grown from cuttings, which root readily in close conditions. Because Basella can be very variable from seed, this is a good way of propagating prized individuals.

Harvesting – The leaves can be selectively taken from the plants once they start to climb; removing basal leaves before the plants have got going will weaken them.

Varieties

There are no known seed strains of Basella, not ones which come true-to-type from seed; a given batch of seed will give either the Ceylon (red leaved) or Malabar (green leaved) sort. Because it is so variable from seed, the best way to perpetuate particular individuals is from cuttings.

Bayam, Calaloo

Latin Name – Amaranthus tricolor
Family – Amaranthaceae
Type – Half Hardy Annual
Hardiness – Zone 5
Height – 1.5m
Rotation – Treat as Brassicas

A tender plant, this tropical Amaranth is popular where it is native as a spinach-like green, braised or steamed. Grows well where summers are hot, or under cover.

Origin & History

From South East Asia, tropical China and Japan, and India, this is a popular "spinach" where it is grown.

Uses

The whole plant can be eaten when young, steamed or boiled, or as a part of Oriental cuisine, usually stir-fried. The young shoots and leaves are the best parts, but the thick side-shoots of mature plants can be pealed and eaten, and are very tender and tasty.

Cultivation

This is a tropical plant, but is worth attempting where summers are hot, or in a polytunnel or under glass. I have grown it outdoors as a catch-crop as one would sow radishes, in high summer. In a warm soil the seeds germinate very quickly, making quick growth to give harvestable plants after only a month. Depending on how big or small the plants you require or prefer determines how it is grown. These notes describe cultivating plants to their maximum size, when they are quite spectacular and very decorative.

Sow seeds indoors or under glass, ideally in a propagator where a constant temperature can be maintained: 20°C will produce the strongest seedlings. They do not like disturbance at the root so are best raised in modules in the same way as onion or lettuce plants, for instance. Plants should be sown

GROWING UNUSUAL VEGETABLES

about 4 weeks before the date of the last frost in your area. As a guide, about the the beginning of May is a reasonable time to sow. Seeds are very tiny and should be barely covered, and kept constantly moist.

Aftercare – They can be planted out as soon as the soil has warmed and any possibility of frost has passed. Any plants raised in modules need to have established sufficiently in their cells if they are to be turned out of them without their roots breaking, so pull up one or two to try them out before committing them to the soil. Covering with cloches for the first week or two really helps them to establish. After then, they like lots of water and enjoy a rich root run. Space the plants according to the size of leaf you want. A spacing of at least 30cm ensures they have lots of room to develop fully, but they can be planted tighter – all that happens is that the plants get a bit drawn and the leaves are smaller, but still a very useful crop. Tighter spacing smothers out the weeds quicker, but they'll need hocing in the initial stages in any case.

Harvest the leaves when required, or take out the tips and side shoots. Taking out the growing point encourages branching and delays flowering and seeding. They set seed very readily (and they do not need to be discouraged to do so as it does not compromise the quality of the crop).

I have known Bayam to self-sow in a polytunnel. The seeds appear to be hardier than the plants (which are cut down instantly by the slightest frost) and I have experienced great flushes of germination under where they were growing the previous year. They are easily hoed off if not required.

Varieties

Where Bayam is a common crop there are several varieties, but none appear to be available to Western horticulture. It is quite variable from seed, with individuals showing variation in the attractive colouration of the leaf veins, often very dark red.

Buckshorn Plantain

Latin Name – Plantago coronopus
Family – Plantaginaceae
Type – Hardy Perennial
Hardiness – Zone 6
Height – 20cm
Rotation – Treat as Brassicas

A British native, this salad plant was once more widely grown before other salad leaves were introduced to European gardens. It is very hardy.

Origin & History

A lot of edible plants originate from the coast (beetroot, asparagus and onions are common examples) and Buckshorn Plantain is no exception. Sea cliffs are a favoured habitat, throughout the British Isles and most of Eastern Europe. It was brought into gardens in ancient times. Unlike other cultivated coastal plants, it has shown little change for being brought into cultivation, and the Plantain of horticulture is little different from the wild plant, with only slightly larger leaves.

Uses

The leaves are quite succulent and fleshy, making a useful textural addition to a mixed salad.

Cultivation

Buckshorn Plantain is very versatile and can be grown in a wide range of conditions. Like any salad leaf, though, it should be grown quickly in a rich soil provided with lots of moisture, otherwise the leaves may tend to be bitter and tough, and they may turn yellow.

Sow the seed onto the surface of the soil in drills 15cm apart, or lightly broadcast over the soil surface. Sowing direct onto the soil surface in rows is quite easy, but not a common practice – plantain seed is very tiny and needs light to germinate. To sow in rows, use a length of straight timber or use a garden line to designate where to make the sowings; you can also take out a shallow drill for guidance, but it must not be filled in afterwards. Sowing can take place at any time of the year, although mid-winter sowings are unlikely to meet with any success, and any that do are susceptible to being smothered by weeds before the seedlings have made progress. Spring or autumn sowings are the most successful. Germination at that time of the year is rapid, but the seedlings do not need any thinning as they are quite tolerant of dense overcrowding.

Aftercare – Weeding can be a little tricky as the plants are initially grass-like in appearance. It is important that weeds are not allowed a head start as Plantain is quite brittle, and hand weeding amongst established plants can result in a lot of casualties, and dirty foliage. Keep them well watered during dry periods.

Harvest the leaves just as soon as they are large enough, by snipping them off with scissors or with a knife. The leaves are very narrow and grow close to the ground. You will quickly appreciate, when harvesting, the need to keep the rows well weeded – cutting the leaves without them becoming contaminated with leaves of other weed plants can be tiresome. They can be cut many times. Although Buckshorn Plantain is perennial, it is best to grow it fresh from seed as the plants soon tire. They are apt to flower and should be allowed to do so if you wish to obtain seed, or you may want to let them self-seed, which they do readily. Allowing them to flower does not compromise the quality of the leaves.

Varieties

There are no varieties of Buckshorn Plantain.

Besides the seaside

For vegetables which originate from the coast, it used to be recommended that salt was added to the soil to improve the plants' prospects. A lot of old gardening literature suggests adding copious quantities of sea salt where beetroot and asparagus is grown in order to emulate their maritime origins. In this age of experimentation and research, though, it has been found that the salt has no benefit to the plants – sea salt is something which is tolerated by maritime plants rather than a necessity. If too much salt is added to soil it is very harmful to the soil's structure, especially on a clay soil. Sea weed, on the other hand – a good old garden standby in days of yore – is an excellent manure. It should be thoroughly rinsed of all salt residues before applying, though, usually by leaving it stacked outdoors to be rinsed by rain.

Cardoon

Latin Name – Cynara cardunculus var. altilis
Family – Compositae
Type – Hardy Perennial
Hardiness – Zone 6
Height – 2m
Rotation – treat as Brassicas

A relative of Globe Artichoke, Cardoon is grown for its blanched leaf stalks. A unique vegetable once very popular and enjoying a deserved revival.

Origin & History

Cardoon is found wild in southern Europe and parts of North Africa. Growing in dry grassland, improved forms have been selected and cultivated since classical times. It is widely cultivated in Spain and parts of Italy, but is now almost unknown in Britain and the US; in Britain it was once occasionally grown by market gardeners, but is now only known as a striking ornamental for the back of the border. Recent interest by chefs in Britain has revived the career of this curious veg.

Uses

The blanched leaf stalks and midrib are eaten as a boiled vegetable, usually served with a sauce: in France with a béchamel; in Italy with a garlic, butter and anchovy sauce, bagna cauda. The flower heads yield a substitute for rennet, and are used for making a particular soft curd cheese, Caillebotte à la Chardonette. Not for nothing is Cardoon Jane Grigson's favourite vegetable.

Cultivation

Cardoons are not particularly hardy; although tolerant of a little frost, they do not survive the harsh winters of continental Europe or the US. For growing for eating, however, they are raised and treated as an annual, the plants discarded after cropping. They are heavy feeders and demanding of moisture, so cultivate the soil

**GROWING
UNUSUAL VEGETABLES**

deeply and incorporate plenty of organic matter. The traditional French technique is to grow them in a trench in the manner of celery, using the earth piled on either side of the trench to later cover the stems to blanch them. The modern method described here requires less labour and yields clean stems.

Sow the seeds in March, two seeds to a 9cm pot. These should be placed 1cm below the compost surface: use a sowing medium for raising, and place the pots in gentle heat. After germination, thin the two seedlings to the single strongest one and grow on with plenty of light and water; feed a little as they develop, if necessary. They can be planted out towards the end of May after hardening them off. They need a lot of room, and should be spaced 60cm apart, 1.5m between rows, or in a block at 80cm stations – they really are gigantic. It is after planting out that they start to make rapid growth: there is little to be gained by sowing too early and potting them on; they will only be more inclined to throw up a flower stem. They are also inclined to do this if they are not given sufficient moisture or if the soil is poor.

Aftercare involves giving them plenty of moisture in dry conditions, and of course regular weeding, although they are robust enough to tolerate a light weed infestation. A weekly liquid feed ensures that they make the growth required of them, and prevents them initiating flower stalks. By early autumn the plants should be touching one another and are ready for blanching. Tie the leaves together at the top with some string or raffia – you may need a step ladder to do this! Then wrap the bunched leaf stalks with cardboard, plastic or similar – anything that is flexible and will exclude the light; sacking, perhaps. Ensure this is done when the leaves are quite dry.

Harvesting – They are ready for the kitchen after 2-3 weeks. The plants should be destroyed after harvesting as they will be too exhausted to be suitable for transplanting to the ornamental border, and certainly no good for growing again the next year for blanched stems.

Varieties

Like Globe Artichokes, Cardoons are very variable from seed, and what is normally sold is generic seed of Cardoon, the offspring from which vary quite considerably. What is important is to use seed of Cardoons which are specifically sold for growing for eating (botanically C. cardunuculs var. altilis) as it is a much less spiky and more succulent type than the florist's Cardoon (straight Cynara cardunculus) usually listed in the ornamental section of seed catalogues. The florist's Cardoon has a much more finely divided leaf than the edible type, and is more likely to flower.

In Italy there is a strain Italian Dwarf, and in France, Plein Blanc Énorme (Plain Giant White).

Blanching

Globe Artichokes are very similar to Cardoons. Can they be blanched?

Yes, they can, but there is little point. Only plants that are raised the same year are any good for growing for blanching; once they start to flower they are useless. Globe Artichokes are slow to make large leaves in their first year, so you might as well grow Cardoon rather than struggle along with slower-growing and smaller Artichokes. And of course once they've been cropped for their leaves, they are no good for growing on for their flower heads. They taste the same, though.

*Stems bound with cardboard
for blanching*

**GROWING
UNUSUAL VEGETABLES**

Celtuce, Stem Lettuce

Latin Name – Lactuca sativa var. angustana
Family – Compositae
Type – Hardy Annual
Hardiness – Zone 7
Height – 50cm
Rotation – Treat as Brassicas

Supposed to be a cross between celery and lettuce, this leafy veg is actually a type of lettuce grown for its long, succulent stem. The leaves are inedible.

Origin & History

Celtuce is a form of lettuce which arose in China, where it is popular. Lettuce has been in cultivation since ancient times, originating in the Mediterranean possibly as a hybrid between the wild Prickly Lettuce (Lactuca serriola) and the Least Lettuce (L. saligna). Following its distribution from its original centres in Egypt, Greece and Ancient Rome, it has been selected for its dense hearts or for the breadth of its foliage, but only in China and Japan is it grown for its succulent stem. Introduced to the West it is known as Celtuce, and some seed catalogues claim a relationship with Celery: only in its use is there a similarity. It is relatively recently that has it come to the attention of gardeners in the West – in America in the 1890s first as Asparagus Lettuce, and much more recently into the United Kingdom, in the 1930s.

Uses

Rather than forming a head or producing succulent leaves, Stem Lettuce runs quickly to seed, sending up a stout and succulent flowering stem which is the part which is eaten, cut into strips and braised or boiled for a few minutes, or cooked au gratin. The leaves are quite coarse, and unpalatable.

Cultivation

Stem Lettuce is grown very much like other lettuce. With leaf and heading lettuce, care has to be taken that the plants do not run to seed. With Celtuce, though, such precautions as supplying sufficient moisture at the early stages of growth to prevent bolting do not need to be heeded as the aim is to allow the plants to run to seed. However, if they are not provided with enough moisture, the quality and flavour of the stems can be compromised. A longer season is needed to allow them time to come to maturity, so they do not lend themselves to be successfully sown as conventional lettuce are. Sowings made after July are unlikely to reach maturity.

Sow seed in shallow drills as soon as the soil is workable. They are more extensive in growth than other lettuces so should be spaced 45cm apart and sown not more than 1cm deep. The seedlings should be thinned soon after emergence to 30cm apart. I find that sowings very early in the year do not succeed so well if direct sown, and I prefer to raise them in modules and plant out the small plants equally spaced at 30cm each way in a block.

Aftercare is standard for most salads crops: they need to be kept free from weeds and well-watered during dry weather to ensure a good quality of stem. They quickly form a leafy rosette after sowing which in no time at all starts to run up to flower. At this stage it is usual to discard a lettuce, but celtuce should be left to grow up to 50cm before harvesting

Harvest by cutting the stem. By then (about 80 days after sowing) the stem will be at its most succulent and tender. They do stand for a week or so, but will turn bitter if they are left for too long. Remove all the leaves as they are no good to eat, and if left on they will quickly turn the central stem flaccid and unappetising.

Varieties

Majesty Long has a greenish-white stem. It is very disease resistant.
Narrow Leaf has leaves only 5cm wide. The pointed leaves droop at the end.
Red (Cracoviensis) has red stems and bronze leaves.
Round-Leaved is the standard sort offered in catalogues as celtuce. It looks rather like a large cos lettuce.

Cornsalad, Lamb's Lettuce

Latin Name – Valerianella locusta
Family – Valerianaceae
Type – Hardy Biennial
Hardiness – Zone 6
Height – 8cm
Rotation – Treat as Brassicas

Cornsalad deserves greater popularity as a winter salad for its hardiness and versatility.

Origin & History

Grown since Roman times, most Cornsalads in cultivation today are of hybrid origin, derived from V. locusta – a Northern European species found growing up to 60°N – and the Italian Cornsalad, V. eriocarpa, of Southern Europe but which has become naturalised further north.

The common name comes from it being a weed of corn fields, often germinating after the wheat has been harvested.

Uses

As a winter salad it is invaluable. Either the plants can be harvested whole, severed at the base, or individual leaves can be taken when needed. Cornsalad is popular on Continental Europe, and the French enjoy whole heads tossed with warmed lardons.

Cultivation

Lamb's Lettuce is very much a winter, spring and autumn plant: summer conditions do not suit it. Although it can be grown through the summer, it does not germinate readily when soil temperatures are very high and the plants tend to run straight to seed rather than putting on useful leafy growth. It is indifferent to soil conditions and will thrive even in a poor soil, although crops will be better where the soil is rich.

Sow – Late summer and early spring are the best times of the year for raising Cornsalad. An August or September sowing simulates what normally happens to it in nature, germinating with the arrival of autumn rains after a crop has been cleared. Sow seed in drills spaced 20cm apart, 1cm deep. Sow thinly; the seeds are relatively large and easy to handle, and with careful sowing there should be no need to thin afterwards. Aim for a spacing within the row of 6-10cm, depending on how leafy the variety is. This same spacing applies to growing equidistantly in a bed, where the seeds can be broadcast and lightly raked in. If you thin, the thinnings can be eaten. The soil can be quite dry at this time of the year, and a light watering after sowing will stimulate the seeds into making a head start. Spring sowing can be in late February to the end of March – sowings made later than this meet with little success.

Aftercare – Sowings made in autumn will grow away trouble-free and, after an initial hoeing to keep down germinated weed seeds, they require no other aftercare. Spring sowings, though, can soon be swamped by weeds and regular weed control will be necessary.

Harvesting – The whole plant can be used all in one go, which is the best strategy with small-leaved varieties, or individual leaves can be taken from the large-leaved sorts. The yield is slow but steady through the winter, then with lengthening days and an increase in day temperatures, a great flush of growth is made near the end of February. It is best by then to take up the whole plants and use them up before they run to seed, which they will start to do within a matter of weeks with the arrival of spring. If they have been grown outside, because they are low growing, the leaves will need washing thoroughly.

Varieties

There are two basic types, large-seeded and small-seeded, and within these groups there are large-leaved and small-leaved varieties. All rather confusing, but bear in mind that large-seeded types are more likely to be the hardiest, while large-leaved are not as weatherproof.

Baval is a particularly generous variety, long leaves and large seeds

Coquille de Louviers has cup-shaped leaves, quite long, favoured in the kitchen. Small-seeded, with small leaves.

Large Leaved is a leafy type, as its name suggests. Small seeded.

Large Seeded also has large leaves, grey-green in colour. The foliage is quite slender and distinctive.

Verte de Cambrai is a very compact variety, most favoured for eating whole. Can be sown quite late into the autumn. Small seeded.

Vit is quick maturing for the first crop of large leaves in the autumn. Large seeded.

Dandelion, Pissentlit

Latin Name – Taraxacum officinale
Family – Compositae
Type – Hardy Perennial
Hardiness – Zone 5
Height – 5cm
Rotation – Treat as Umbelliferous

A common weed, it is actually worth the effort in cultivation for its blanched leaves and for its roots; in cultivation they grow thick and long, excellent for hot beverages.

Origin & History

One of the commonest and most cursed weeds in Britain and northern Europe, the Dandelion is actually a useful plant, popular in France and Italy. The leaves are quite bitter in their green state, but this can be attenuated by blanching in the garden by the removal of light, and by further blanching in the kitchen by placing in boiling water for a few seconds. Only recently have its roots become valued.

Uses

It is recognised as a fine salad plant in places where it is popular; in France it is combined with bacon. The leaves are very rich in vitamins and minerals. The roots can be roasted and ground up and used as a hot beverage. Infused with water, dandelion root gives a coffee-like drink, rich and aromatic and free from caffeine.

Cultivation

It may seem fatuous to give growing instructions for Dandelion, but if you are to get good results after going to the trouble of sowing and growing them (and perhaps suffering derision from your gardening neighbours) then it is worth knowing about a few things.

Sowing – This can take place at any time during spring and summer, but to get the biggest roots and leaves the seeds are best sown in April. For the same reason, thinning is beneficial after germination. Seed is surface sown.

Aftercare – You will need to remove the flowers to prevent them seeding. To blanch the leaves, the roots can be lifted and potted, placed under the greenhouse staging or in a cupboard and all light excluded by whatever means you might have at your disposal: plastic bag, inverted plant pot, ceramic dish inverted over them etc. Otherwise they can be blanched where they grow by blackening them out. Unlike with the former method, though, it is not possible to obtain blanched leaves out of season this way.

Harvesting – The roots need to be completely removed if you are avoid them persisting – a small piece of root left deep in the ground will shoot and continue to grow. By growing them in a well-worked soil it should be possible to dig them up intact.

Varieties

Cultivated Dandelions are quite different from the wild sort, with considerably larger and more luxuriant leaves, and fatter roots. Broad Leaved and Thick Leaved are two varieties commonly offered, differing little from one another.
A Coeur Plain is the real McCoy French variety which is occasionally available and should be sought.

Améliore Géant is another French variety worth seeking, by far the most superior strain.

Dandelions give off, as anyone who has attempted to be rid of them will have noticed, a milky sap. In Russia there is another species of Dandelion, Taraxacum koksaghyz, which is grown and gathered for its latex as a source of rubber.

Dandelions do not need to be pollinated in order to set seed. Indeed, the seeds are often developing before the flowers have even opened, which is why they are so quick to disperse their seeds after their flowers have faded. This is known as apomixis. It means that dandelions are effectively clones: every individual is genetically identical, as though they had been grown from cuttings. Each one also has only half the usual set of chromosomes that most other organisms do; they are haploid. And you thought they were a weed ...

Good King Henry, Mercury

Latin Name – Chenopodium bonus-henricus
Family – Chenopodiaceae
Type – Hardy Perennial
Hardiness – Zone 5
Height – 75cm
Rotation – Treat as Permanent bed

This perennial is one of the earliest plants to emerge in the spring, to give succulent young greens at a time when they are most appreciated.

Origin & History

Also called Lincolnshire Asparagus. An ancient vegetable possibly introduced by the Romans. It grows on roadsides and on wasteland, concentrated in areas near former Roman settlements, which suggests its origins: it does not readily spread itself widely. In former times it was eaten as a spinach or early salad substitute. It has never been grown as a commercial crop mostly because of its habit of wilting soon after harvest, which spinach does not do so readily. The only way to enjoy Good King Henry, therefore, is to grow it yourself and enjoy it freshly picked.

The name is an anglicisation of the German Güter Heinrich, Good Henry. He was a Teutonic elf, the equivalent of the British Robin Goodfellow.

Uses

It is principally for the fresh emerging shoots that it is grown. Picked young enough, as the flower buds are starting to show, then boiled or steamed and served with butter it tastes very like asparagus. As the plant develops, individual leaves can be taken.

Cultivation

Good King Henry is a very hardy plant with great longevity, and once established it can be left to its own devices. If it is to be regularly harvested, though, it should be kept well fed and/or frequently mulched to feed it. It can be grown from seed or, more readily, by dividing established crowns.

Sowing – Seed is not easy to germinate. Good King Henry is a very "wild" plant and requires, like other crops which are little removed from their wild ancestry, a period of pre-treatment before it will emerge. The mechanism for breaking dormancy within the seeds (vernalisation) is complicated, but as far as the gardener is concerned, dormancy is easily overcome by sowing in the autumn and letting winter weather work on the seeds. Sow in October or November in a nursery bed outdoors. The drills need not be widely spaced, since they are not sown at the plants' final spacing – about 15cm between the rows is fine. Cover with about 1cm of soil and then leave them. Nothing will happen until the spring, when they will germinate as soon as the weather is conducive. If you only want a few plants, seeds can be sown in pots and overwintered in a cold frame. That way, there's less likelihood of competition from weeds when they germinate.

Propagating from divisions is a ready method of quickly establishing plants but is a slow method of producing plants in quantity. While dormant, dig up an established clump and split it, using two garden forks inserted in the crown back-to-back to lever against one another to prise the clump apart. A good clump can be divided into four or five pieces. Each should be replanted, at the same spacing as that for planting out seedlings.

Aftercare – Germination usually coincides with an upsurge of weeds, so you will need to patrol the sown rows and take out the weeds. This is easy between the rows but a bit more complicated to discriminate between the weeds and the Good King Henry seedlings. It might be necessary to let them get bigger before you can tell them apart. If grown in pots transplant the seedlings when they are a good size, when 5-6 true leaves have formed, to their final stations. Space each about 40cm from its neighbour. This spacing may seem wide at first, but it is necessary to give them plenty of space for when they are fully established.

Harvesting – The youngest shoots emerge very early in the year, as early as the beginning of March if the winter has been a mild one. They are good to eat in their natural green state, but they can be blanched in the field by inverting some sort of heavy container like a bucket or a large plant pot with the drainage hole blanked out or similar – anything to exclude the light – over the developing shoots. They will become drawn and quite white after a couple of weeks, which in some minds improves the flavour.

Varieties

There are no known varieties.

Mercuries

Good [King] Henry is named in contrast to Bad Henry or Dog's Mercury. Both are sometimes called Mercury and they are similar plants, both of them among the first to emerge in spring hedgerows and roadsides. Dog's Mercury, Mercurialis perennis, is quite poisonous and should not be confused with it: Good King Henry's triangular leaves make it very distinct.

Herb Patience

Latin Name – Rumex patentia
Family – Polygonaceae
Type – Hardy Perennial
Hardiness – Zone 6
Height – 2m
Rotation – Treat as Umbelliferous

This ancient herb was popular in former times as a green. It has particularly attractive red-veined leaves – an asset to the ornamental kitchen garden.

Origin & History

Herb Patience is native to Eastern Europe, Turkey through northern Asia and into North Africa. It is naturalised throughout most of the northern United States, and indeed through most of Northern Europe, including Britain, usually as a garden escapee from its former use as a pot herb. It is a similar plant to the pernicious weed Dock, but much taller and distinctive for its red-veined foliage; very much more refined. It is very hardy and perennial, and is a particularly good stand-by green, emerging early in the spring when few other greens are available.

Uses

The leaves are picked and eaten like spinach. Unlike its relatives, such as Sorrel, the leaves are quite bland in flavour, but pleasant.

Cultivation

Herb Patience is very easy to grow, and will naturalise quite readily in derelict land. It does not self-seed as readily as its near relatives (especially Dock) so does not become a nuisance where it is left to grow unfettered. It is possible to remove the flowering stalks to discourage seeding. Any sort of soil suits it, in a position in full sun. But like any leafy crop, a rich soil and plentiful water ensures a good yield of leaf.

Sowing – Should be in autumn, ideally, or again in early spring. The seed does not germinate readily through the summer and will remain dormant if sown then, emerging in the autumn with the onset of autumn rains. Sow direct into drills in early April (or for autumn sowing, in September) spaced 20cm apart. Sow the seed thinly – the seeds are winged and will blow away easily, so choose a calm day to do this. Bury the seeds about 1cm deep.

Aftercare – Thin the seedlings if they appear to becoming excessively overcrowded, although they don't mind a bit of jostling with their neighbours. Keep them regularly hoed at first to keep down germinating weed seeds, but they do withstand quite heavy competition once they have got going.

Harvesting – The leaves can get very large, up to about 30cm, but they are better picked before they have reached this size, for the tenderest leaves. The best leaves are produced at the beginning of the season, before midsummer when they begin to get tough. Herb Patience will go on cropping for many years.

Varieties

There are no known varieties.

Pot Herb

It's a funny term, pot herb, and a rather old-fashioned one. It should not be taken to mean that the herb is suitable for growing in a pot (although many many pot herbs are) but rather that they are grown for the cooking pot. There's also pot marigold, the marigold of cottage gardens: it does not grow well in a pot at all, where it tends to remain rather stunted.

Kangkong, Water Convolvulus

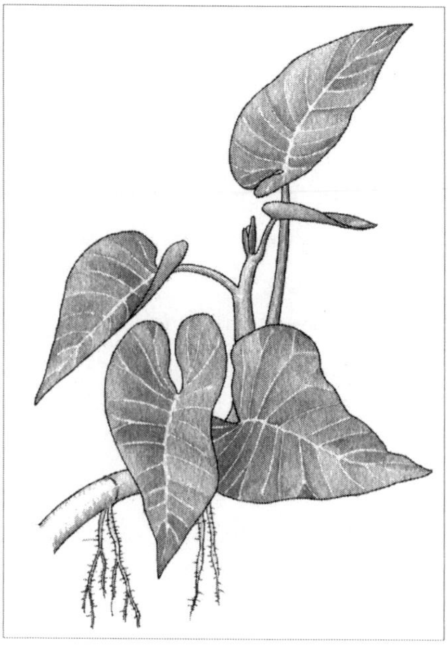

Latin Name – Ipomoea aquatica
Family – Convolvulaceae
Type – Half Hardy Perennial
Hardiness – Zone 9
Height – 50cm
Rotation – Treat as Brassicas

A common tropical plant, this semi-aquatic novelty is a tasty vegetable. It does not need to be grown in water: a wet soil will do.

Origin & History

Probably originating in India, Kangkong now grows all over the tropics. It mostly grows in water but will also grow in wet soils, creating large colonies by sending out long rhizomes. It has become a serious pest in Florida. In seasonally-dry areas of the tropics, it provides fresh greens during the dry season.

Uses

It can be eaten raw or cooked. Raw, the young leaves and tips of the trailing stems are crisp and have a pleasantly slippery, mucilaginous texture to them, and a sweet flavour. Cooked, in stir-fries with garlic and chillies, the stems retain their crispness while the leaves wilt to a spinach-like consistency.

Cultivation

Although it is tropical, Kangkong is quite easily accommodated in a temperate climate, although it will grow better, where cool summers are experienced, under glass or in a polytunnel. It does not need to be grown in water but does need to be kept wet. I have grown it equally successfully as an aquatic (in an old sink) and in wet soil. Kangkong is daylength-dependent and will almost cease growth with shortening days, when it will flower. It is best treated as an annual, raised fresh from seed each spring.

Sowing – The seeds are large and can be easily space-sown; their germination is excellent. A loam-based growing medium is best, one which will not rapidly decompose and ferment when submerged. Sow seven seeds (six around the edge, and one in the middle) to a 23cm/2 litre pot; push them just under the surface. Stand the pots in a tray of water and germinate the seeds at 22°C or above. Because kangkong reacts to daylength, it is best to sow early in the year to give the plants opportunity to produce a good crop before they cease growing after mid-summer.

Aftercare – They germinate quickly and growth is very rapid. If you are growing them in water, plant the potfuls out into a suitable container – an old sink is good, or a temporary pool dug in the ground and lined with polythene – into a good layer of loam-based medium in the bottom, then top the pool up with water. The water should stay warm enough (around 25°C) from the middle of May under glass, for rapid growth. If grown in the soil, plant out spaced around 15cm each way, usually in a block or in rows 25cm apart, 10cm within the row. Seed can be sown direct at these spacings, sown in May. Keep the soil constantly heavily watered. Water retention can be improved by adding copious quantities of organic matter.

Harvesting – Take the tips of the runners when needed. Kangkong does not keep well and will rapidly wilt, so should be picked as fresh as possible.

Once the plants start flowering, there is little chance of them making further progress for the rest of the season and they should be discarded. Kangkong is perennial but it does not overwinter well in temperate areas. Even if the minimum temperature can be maintained, light levels are too low to sustain growth.

Varieties

There are no named varieties, but there are two types: a white-stemmed and a green-stemmed form. The former is considered to be the superior sort in the kitchen, but the green-stemmed type is the more robust of the two.

Land Cress

Latin Name – Barbarea spp.
Family – Cruciferae
Type – Hardy Biennial
Hardiness – Zone 6
Height – 20cm
Rotation – Treat as Brassicas

With a flavour and appearance similar to watercress this is an easily grown alternative. It is particularly hardy, yielding fresh salad greens through the winter.

Origin & History

There are about 14 species of Land Cress, differing only very slightly from one another. They are all of them wintergreen and edible. The main species are BB. praecox, verna and vulgaris, from Central Europe and Northern Asia, and the American species B. orthoceras. This latter is the true American cress, although all species can be seen listed as American cress from time to time. Land Cress was once widely grown in Europe, at least from the 17th century, but its widespread cultivation had all but died out in Britain by the 18th century. It continues to be a popular and well-known green in the US, and is occasionally seen in local markets on the European continent. It is a common wayside plant in Britain, a garden escape.

The Latin name Barbarea is named for St Barbara. St Barbara's feast day is 4th December, and it is said that eating it on that day will bring good luck.

Uses

Land Cress is one of the hardiest of greens, providing pungent leaves right through the winter. Eaten on their own they are quite strong, but the leaves combine well with other winter salad leaves, such as Mizuna, and they make an excellent ingredient in soup, in place of Watercress. It is particularly rich in vitamin C.

Cultivation

Land Cress is totally adapted to growing through the winter, and spring or early summer sowings will fail: germination will either be poor or non-existent, and the plants will rapidly run to seed. Successful sowing is in July and August, into land which is well cultivated and nourished, preferably in a damp but not waterlogged spot. Water availability is not, though, usually an issue with overwintering crops! It enjoys full sun but will tolerate shade, too. It will grow well under deciduous trees, where it will receive enough light through the bare boughs.

Sowing – Sow into drills 20cm apart, and barely cover the fine seed. If you take pains to sow thinly the plants will not need thinning later; they do tolerate a fair amount of overcrowding, though, so the seedlings will only need thinning if they are excessively crowded after emergence.

Aftercare – Hoe off weed seedlings between the rows after the seedlings have emerged, at the beginning of autumn so that they do not get an opportunity to establish over winter.

Harvesting – Leaves can be taken through the winter as and when needed. Land Cress should not be cut all in one go, which seriously weakens the plants, but a few leaves should be taken from each at each cutting. Harvesting can start in late autumn and continue right through the winter. They will run to seed with lengthening days in the spring, at which point the leaves start to get unpleasantly pungent. Plants should be taken up before they set seed: Land Cress will self-seed voraciously if given the opportunity.

Varieties

There is a variegated form of Barbarea vulgaris, B. v. 'Variegata'. which unlike many variegated plants reproduces true from seed.

Leaf Celery, Zwolsche Krul

Latin Name – Apium graveolens var. secalinum
Family – Umbelliferae
Type – Hardy Biennial
Hardiness – Zone 6
Height 40cm
Rotation – Treat as Umbelliferous

Related to celery, this sort is grown for its leaves. An excellent addition to soups and stews, or used in Oriental cooking.

Origin & History

For years I've seen Zwolsche Krul listed in some seed catalogues and wondered what on earth it is. Actually it is the same species of celery, but one which has been selected to be smaller in stature, quite green and the whole plant is eaten, rather than just the succulent midrib. The name Zwolsche Krul comes from the Dutch, and it is unclear whether Leaf Celery came from Europe originally, or that it came from China via Holland. Certainly plants grown from seed marketed as Zwlosche Krul show strikingly similar characteristics to that marketed as Leaf Celery or Chinese celery. So it may likely be a case of what natural historians (but not necessarily economic botanists) call covergent evolution.

Celery itself is a native of Europe and the British Isles, in marshy places sometimes near tidal waters, always near the sea. The French and the Italians developed stem celery from the 17th century, and in 1699 John Evelyn wrote of it in his Acetaria as "sellery ... was formerly a stranger with us (not very long since in Italy) is an hot and more generous form of Macedonian persley, or smallage."

Uses

Leaves and stems have a strong celery flavour. Wherever celery is used as a flavouring ingredient, for instance in soups and stews, sauces, Leaf Celery can be used instead. The stems can be eaten as a vegetable, or stir-fried with sugar and sesame oil, and a drop of soy sauce. It can be eaten raw, but the flavour is quite a lot stronger than blanched celery and should be used sparingly in a salad.

Cultivation

Leaf Celery is a lot easier to grow than celery. Whereas celery usually requires some sort of blanching technique and a long season to develop, Leaf Celery does not. It can be sown successionally through the summer, from May until July. An August sowing can be made to provide leaves and stems the following spring, from plants protected under cloches or grown in a polytunnel. So, as an easier-to-grow alternative to celery, Leaf Celery is just the thing. All celery grows at its most succulent, and with the least string, if grown in a wet soil, even one that is waterlogged for most of the year, and with lots of organic matter.

Sowing – Leaf Celery seeds are very tiny, so small that it is not practical to sow them direct outdoors. Germination is slow and erratic, resulting in the seedlings rapidly becoming overcome by weeds by the time they have emerged. They require constant moisture for germination, too, and that is not so easy to provide in the field. So it is better to sow in modules indoors. Sow several seeds per cell (there's no chance of sowing them individually) and leave them uncovered. Use seed-sowing medium. Cover the cells with damp newspaper to keep in the moisture and carefully watch for germination; remove the newspaper when seedlings emerge. Seeds germinate best at around 16°C: if the temperature drops for prolonged periods below 14°C while they are developing, any sort of celery is likely to later run quickly to seed. The opportunity for this temperature drop is easily avoided if sowing is delayed until a little later in the spring: unless the weather turns seriously inclement, sowings after the beginning of April should not require additional heat. Seedlings will of course need thinning to leave one in each cell soon after they have emerged, and they require regular and quite heavy watering.

Aftercare – Plant them out at a much closer spacing than other celeries, 10–15cm apart. They are most naturally suited to being grown in a block in a deep bed, alternatively in rows spaced 30cm apart. They are slow to develop initially and will need regularly weeding and frequent watering – if they are left short of water for too long, they become tough and stringy.

Harvesting – Leaf Celery can be harvested when quite young, about 6 weeks after planting. Cut individual leaf stalks as required, or cut the whole thing about 2cm above ground level; they will regrow but the second crop is usually poor.

Varieties

There are several varieties, some originating in China, others in Holland.

Afina has a clumping habit forming many dark green stems. Good regrowth after cutting.

Dinant is one of the hardier varieties, for overwintering.

Heung Kunn, also known as Kintsai, under which name it is often listed in catalogues. The commonest variety in China, where it is a popular vegetable.

Par-Cel is another confusing catalogue listing (like Zwolsche Krul) this is often described as being a cross between a celery and a parsley – which it isn't, it's a type of Leaf Celery.

Milk Thistle

Latin Name – Silybum marianum
Family – Compositae
Type – Hardy Annual
Hardiness – Zone 7
Height – 30cm
Rotation – Treat as Brassicas

Thistles are not just for Eeyore: this highly ornamental thistle is good eating — the thorns wilt away on cooking.

Origin & History

Milk Thistle has been in cultivation as an ornamental for many centuries. It is naturalised in many parts of the world — East Africa, California, the South American pampas — having been introduced to those parts from the Mediterranean and Afghanistan. It favours dry, sunny situations and will overwinter as a biennial where summers are hot and winters low in rainfall, but usually grows as an annual. It is best treated as such in cultivation.

Uses

Lightly steam or boil the leaves for several minutes. The spines do not need to be removed, and will soften on cooking. Eat like spinach. The leaves tend to reduce down a lot on cooking, so cram plenty of fresh leaves into the pan to allow for this.

Cultivation

Milk Thistle is a robust plant and grows well in a rich soil. Poor soils will produce a crop — indeed it prefers a freely-draining soil in its habitat — but as with all leafy vegetables, thorough cultivation and a soil which is in good heart will produce better, more succulent and worthwhile yields. It enjoys a sunny site. I have grown excellent crops of Milk Thistle in a soil which was heavy and poorly drained.

Sowing – Seed direct into drills in spring through to early summer. Space drills 30cm apart and sow the large, shiny seeds 15cm apart in the row. Sow 2cm deep and cover the seeds, and firm them in lightly with the back of a rake.

Aftercare – is minimal. Hoeing between the rows soon after the seedlings emerge keeps down weed competition, although this is not too critical: Milk Thistle will withstand a fair amount of competition. No thinning of the seedlings should be necessary if they have been space-sown.

Harvesting – The first leaves can be taken as soon as they are large enough.
Otherwise, cut the whole rosette as soon as it is of a good size, usually about 10 weeks after sowing. Take great care harvesting the leaves as they are extremely spiny, and stout gloves are essential. Milk Thistle tends to run to seed easily, at which point the plants can be discarded. However, the flowers are very ornamental, scented, and the feathery seed heads are enjoyed by finches.

Varieties

There are no known varieties.

Miner's Lettuce, Winter Purslane

Latin Name – Montia (Claytonia) perfoliata
Family – Portulacaceae
Type – Hardy Perennial
Hardiness – Zone 7
Height – 25cm
Rotation – Treat as Brassicas

One of the hardiest of winter leaves, this attractive salad leaf can be grown all the year round. Succulent and tasty, it adds diversity to salad greens.

Origin & History

This diminutive plant originates in the United States, on the Western seaboard from Baja California to British Columbia. It is well adapted to dry conditions, thriving in deserts by subsisting on winter moisture in shady places. In areas where it has been introduced, it thrives in similar situations – in Northern Europe and Britain in sandy areas such as East Anglia.

The name Miner's Lettuce dates from when it was eaten by miners in the gold rush of the 1850s as a prevention against scurvy.

Uses

Eaten raw, the leaves are succulent and juicy, with a pleasant crispness. They do not lend themselves to being cooked, turning to mush.

Cultivation

Although it most frequently inhabits shady places where it is naturalised, it is quite happy in an open situation; it is tolerant, too, of quite heavy winter rains, and tolerant of heavy soil as long as it does not remain too waterlogged.

Sowing – This is usually in late August/early September, but sowings can be made in spring; it is as a winter vegetable, though, that it is most valued. The seeds are very tiny, shiny and black so they are not easy to sow with any accuracy. Because it tolerates shade, good use can be made of a shady patch under trees where little else useful will grow. In this case, simply broadcast the seeds under the tree and rake them in. Otherwise, take out shallow drills, barely making an impression, and sow carefully. Only the merest covering of soil is required. Rows can be spaced narrowly – 20cm – but be sure to leave enough room to run a hoe through to keep the weeds down. To assist sowing, the seeds can be mixed with a little sand to help distribute them evenly.

Aftercare – The seedlings don't really need any thinning once they have emerged as, even if they have become very overcrowded, they are well able to jostle with one another. If you're after really large leaves, though, thin them to 10cm.

Harvesting – You can start picking leaves as soon as they are large enough, but don't take too many at first or the plants will be hindered. Snip them off with scissors or sharp knife as they are needed. Plants will continue cropping right through the winter. As days lengthen in the spring, they will start to flower: a different leaf form is produced, almost circular and enclosing the flowers – what is known as 'perfoliate'. These can be eaten as readily as the leaves, and make an attractive presentation on the plate. Cropping can continue into the summer, but falls off during the hottest weather. Miner's Lettuce will readily self-seed if it is allowed to do so.

Varieties

There are no known varieties of Miner's Lettuce.

Which?

Montia, Claytonia – Which? Miner's Lettuce can be seen listed in seed catalogues and some gardening literature under two different Latin names, Montia and Claytonia. Which one is correct? For a long time, Winter Purslane was classified as in the genus Claytonia, but botanists have decided that it does not show sufficient similarities to other plants in that genus, so have put it, and two other species, into a distinct and separate genus, Montia. But the gardening community is a conservative one, and the old name has stuck in many quarters; it is sometimes called Claytonia as a common name. Montia, incidentally, is named after Guiseppe Monti, an Italian botanist who died 1790.

Mitsuba, Japanese Parsley

Latin Name – Cryptotaenia japonica
Family – Umbelliferae
Type – Hardy Perennial
Hardiness – Zone 6
Height – 30cm
Rotation – treat as Umbelliferous

A native of Japan, it has come to be used there in the same way as parsley. It has a flavour something like celery and angelica.

Origin & History

It has been cultivated for many centuries in Japan, where it is thought to be native. Like many plants which have been long domesticated, its true origins are obscure.

Uses

Mitsuba is flavoursome, likened to a mixture of parsley, celery and angelica. It can be eaten raw, but is better cooked, steamed for no more than two minutes. It forms the basis for many Japanese dishes including sukiyaki, and for seasoning clear fish soups. The leaves and stems are often preferred blanched in the field to give white stems.

Cultivation

Like many Oriental greens, Mitsuba likes conditions in spring and autumn, remaining dormant in winter and growing poorly, and usually running to seed, in high summer. It is a plant of woodland margins and clearings, and is one of few vegetables which will thrive in shade. Indeed, if grown in full sun the leaves tend to turn yellow. It does not require a rich soil, but will reward good fertility. The way it is grown depends on how it is to be used, and specialised techniques are used to produce the commercial blanched product in Japan. It is usually, though, grown for its green leaves, which is very straightforward. Plants are always raised from seed.

Although it is perennial, Mitsuba is usually treated as an annual, the root discarded after harvesting.

Sowing – The seed requires warmth for germination. Although it will germinate in a colder soil, germination can be poor and the development of the seedlings hindered, with them often running to seed. Sowing in late spring or early autumn gives the best results. Seed should be sown direct, into drills 20cm apart, and thinly. Thin to leave plants spaced 3cm apart. The seed can also be broadcast in a deep bed.

Aftercare – The rows should be weeded and the plants kept watered during dry weather.

Harvesting – Leaves are good for eating after about 60 days. Older plants are not so good, the older leaves becoming rigid and erect. A good guide is to harvest while the stems are still supple.

To grow for blanching – raise the plants from a spring sowing and allow them to develop a sizable root. They are grown at a much wider spacing than those grown for green leaf at about 20cm apart. They will die down through the winter if left outside, and in early spring will recommence growth. The new shoots can be blanched by covering with 20–30cm of soil, or with some darkening material such as a black polythene cloche or inverted pot. Blanching takes several weeks, at the end of which light should be admitted to allow the plants to green slightly before harvesting.

Varieties

There are two main types preferred in Japan:
Kansai has green stems and is the sort normally grown as a green crop.
Kanto has whiter stems and is the sort usually preferred for blanching.
When buying seed in the West, no distinction is usually made between the two types.

New Zealand Spinach

Latin Name – Tetragonia tetragonioides
Family – Aizoaceae
Type – Half Hardy Perennial
Hardiness – Zone 9
Height – Trailing to 1.5m
Rotation – Treat as Brassicas

A perennial grown as an annual, this spinach relative has the advantage over its cousin of being tolerant of hot, dry conditions.

Origin & History

New Zealand Spinach was first brought to Europe from New Zealand, hence the common name, but is widely distributed in the wild, in coastal habitats of China, Japan, South America, Australia and most of Polynesia. It also grows along the Californian coast of North America all the way to Oregon and is considered to have been naturalised there.

Captain Cook's voyage first brought it to Europe, collected by the famous collector Sir Joseph Banks in 1770 from Queen Charlotte's Sound. It was first grown at the Royal Botanic Gardens, Kew, as a botanical curiosity. There is no record of it having been used as a vegetable until 1819. It still remains under-utilised as a vegetable to this day, in spite of its ease of growing, adaptability and high yield.

Uses

As a spinach substitute, boiled or braised, or steamed.

Cultivation

New Zealand Spinach is a creeping plant, and extensive. It has a reputation for enjoying dry and hot conditions but these conditions are not a requirement and it will grow well in most summers, even a wet British one. Hot and wet conditions are, oddly, the only conditions it does not tolerate. Being of coastal origin, it enjoys full sun and a well-drained soil (gravel, in habitat). In cultivation, better yields and more robust plants result from a well fed soil.

Sowing – The seeds are large and quick to germinate. There's no value in raising plants from seed under glass and planting them out – they grow away quickly from a late sowing into warm soil and benefit from not having their growth checked through root disturbance. Sow them direct at stations spaced at least 50cm apart. Plant 2-3 seeds per station, and thin to the strongest plant if more than one germinates.

Aftercare – Keep them weeded at first, but they rapidly start vining and all but the worst weeds are smothered out. No extra irrigation is needed in periods of drought, but for better yields of fresh leaves it is wise to give some extra water when necessary.

Harvesting – The tips of the shoots are removed when required and as soon as the plants are large enough, and through the whole growing season. Regular pruning of the shoot tips by harvesting encourages the plants to become bushy, which is a great advantage in a crowded vegetable patch – New Zealand Spinach can rather rampage if left unchecked.

New Zealand Spinach is naturally perennial, but will be destroyed by hard frosts. It may, though, in a mild winter, continue cropping until very late in the year.

Varieties

There are no known varieties.

Ice Plant

New Zealand Spinach is lightly covered in curious dewdrop-like glands, giving it the appearance of being covered in a light haw frost. There's a plant similar to New Zealand Spinach which is smothered in these glands, making it look deep-frozen and giving it the name Ice Plant, Mesembryanthemum crystallinum. Originating in Namibia and the southern Cape of Africa, it is demanding of drier conditions than NZ Spinach and normally grows through the winter in its native habitat and is quite intolerant of frost, despite what its name might suggest. Since it differs so little from its cousin, it is seldom worth attempting in cooler climates apart from for its novelty value.

Orache, Mountain Spinach

Latin Name – Atriplex hortensis
Family – Chenopodiaceae
Type – Hardy Annual
Hardiness – Zone 6
Height – 2m
Rotation – Treat as Brassicas

This spinach-like green exists in a kaleidoscope of colour forms. Ridiculously easy to grow, it was once widely grown and deserves to be again.

Origin & History

The origins of Orache are obscure, hence its Latin name (hortensis = of horticulture, that is, arisen in cultivation). Wild species similar to the cultivated orache exist in Siberia and central Asia. It has been grown in Europe since the middle ages, extensively until the 18th century. It is now seldom grown as a commercial crop except in parts of France and Germany. The coloured forms are popular as ornamentals.

Uses

The flavour and texture is very similar to spinach, and wherever spinach is used, orache can be used instead.

Cultivation

Mountain spinach is grown in the same way as ordinary spinach. In fact, like spinach it easily runs to seed if it is deprived of water for too long, or during prolonged hot weather, unlike some of the other spinach substitutes such as New Zealand spinach. It enjoys a rich soil and a position in full sun and, of course, plentiful water.

Sowing – Sow in drills spaced 30cm apart, depending on the ultimate size of the plants being aimed for. It is possible to sow orache around mid summer and cut it several weeks later, before the plants have fully developed and while they are young and tender, in which case they can be sown very close together.

Aftercare – Keep between each row weeded by regular hoeing. Ensure the plants get plenty of water to grow big succulent leaves and prevent them running prematurely to seed.

Harvesting – Either cut very young plants whole, or use thinnings, or take a few leaves from each plant when needed.

Like spinach, sowing at two weekly intervals through the growing season, from April to August, will ensure a continuous supply of fresh leaves.

Varieties

There are three colour forms, red, green and golden. The golden variety is less vigorous than the other two.

Pink Purslane

Latin Name – Montia sibirica
Family – Portulacaceae
Type – Hardy Perennial
Hardiness – Zone 7
Height – 30cm
Rotation – Treat as Brassicas

Very similar to Miner's Lettuce, this pink-flowered, rosette-forming salad is pleasing on the plate and in the ornamental salad garden.

Origin & History

Pink Purslane is very similar to Winter Purslane both in its appearance and in the places it inhabits. Pink Purslane extends all the way up to Alaska and inland from the western seaboard of the US to the mid west, inhabiting moist shady spots and well-drained sands and gravels on river banks, and in Europe it has become naturalised in these habitats. It is a relatively new discovery as an edible, having been grown for many years as an ornamental, freely naturalising in woodland and waterside gardens.

Uses

The leaves are succulent and refreshing as a raw salad leaf, pleasantly crisp. They can be briefly steamed or boiled like spinach.

Cultivation

Cultivation is identical to that of Miner's Lettuce. Like Miner's Lettuce, it resents waterlogging. It will thrive in quite poor soils, and is invaluable for growing in shady or difficult spots.

Varieties

There are no known varieties of Pink Purslane.

Salad Mallow

Latin Name – Malva verticillata var. crispa
Family – Malvaceae
Type – Hardy Annual
Hardiness – Zone 6
Height – 1.6m
Rotation – Treat as Brassicas

This relative of Marsh Mallow is grown for its leaves; picked young
they're delicious, with a distinctly "mallow" texture.

Origin & History

Salad mallow is a common plant
throughout northern Europe, and is
naturalised over most of the northern
hemisphere. It was once commonly
cultivated in European gardens, but is now
only purposely grown in parts of China,
along with M. verticillata.

Uses

Mallow has a curious jelly-like texture to
its leaf – mucilaginous is the usual
description for this; very pleasantly so.
Young leaves can be eaten in a mixed
salad, or lightly steamed and eaten in place
of spinach, or in soups.

Cultivation

Salad mallow is very easy to grow,
adaptable, and quick to mature. It can be
sown throughout the growing season, early
spring to autumn, for a succession of
young leaves and shoots. It is a stemmy
plant, not growing as a rosette like, for
instance, lettuce, and will still yield good
leaves when it has become quite tall. It
therefore needs to be carefully sited so that
it does not cast shade over other crops. It is
tolerant of poor conditions, but like any
salad plant it will not give of its best unless
it is given a rich, well-cultivated soil and
provided with plenty of moisture.

Sowing – Seed into shallow drills, 2cm
deep and spaced 30cm apart. The seeds are

quite large and can be spaced 10cm apart, or they can be sown at a rather arbitrary spacing and later thinned. Or they can be broadcast-sown over a deep bed.

Aftercare – Germination is rapid and development is quick. You can use the first thinnings by pulling the whole plant, to eventually leave plants at 20cm stations, or wider if really big plants are sought. However, if they are allowed to grow really large, the leaves can actually grow too broad to be useful, particularly as a salad leaf. It is better to grow them quite densely to reduce their leaf size.

Harvesting – The leaves can be taken at any stage, as soon as they are large enough.

Snip or pinch off however many leaves are needed, a few from each plant at each picking. Flowers are freely produced which will in turn yield seed: the plants should be uprooted before seed ripens to avoid being over-run with volunteers. Because it is so quick growing, Salad Mallow is a useful catch-crop, filling in a gap for a couple of months between crops.

Varieties

There are no known varieties. It is thought that Malva crispa is actually a varietal form of Malva verticillata, with curly and broader leaves. Both species can be grown and used the same way.

Marshmallow

Can I make marshmallow with this plant?
No. In fact the confectionery marshmallow is no longer made from the true marshmallow, Malva officinalis, but is now instead made of sugar, water and gelatin.

Scurvy Grass

Latin Name – Cochlearia officinalis
Family – Cruciferae
Type – Hardy Biennial
Hardiness – Zone 6
Height – 50cm
Rotation – Treat as Brassicas

Not a grass, but a broad-leaved herb once highly valued as a concentrated source of vitamin C.

Origin & History

C. officinalis originates in coastal habitats throughout northwest Europe, into Finland and the Baltic, growing on cliffs and rocky shores and occasionally in dry salt marsh.

Scurvy Grass, as its name would suggest, is high in vitamin C and was a popular salad vegetable in the mid-17th century. The leaves were renowned amongst sailors for their anti-scorbutic (that is, as a prevention for scurvy) properties, and they would eat them steeped in ale. Ships were in a habit of growing pots of Scurvy Grass on long voyages. John Evelyn, in his Acetaria: A Discourse of Sallets (1699) writes of Scurvy Grass, "Cochlearia, of the garden,

but especially that of the sea, is sharp, biting and hot; of nature like nasturtium, prevalent in the scorbute. A few of the tender leaves may be admitted in the composition." Medicine in the 17th century was a doctrine of humours: hot, wet, cold and dry needed to be kept in balance according to the character of a patient, and each food contributed to one or more of these humours and neutralised others. The scorbute referred to by Evelyn was a newly discovered 'humour', that contributed to scurvy. Scurvy Grass appears in prescriptions for "scurby" written by William Shakespeare's son-in-law, Dr John Hall.

Uses

The leaves are slightly acid, salty and a little bitter, similar in flavour and sensation to watercress or Nasturtium. They make an interesting contrast added to a mixed salad.

Cultivation

Although Scurvy Grass originates from a very specific maritime habitat, it is extremely adaptable in cultivation and is very hardy. Some notes suggest an open, sandy soil but I have had success growing it in a heavier soil, and one which has been periodically waterlogged. It is very hardy and is a useful winter green grown from a late summer sowing. An alkaline to neutral soil suits it best, though, or the leaves are apt to turn yellow. It is not heavy feeding and will grow in poor soil, but enjoys full sun.

Sowing – Seed in very shallow drills, barely an impression in the soil, or broadcast thinly over the soil surface. Sowing should be in March for an early summer crop, or in late August/September for a late autumn/winter crop; mid-summer sowings do not meet with much success – germination tends to be poor and the plants run to seed. Space the drills 20cm apart, and thin the seedlings to just 5cm apart, or they may not need thinning at all if they were sown sparsely. Scurvy grass will grow to 50cm when in flower, but is a small plant in its vegetative state.

Aftercare – They are apt to be quickly smothered in weeds, being small, so should be kept regularly hoed – soon after germination is a good time, and at regular intervals while they are growing. No extra irrigation is usually required.

Harvesting – They can be cut as soon as the plants are large enough, with scissors or a sharp knife at ground level. They do not withstand many harvests and should be pulled up and discarded after the second cut. Overwintered plants start to run to seed with lengthening days and will become unpalatable by the beginning of April. Spring-sown plants will also run to seed, but later than plants which have overwintered.

Varieties

There are no known varieties of Scurvy Grass.

Sea Beet

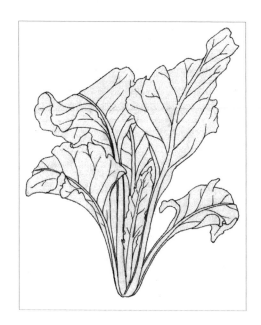

Latin Name – Beta vulgaris ssp. maritima
Family – Chenopodiaceae
Type – Hardy Perennial
Hardiness – Zone 5
Height – 50cm
Rotation – Treat as Umbelliferous

This relative of beetroot and Swiss chard is worth growing for its productive and tasty leaves.

Origin & History

Sea Beet is the parent of beetroot and Swiss chard. It is a coastal plant native of Britain, the Mediterranean and western Asia where it tends to occupy cliffs and rocky crevasses. It is very adaptable in cultivation, tolerant of most soil types and conditions. Where it has been grown (and it has been grown since Prehistoric times) it has been selected for bigger roots to give beetroot, mangel and sugar beet, or for bigger leaves and a broader midrib to give Swiss chard and seakale beet. Wild Sea Beet, when brought into cultivation, grows robustly to yield large quantities of succulent leaves.

Uses

As a spinach substitute, lightly steamed or boiled. They can be puréed or added to soups and used anywhere where spinach or Swiss chard might be used.

Cultivation

Sea Beet is grown in basically the same way as chard. The plants are extensive and need to be given plenty of room, and respond to a rich soil which has been well cultivated.

Sowing – Direct into drills from March onwards. The seeds (more correctly, seed clusters) are quite large and can be space-sown at intervals of 10cm in rows spaced

40cm apart and covered to a depth of 1cm. If you're growing them in a deep bed, sow them at an equidistant spacing of 30cm. Like beetroot, each seed cluster gives rise to two or more seedlings, rarely only one, so after germination thin the seedlings to leave the strongest individual at each station.

Aftercare – Sea Beet grows quickly and is very robust, so after an initial hoeing to keep weed seedlings down they tend to smother out any further weeds. They will need further thinning until a spacing of 30cm within the row is achieved; the thinnings can be eaten. They respond well to irrigation.

Harvesting – Leaves can be gathered when required, a few broken out at the base from each plant. The harvesting season is very long, and leaves can be taken as long as there are leaves to be had – it will keep green right into the depths of winter.

Sea Beet is perennial and will throw up seed heads the following year. These are spectacular and will yield useful seed and the plants are not harmed. However, leaf production is compromised if plants are allowed to flower, and it is probably better (and it is certainly very straightforward) to keep growing new plants from seed annually.

Varieties

There are many varieties of Sea Beet, but of course all these varieties are themselves different vegetables: beetroot, chard etc. What is interesting about Sea Beet is how robustly the plants will grow with good cultivation, even offspring from rather suspect plants. For instance, in its shoreline habitat Sea Beet tends to be rather stunted in stature, but if seeds are gathered from these plants and sown in rich conditions and supplied with lots of water, they can reach impressive proportions.

Sea Kale

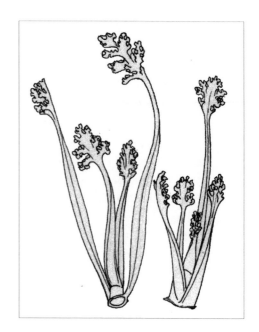

Latin Name – Crambe maritima
Family – Cruciferae
Type – Hardy Perennial
Hardiness – Zone 5
Height – 75cm
Rotation – Treat as Permanent bed

This British native has been cultivated for centuries and was once a favourite of royalty. It does not store or travel well, so grow your own to enjoy it fresh.

Origin & History

Sea Kale is a prominent feature on shingle beaches, particularly around southern Britain and the northern European coastline, parts of the Baltic and Atlantic coasts. It has coarse, leathery leaves which are bitter to eat, but the blanched shoots are particularly tender and succulent, and quite sweet. It is highly probable that its edible qualities came to light after locals discovered the shoots growing up through a thick covering of shingle following winter storms. Sea Kale became a preferred food for royalty, particularly the Prince Regent who took advantage of the abundance of wild Sea Kale on Brighton beach. It is a strictly seasonal vegetable, only the first shoots appearing in late winter/early spring can be blanched. It is also a particularly English one, no other countries are recorded as making use of it.

Uses

Cooked like asparagus, to which it can be closely compared in flavour and texture. It is delicious served simply, with butter or a light sauce, and seldom as an accompaniment to anything else. A real vegetable delicacy.

Cultivation

Despite its coastal origins, and its very specific habitat (it is only ever encountered in the wild growing in shingle), it is actually very easily accommodated in cultivation. Sea Kale is perennial, living for many years, and should seldom be disturbed once established, so siting needs to be carefully considered. It demands full sun and a soil which is well drained but rich. This last requirement is surprising considering the what-one-would-consider impoverished conditions of a shingle beach. Plants need two to three years to grow to maturity from seed, and at least a year to establish grown from a young plant. Because it is perennial there are two methods of propagation, from seed and from root cuttings, or what are known in the trade as 'thongs'. Seedlings can be quite variable, so the latter method is the only one to use if you wish to propagate a particularly good individual or named clone.

Sowing – The seeds may seem unusually large, and variable in size. This is because they are not seeds at all, but fruits containing individual seeds. Each is quite corky and floats well, and is impervious to sea water. These durable fruits are a highly successful means of reproduction for the wild plant. They are easy to sow individually but germination is poor and quite erratic.

Sowing Indoors – Although Sea Kale is quite hardy, raising plants indoors and starting them early gives them a longer season, and therefore a better chance of really strong plants that can be blanched sooner. Sow in early spring, from March onwards but no later than late May, into 15cm dwarf pots. A seed-sowing medium is recommended. Sow the seeds spaced about 0.5cm apart. High temperatures are not required; around a minimum of 12°C suits them. As the seedlings emerge, prick them out into individual pots, 9cm diameter. They establish quickly and should be given lots of light and air. They can be planted in the garden from May onwards, into their final positions, 75cm apart. They do not grow very big in their first year, and other crops can be grown between the plants to make good use of space.

Sowing Outdoors – Sow into a well-drained seed bed from mid April onwards, spacing the seeds 2cm apart and 1cm deep. When they're handleable, transplant the seedlings to a nursery bed spacing them 30cm apart.

The young plants need to be kept well weeded, but do not require watering – Sea Kale is very resistant to drought and dry spells do not affect the quality of the crop. At the end of the first year, seedlings which have been lined out in a nursery bed should be transplanted to their final positions. They should be grown on for a further year before blanching is attempted.

From root cuttings – Sea Kale possesses a fleshy crown, much branched, and the fleshy roots are a ready means of propagation. Dig up a plant while dormant and rim off the roots, leaving stumps 10–15cm long still attached to the crown – the crown can be replanted and will suffer little from the experience, although it should be allowed to settle for a year before blanching again. Each root is then cut to 10cm long pieces, and cut with a straight cut to mark the top and a sloping cut to mark the bottom. This ensures they are planted the right way up. Line these cuttings out into a nursery bed 30cm apart. Like plants grown from seed, they should be planted out in their final positions (75cm apart) at the end of the first year, while dormant.

Harvesting – Sea Kale starts into growth from the end of February. The season for blanched shoots is very short, from March into the beginning of April but no longer. Mounds of shingle are not required, and in fact a more satisfactory job is done using a totally light-excluding cover such as black polythene, an inverted bucket or similar. (Be careful about choosing plastics for blanching: some lightly-coloured or white plastics may admit some light). The aesthetically-conscious may want to invest in a specific ceramic Sea Kale forcing pot, with a fitted lid for inspection, but it is not necessary. The pots though, are extremely durable and not likely to blow away. They were popular in the 19th century when

Sea Kale was quite widely grown. Whatever modern equivalent is used must be well weighted or anchored to prevent it being blown off. An old chimney pot or ceramic drainage tile is highly recommended. The shoots are ready about three to four weeks later. The best shoots are no longer than 10–15cm long. Do not be put off if there are signs of flower buds – they're all edible – they should be entirely white, usually with a hint of red and purple. Green shoots, even ones which are only slightly green, are quite bitter. Cut the shoots off at their base, but leave enough shooting potential for the plant to regrow.

Leave the pots off for the rest of the season for the plants to rebuild their energies for blanching again the next year. They will flower and the flowers can be left on; they will not weaken the plant and are beautiful.

Variations

It is possible to raise Sea Kale and crop blanched shoots within 12 months of sowing. Small shoots result and it is destructive to the plants but it is possible to have blanched shoots in winter using this technique, and by holding the dormant crowns in refrigeration it is possible to harvest late, into May.

Raise the seedlings as above and line them out in the garden at 30cm spacing, or propagate some budded thongs.

Lift the crowns and bring them indoors from December, pot them into damp sand or soil and keep them completely dark, usually in a warm cupboard, to encourage their shoots. The roots should be discarded after harvesting.

Varieties

There are several seed–raised varieties listed. However, Sea Kale is extremely variable from seed and these variety names are, I suspect, to be treated advisedly. Lily White is regarded as possessing less of the purple colouration which predominates in the wild sort. However, I have grown seedlings from this and the wild sort and have noticed no difference. Ordinary Pink Tipped is almost certainly the wild type, with a pink tinge to it when blanched.

Angers is a named clone, propagated entirely from thongs. Bred at the University of Brittany in France, it is a big improvement on its predecessors, productive and easy to blanch.

Germination Tip

The seeds of sea kale appear to be quite large. In fact, what is usually supplied by seedsmen are the corky fruits, each containing a single seed: these fruits are buoyant and impermeable to sea water, which is how sea kale disperses itself. These fruits can be sown as they are and the seeds will germinate well, albeit slightly erratically. They can be helped to germinate more evenly if the seeds are first extracted from the fruits. The seeds within are brittle and easily crushed, so it is not advisable to thresh the seeds as one would perhaps other kinds of seeds — by flailing or lightly crushing the pods — but instead they need to be carefully extracted by hand. It is very time consuming but it is worth it if you want as many plants as possible to germinate from a single packet of seeds. Since the seed is very expensive to buy (sea kale is very shy to set seed), this is a good economy.

Shungiku, Chrysanthemum Greens

Latin Name – Chrysanthemum coronarium
var. spatiosum
Family – Compositae
Type – Half Hardy Annual
Hardiness – Zone 8
Height – 80cm
Rotation – Treat as Brassicas

The popular Annual Chrysanthemum can be eaten in salads or as a steamed green. A delicious, fragrant vegetable with the bonus of attractive flowers.

Origin & History

Although widely grown as a green vegetable in China, Japan and Vietnam, Shungiku originates in the Mediterranean and Portugal. How it came to be eaten in the East but not in its native area is not recorded. In its habitat it is an overwintering annual, germinating in early autumn and overwintering to flower the next year, withering by mid summer. In cultivation, though, it is a summer annual, grown from spring and summer sowings. It does not tolerate high summer temperatures and is not well-suited to Continental summers.

Uses

Lightly steamed it is a delicious accompaniment to other dishes, particularly in Oriental cooking. It is pleasantly fragrant.

Cultivation

Shungiku should be grown quickly and eaten young. The flowers and foliage are ornamental and so it can be successfully combined with other plants in an ornamental garden. It does not demand a rich soil but plenty of organic matter incorporated will ensure good water retention to give more succulent shoots.

Sowing – Sow direct where it is to grow from April onwards, through to July. It is quite hardy and will tolerate some frosts, but March sowings tend to stagnate while the soil remains cold and should not be attempted. Sow in rows 30cm apart, shallowly in drills and thinly, or broadcast the seeds in blocks and lightly rake it in.

Aftercare – No thinning should be required unless the seedlings emerge particularly densely. Keep well watered and hoe between the rows soon after germination to keep annual weeds down.

Harvesting – Growth is very rapid and the first harvest can be made about six weeks after sowing during high summer, a bit longer at other times. Take off the topmost succulent shoots about 20cm long and leave the lower parts to resprout. Plants will rapidly run to flower and are still edible if they do so — remove the leaves when required, leaving the woody stems.

Varieties

There are no named varieties of shungiku, but there do appear to be two different sorts on the market: one with finely divided leaves, and another sort with leaves which are simpler in structure and much broader, more suitable for the pot. Ornamental varieties of C. coronarium, such as Eastern Star or German Flag, can be eaten, but the yield from them is meagre.

Summer Purslane

Latin Name – Portulaca oleracea var. sativa
Family – Portulacaceae
Type – Half Hardy Annual
Hardiness – Zone 8
Height – 40cm
Rotation – Treat as Brassicas

This fleshy salad plant is tender and tasty, adding zest to a salad. Quick and easy to grow, it is drought tolerant and loves summer heat.

Origin & History

Occurring in most of Europe and parts of North Africa, it is also naturalised in parts of North America, and the wild form has found its way into southern Britain. The cultivated form is quite different from the wild type, fleshier and more upright in habit.

Uses

As a summer salad crop. Young shoot tips are added to salads raw, or can be lightly boiled or steamed and eaten like spinach, or added to soups. Much of the pleasant succulence in the raw form, though, is lost on cooking. Some reports are of the leaves being peppery, but in cooler temperate climates this is not developed.

Cultivation

Purslane is best sown into a warm soil and grown quickly. It can be raised under glass and planted out after frost, but there is little to be gained from this extra effort – Winter Purslane / Miner's Lettuce can be enjoyed earlier in the year instead, having as it does nearly the same texture and flavour as Summer Purslane. Purslane enjoys full sun, although it is tolerant of a wide range of conditions, but not waterlogging. It will tolerate a poor soil but, like any crop, gives better results in fertile conditions.

Sowing – Sow the seed when the soil has warmed, from about mid to late April onwards to early June in most cold temperate areas. The seed is very fine and should be barely covered. Take out drills 30cm apart and sow thinly into shallow drills, the merest depression with a cane or stick being all that is necessary.

Aftercare – Thin the seedlings to leave 15–20cm between plants, hoe to keep down weeds. Thinnings can be eaten. No watering is required after germination, but a light irrigation of the sown seeds will bring them on to germinate more evenly if the weather is dry.

Harvesting – Snip off with scissors or cut the shoot tips when the plants have reached a reasonable size – about 20cm as a guide, but not when the plants are so small that they are weakened. If they are kept regularly cropped, more tender shoots will be produced and the plants become bushier. They will flower towards the end of summer, and these flowering shoots can be eaten, too.

Varieties

There are only two types, neither of which can be termed a variety – there has never been enough variation within this species as a basis for the selection of new types. Green Purslane is the type commonest in Northern European gardens as it is tolerant of low light levels.

Golden Purslane has less chlorophyll than the green type so therefore requires higher light levels. It is the type most favoured on Continental Europe, where conditions better suit it.

Turkish Rocket

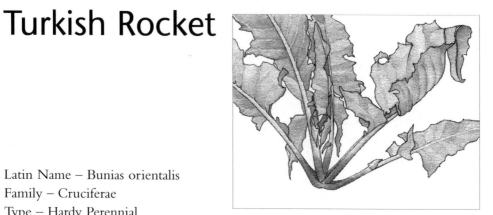

Latin Name – Bunias orientalis
Family – Cruciferae
Type – Hardy Perennial
Hardiness – Zone 7
Height – 40cm
Rotation – Treat as Brassicas

This hardy salad leaf grows anywhere and is perennial, yielding leaves early in the season when they are most appreciated.

Origin & History

This perennial herb is popular in Russia and Poland, where it is native. In Russia it is called Sverbiga. It occurs naturally in waste ground and is naturalised throughout Britain and Europe.

Uses

Large quantities of leaves are produced early in the year when they are most useful and appreciated. They can be eaten young in salads or boiled as greens, or lightly steamed. The young spring shoots are particularly prized, succulent and tasty eaten like broccoli.

Cultivation

Very easily grown, it withstands heat and drought well, and cold winters. It can be treated as an annual or as a perennial and will self-seed. Plants can be allowed to flower without them weakening. The flowers are quite attractive and highly scented, attractive to bees. A sunny situation suits it best, in soil of medium fertility.

Sowing – Sow in rows, direct where they are to grow in drills 40cm apart, sown 1cm deep. The seeds are quite large and can be spaced 10cm apart. In a deep bed, the seeds can be sown at 30cm stations, equidistantly.

Aftercare – Seedlings grow rapidly and will need to be thinned, leaving them at a final spacing of 30cm. The thinnings can be eaten. Some weed control by hoeing soon after germination is necessary, but the plants soon make a dense covering of foliage, smothering out most regrowth.

Harvesting – Leaves should be taken as and when needed. Turkish rocket is most valued as an early spring vegetable. The whole head of overwintered plants can be cut for the kitchen. The roots should then be discarded to make way for another crop, or they can be left to regrow.

Varieties

There are no known varieties. Sometimes seed of the common rocket, Eruca sativa, is passed off as Turkish rocket. The two are easily distinguishable by their seeds: those of rocket are small, variously brown and black, whereas seeds of Turkish rocket are quite large – in fact, more correctly they are a small woody fruit containing a seed.

Rainsplash

One drawback with growing salads through the winter is that they can get very dirty. Heavy winter rains can fall onto bare ground around the crops and splash mud up onto the leaves. They can get filthy, and moreover a gritty soil can molest the leaves, leaving them ragged. For really high quality winter salads they're best grown in a polytunnel, or under a cold frame or cloches. They'll not be any warmer in the depths of winter, but they will be clean.

Walking Stick Cabbage

Latin Name – Brassica oleracea var. acephala
Family – Cruciferae
Type – Hardy Biennial
Hardiness – Zone 6
Height – 2m+
Rotation – Treat as Brassicas

This curious selection from the common cabbage is grown for its
remarkable height. The woody stem can be cut and dried, polished
and made into a walking stick.

Origin & History

Also known as the Jersey kale, Walking
Stick Cabbage is a type of kale that is
peculiar for its height. Many varieties of
kale grow tall, but this selection can, with a
bit of care and attention, produce a single
stem to 2m. Its origins are unclear, but
long-stemmed varieties appear in literature
dating back two centuries.

Uses

The leaves of walking stick cabbage can be
eaten like any other kale, usually boiled,
steamed or braised. It is particularly hardy
and, like all kales, it is an excellent winter
veg. However, it is mainly grown for the
stem.

Cultivation

Walking Stick Cabbage is grown like any
other kale. Kales are best sown quite late
into the spring, or even into early summer
– indeed, if they are sown very early in the
year they tend to run to seed. After the end
of April is a safe time. Traditionally they
were sown into a nursery bed, then
transplanted, bare root, to their final
positions. This is a good method as far as
making economic use of resources is
concerned (i.e. it does not involve pots,
compost or time spent watering). However,
by growing them in small pots or cells,
transplanting shock is completely
eliminated. This is particularly important
with walking stick cabbage if it is to grow
a really long, thick stem by the end of the

year. Because they are raised later in the season, kales are a good follow-on crop from early potatoes, for instance. Walking Stick Cabbage especially benefits from a well-cultivated soil to which lots of organic matter has been added. A sunny site is recommended. While a very long stem will be produced if it is grown under semi-shade near trees, it will likely be curved and will certainly be weak and spindly, no good as a walking stick at all.

Sowing – Sow from the end of April to early June, direct into cell trays of seed-sowing medium and cover lightly. Or you can sow them thinly into dwarf 15cm pots and prick out either into cells or into individual 9cm pots after they have germinated. The latter container is best if you want to get them growing robustly from the start. Seed can also be sown thinly into a nursery bed, rows spaced 20cm apart. Once the seedlings have made 3-4 true leaves, they are levered out with a fork for transplanting, leaving as much intact root on them as possible.

Aftercare – Plant them out at a spacing of 50cm each way, or even 80cm or 1m if you can spare the space, for really stout stems. It is important to plant Walking Stick Cabbage firmly. This is advice given for all Brassicas – if they are not planted into a firm soil they tend to get very easily blown over – but it particularly applies to a crop as tall as Walking Stick Cabbage. They can be planted quite deeply and they will root adventitiously from the stem, which further

helps them to anchor. Give them a good watering in with a watering can without a rose fitted, using the force of the water to wash the soil well around the roots, then tread either side of each plant with the heal of your shoe to really get them firmed in. Firming of the soil like this is contrary to the ethos behind the deep bed method of cultivation: if you are reluctant to firm your soil, it is possible to plant them loosely but then they will need the support of a cane, or a stout stake. Keep the plants free of weeds, and a mulch with organic matter is particularly beneficial.

Harvesting – A few leaves can be taken from each through the season. Sometimes the most succulent leaves can be gathered from a kale around the growing point, and indeed the growing tips themselves can be harvested, which encourages branching. But with Walking Stick Cabbage it is important that the growing tip is not taken so that the stem can keep extending. If you wish to make a stick, the stem is at its woodiest, and therefore sturdiest, by the middle of winter. Cut the whole length of stem and leave it to dry somewhere warm and, of course, dry. It can be polished and varnished after it has completely "cured", and fitted, perhaps, with a brass finial.

Varieties

Walking Stick Cabbage is the variety name, or sometimes listed in catalogues as Jersey Kale.

Watercress

Latin Name – Nasturtium officinale
Family – Cruciferae
Type – Hardy Perennial
Hardiness – Zone 6
Height – Trailing to 80cm
Rotation – Treat as Permanent bed

Watercress is one of the most vitamin-rich greens known. It does not
need to be grown submerged in water and will grow equally well
kept wet at the roots.

Origin & History

Watercress is a common plant of brooks,
streams and rivers' edge throughout
Britain, central and southern Europe and
western Asia. It has been gathered as a wild
plant for many centuries, but it was only
brought into cultivation during the 19th
century, at first in natural shallow river
inlets (most famously at Chesham,
Buckinghamshire, originally called
Cresham) and then later in artificially-
created pools fed by running water. The
running water ensures that the pools do
not freeze solid, to provide a year-round
supply of cress, and to ensure the freshness
of the water – stagnant water can
contaminate the crop, endangering the
consumer. Watercress is very sensitive to
water-carried pollutants, such as slurry or
sewage, and requires a high pH of 7.2 or
above, so chalk streams are favoured.

There are two types of cress, both of them
found wild: Nasturtium officinalis & N.
microphyllum. The latter is often
distinguished as One-Rowed Watercress
(the seeds are in one row within the pod)
The completely sterile naturally-occurring
hybrid between the two is called Brown or
Winter Watercress; it is quite hardy and
turns brown through the winter. It was the
form most commonly cultivated up until
World War II, before it became plagued by
virus disease. Watercress is now mostly
grown from seed, to avoid viruses

transferred from N. officinale, and grown in pools fed by chalk springs. Watercress has been introduced to New Zealand and North America, where it has become a pest.

Uses

Although mostly used as a garnish it is an excellent vegetable in itself, in soups or as a sandwich filling or as a salad And it is extraordinarily vitamin-rich, containing every important vitamin and considerable quantities of iron.

Cultivation

If a source of running water is to hand then it is simplicity itself to grow watercress: sow the fine seed about 15cm above the low water line of a stream, river or brook and it will more or less look after itself. The risk with gathering watercress from the wild is the risk to humans from water-borne diseases and parasites. It should only be taken from sites which have been proven to yield clean watercress, and then taken only in small quantities to ensure its continuation. You also need to be sure that what you are gathering is watercress! (see below) With a little ingenuity, though, it can be grown in the garden. Bear in mind that it requires running water (which is the same as freely-draining water), never stagnant water which is a danger to the watercress and to you.

Preparation – Dig a shallow pit or trench 30cm deep and 60cm wide and put a 10-15cm layer of organic matter such as manure or compost in the bottom. Replace 10cm of the top soil deep to cover the organic layer. Soak the ground thoroughly. Is is wise to create this bed in the previous autumn or winter to allow the organic matter to settle and for the pit to become naturally inundated over winter. Be sure, though, that it does only become inundated, not waterlogged: the water should drain gradually, albeit very slowly through the winter.

Propagation of watercress is from seed, which ensures virus-free plants but takes a bit longer, or from cuttings which can be obtained by using cress bought from the greengrocer.

From cuttings: In spring insert the shoots 15cm apart into the bottom of the prepared trench.

From seed: Sow into shallow drills 15cm apart, and thin the seedlings to 15cm apart when they are large enough to handle.

Aftercare – The trench needs to be inundated with water on a daily basis, twice during really hot weather. It is not necessary to fill it to the top with each watering, but aim to submerge the plants a few centimetres before the water drains. When the plants have made a few centimetres of growth, put a shallow layer of gravel around the base of them to prevent the leaves getting dirty from water splash.

Harvesting – Shoots can be cut as soon as the plants are large enough. The more they are cut, the more leaves are produced and on bushier plants. Watercress can be cut nearly all the year round when grown in running water, but does get damaged by frost in extreme weather. It is possible to grow it under glass through the winter, in shallow pots with the base immersed in water. The water should be changed daily. Growth will be slow but they stay green, unlike plants outside which may get to look very sorry for themselves. They will green up again come the spring and can be cropped for many years. Cold winds can be damaging and it might be wise, during the most extreme winter weather, to cover the trench with a lid of some sort.

It is possible to grow small quantities of cress in old polystyrene boxes, the type that fish gets sold in and which can usually be obtained for free. They have a large capacity and drain very slowly. Fill it with potting medium and sow on the surface or insert a few cuttings, and of course keep the boxes well watered throughout the year.

Varieties

There are no known varieties. Wild watercress will do just as well in cultivation, and is just as good to eat, as the sort bought from the grocers, or grown from seed.

Look Alike

Be sure, when gathering watercress from the wild, that you're picking the right plant. Fool's Watercress (Apium nodiflorum) is a relative of celery and looks like watercress for most of the year. Its flowers, though, are more like those of hedge or cow parsley – an umbel; watercress flowers are more like those of lady's tresses or Alyssum – a white cross-shaped flower. Fool's Watercress is not edible, but fortunately nor is it toxic.

Wild Rocket, Italian Meadow Rocket

Latin Name – Eruca selvatica
Family – Cruciferae
Type – Hardy Perennial
Hardiness – Zone 7
Height – 50cm
Rotation – Treat as Brassicas

This wild relative of rocket is very hardy and ornamental, with attractive scented flowers. Unlike common rocket, the leaves are still good to eat when the plants flower.

Origin & History

From the Mediterranean, this is one of many species of the Eruca family which are edible, and good to eat.

Uses

As a salad leaf. The leaves are hot and should be combined with bland-tasting leaves such as lettuce, or the aromatic leaves of shiso. The leaves are slightly tougher than common rocket but have an excellent quality all of their own, preferred by many chefs.

Cultivation

Wild Rocket is very easy to grow, and freely self-seeds. Although it perennial, it is better grown as an annual. It will come through all but the most severe winters intact, but the plants rarely recover sufficiently from a bad winter to yield a useful crop the following year and are best grown fresh from seed each year. They like full sun, but will tolerate semi-shade and a rich soil will yield better quality leaves, although a poor soil is tolerated. This sort of rocket is better suited to growing in containers than common rocket.

Sowing – Sow in spring, as soon as the soil is workable, in drills 20cm apart, 0.5cm deep. Seed is very fine and care has to be taken that it is not sown too densely, or too deep – a drill which is little more than a slight impression in the ground is sufficient, and the seeds barely covered.

Aftercare – Keep the area between rows free of weeds by regularly hoeing. Development is quite rapid and the plants are able to look after themselves amongst a light infestation of weeds. Unlike common rocket, it does not require frequent watering to maintain the quality of the leaves. Wild Rocket will run to seed in mid summer and can be allowed to do so. The flowers do not take anything from the plant, they are highly scented and enjoyed by bees. The plants self-seed readily, and it's a good idea to remove the flowers after they have gone over to prevent them setting seed and potentially becoming a nuisance.

Harvesting – Leaves are taken when they are required. Rather than cut the whole plant, it is less destructive to take a few leaves from each. Plants will keep producing right through the summer, into early winter in some years. They do not need to be successionally sown for a successional crop.

Varieties

There are no known varieties.

Differences

The term rocket itself comes from the French roquette; in Italian, rucola; in Russian, eruka posevnaya, hence the Latin name Eruca. The common rocket is Eruca sativa (or in some references Eruca vesicaria spp. sativa). This is the sort once very commonly grown in Britain and now enjoying a revival (albeit a rather over-priced one considering the ease with which it can be grown). It is an annual and runs to seed quickly but makes a good catch-crop between crops, maturing in 40 days. Wild rocket is the sort described above. Nominally Eruca selvatica, its true nomenclature is obscure. Olive-leaved rocket is Eruca vesicaria, the true species as opposed to the subspecies E. vesicaria spp. sativa under which name common rocket was once widely known.

Turkish rocket is a different genus altogether, Bunias, but with culinary characteristics very similar to the Eruca species. All of these can be easily (and are frequently) confused with one another, but none should be confused with the ornamental Hesperis matrionlis – a food plant of the Orange Tip butterfly, but not good eating for us.

Roots

Plants grown principally for their roots, but some have the added bonus of edible leaves, like Madeira vine. Some of these are ancient vegetables — bulbous rooted chervil, skirret and Hamburg parsley — which have been displaced by the potato. As an alternative to radish, rampion is a vegetable of folklore. The poor relations of the vegetable garden, scorzonera and salsify deserve to be widely grown.

The Andean tubers (mashua, oca, ulluco, yacon) share their origins with the potato and are particularly well suited to growing in cool temperate climates. With a little more selection and careful cultivation they could become viable, blight–resistant alternatives.

Roots from the tropics are becoming increasingly better known, and many, such as Water Chestnut and Sweet Potato, can be attempted in cooler climates.

American Groundnut, Potato Bean

Latin Name – Apios americana
Family – Leguminosae
Type – Hardy Perennial
Hardiness – Zone 3
Height – Climbing to 4m
Rotation – Treat as Legumes

From North America, this was a staple food of the native people and a life-saver for early settlers to the continent. It has great potential for selection for better yields.

Origin & History

Native to North America, from New Brunswick to Colorado and south to Texas and Florida, this tuber was eaten by the native Americans long before the first Europeans arrived. It is rumoured to have been a life-saver for the Pilgrim Fathers, who were sustained by a diet of Groundnut through their first winter in the New World. Some authorities suggest that this was the "potato" brought to England by Sir Walter Raleigh. There are reports of it being grown as a crop in France in the 19th century, but it has since fallen out of favour. Recent breeding work in the US should revive its fortunes as an edible plant.

Uses

Boiled, baked or roasted, the flavour is similar to potato but slightly sweeter. The Menomini made a preserve from the boiled tubers mashed and mixed with maple syrup. The seeds can be used like peas or beans.

Cultivation

Groundnut is not difficult to grow. On the contrary, it persists very successfully if left unharvested, and it seldom makes a nuisance of itself. The tubers develop on long rhizomes, appearing as swellings along the rhizome's length like a string of pearls. They enjoy a rich soil and position in full sun or dappled shade. Because they climb, they generally find their way to where they prefer to grow. They can be grown from seed, but growing from tubers ensures that you are growing successful cultivars from named material. Plants grown from seed may take 2-3 years to reach maturity. Potato Bean is unusual in that tubers can be eaten at different stages, the "daughter" tubers (the tubers produced the same year as planting) as much as the "mother" tuber (the tuber which is planted and from which the "daughter" tubers are produced, and which may be several years old). A heavy, wet soil, to which lots of organic matter has been applied, suits Groundnut best. It is originally a plant of marshy places but is quite adaptable in cultivation.

Planting – Space the tubers 30cm apart in double rows, each block set 50cm apart. In fact, an arrangement like that used for growing runner beans is best, with wigwam or row supports of bamboo canes provided for them at planting time. Planting is from May. This may seem late for a hardy plant like Groundnut but it coincides closely with their time of emergence – they have a very long dormancy and it might be as late as early June before they start to appear above ground. Plant the tubers deep, about 7-10cm.

Aftercare – Groundnut produces vigorous twining shoots which need to be encouraged onto their supports when they first emerge to prevent them finding their way into neighbouring crops (or clustering around each other) and becoming a nuisance. If the soil is well-drained, the vines will need copious watering during dry weather and they are apt to drop their leaves if left short of water for too long. Heavy weed infestations are tolerated but for the best tubers and the biggest yields, weeds should be kept down, regularly if possible. Near the end of the season, in August and September, flowers are produced. These are highly scented and decorative and can be left on without them weakening the plants. They seldom set seed in short summer areas.

Harvesting – The plants die down to indicate that tubers are fully formed. They are best stored in the ground, and will shrivel if they are dug and stored anywhere dry and warm. Indeed, this can be fatal for the tubers, and they seldom regrow from tubers which are replanted after they have been allowed to become excessively dehydrated. If particularly harsh weather threatens to freeze up the ground or make it too waterlogged for harvesting, they can be lifted and stored in plastic bags with a few slits cut into them for ventilation.

Varieties

Many new varieties are being developed by Louisiana State University, for heavier yields and, most importantly, for bigger tubers.

Aquarius – The variety with the largest tubers of any, but not the most productive. Large tubers are more useful in the kitchen.

Corona is imilar to the above but tubers produced more abundantly.

Draco is not as high yielding as most varieties, but markedly more flavourful and abundant.

Gemini is particularly high-yielding variety.

Lyra-Large tubers comparable to Aquarius, but with smoother skin which is another important consideration for the kitchen.

Orion has good yields of tubers produced close to the mother tuber, making harvesting easier.

Serpens is an old selection from the wild type, not significantly an improvement but mother tubers can reach a considerable size.

Sirius has abundant tubers produced close to the crown.

Groundnuts

American Groundnut should not be confused with peanut, Arachis hypogea, also sometimes called groundnut. Peanuts are a true nut; they're called groundnuts because, once the flower has been pollinated, the developing seed pod is thrust into the ground where it develops and ripens. Peanuts cannot realistically be grown without artificial heat, but they do occasionally meet with success grown by children (see Introduction).

Babbington's Leek

Latin Name – Allium babbingtonii
Family – Liliaceae
Type – Hardy Perennial
Bulb Hardiness – Zone 6
Height – 1m
Rotation – Treat as Onion family

This British native is a useful substitute for garlic. A striking addition
to the vegetable or ornamental garden, it produces bulbils on the ends
of the flowering stalks.

Origin & History

Babbington's Leek is a very interesting
plant, found naturalised in sand dunes in
the southwest of England, the north
European coast and in Ireland, having
probably escaped from gardens. It is in fact
a very rare plant in the wild, and is
afforded protection under law wherever it
is found. Some references name it A.
ampeloprasum var. babbingtonii, classifying
it as a subspecies of the cultivated leek, and
it is sometimes offered under that name in
catalogues. However, recent work to classify
this plant has placed it as a separate species:
it actually has more in common with garlic
(Allium sativum) than it does with the
garden leek, particularly as far as its

strength of flavour and use in the kitchen is
concerned.

Uses

It can be used wherever garlic is used. The
underground bulbs are very large, like
jumbo garlic but stronger in flavour.

Cultivation

The long, erect flower stalk of Babbington's
Leek carries a mass of small bulbils as well
as flowers, rather like Egyptian onion. It has
never been known to set seed and these
bulbils can be used for propagation. It can
also be propagated from the daughter bulbs
which form as offsets from the main basal
bulb, in the same way as garlic is grown

from cloves. Babbington's leek is very accommodating in cultivation and will grow in most soils, even one which is waterlogged for part of the year. It is undemanding of fertility and tolerant of weed competition so can be grown on waste ground in the poorest of soils. Its only demand is a position in full sun. Unlike other garlics it is entirely hardy and it does not need to be lifted and dried, so it can be grown in a permanent bed and lifted when required.

Planting – Babbington's Leek will stand close planting, and indeed gets quite crowded after a few years from the bulbils falling naturally from the flower stalks and growing under the parent plants. But plant at a widish spacing to start with, when creating a new bed. Push them into the soil so that they are buried with their tips about 1cm below the soil surface, and space them about 10cm apart. If planting a permanent bed, putting them in at an equidistant spacing in a block is an efficient use of space.

Aftercare – Very little, attention needs to be given to Babbington's Leek. The plants grown from the bulbils will be quite small

at the end of their first year and should be left to develop for about another year before attempting to harvest them. A quicker result is achieved if they are propagated from daughter bulbs, which tend to be a bit bigger than bulbils so give a better head start. Underground bulbs have a very hard outer skin and it is a good idea to slit this hard coat just before planting to liberate the developing plant.

Harvesting – They should be ready after late summer, when the bulb has had a chance to bulk up and when the bulbils have fully formed. Dig up the bulbs when needed. They can be lifted and stored if required. Babbington's Leek bulbs have remarkable longevity, and it is possible to store them for over a year, after which they still have enough vitality to grow away when replanted.

Varieties

There are no named varieties, but there is a form with red bulbs and bulbils. It remains rare.

Bulbous Rooted Chervil

Latin Name – Chaerophyllum bulbosum
Family – Umbelliferae
Type – Hardy Biennial
Hardiness – Zone 7
Height – 15cm
Rotation – Treat as Umbelliferous

At one time grown by the field-full, this once popular root deserves the attention it demands in cultivation for its gourmet flavour.

Origin & History

A native of Southern Europe, introduced to British gardens in 1726 and, like a lot of vegetables were when first introduced (runner beans and tomatoes, for example), initially grown as an ornamental. It is popular in France and Italy where its roots, similar in flavour and appearance to short parsnips, are highly prized for their sweet and floury flesh – which has often been described as 'farinaceous'. It was once grown widely in Britain on a field scale but has never been high yielding. In Watson's 'The Gardener's Assistant' (1902) an estimate of total yield is given: "The produce is from 60 to 70 pounds per square pole or perch, or a dish from about a square yard." Detailed advice is also given about overcoming its dormancy. William Cobbett, Parliamentarian and gardening guru writing in 1829 in his 'The English Gardener,' makes no mention of it at all despite it becoming the vogue throughout Europe at the time. He mentions the herb Chervil, though (Anthriscus cereifolium), with which this bulbous sort should not be confused as it is quite a different plant of a different genus, but of the same family.

Uses

As a vegetable delicacy, lightly steamed with only the merest hint of seasoning, eaten on their own or as an accompaniment to fish or roast meats.

Cultivation

Bulbous Chervil would be a very simple crop to grow and surely a more popular one if it were not for its recalcitrance in germinating from a spring sowing. No amount of selection over the years has resulted in a seed strain which will germinate without any pre-treatment. Work continues to overcome its dormancy, notably at Horticulture Research International, Warwickshire where Brian Smith championed this crop for many years. They have so far been unable to "break the code" but do offer the following cultivation notes which I have also had success with. These notes differ little from the recommendations given in 'The Gardeners Assistant' a century ago.

To germinate, the seeds need to undergo a period of warmth followed by a period of cold. This is known as vernalisation (literally, experiencing winter). It's a process familiar to any gardener who has attempted to raise trees and shrubs (and some ornamental perennials) from seed but is perhaps not so familiar to the vegetable grower. The simplest method is to sow the seeds in autumn, preferably early autumn (September, October) while the soil is still quite warm. The seeds will take on water but they will not immediately start to emerge. Instead, the water activates some of the enzymes within the seed which starts its internal clock ticking towards spring. Warmth is the first trigger which gets the process started, then a period of cold is the second which shuts some enzymes down and activates some others; these sensitise the seeds to the arrival of spring. When spring arrives, the seeds can be seen to emerge. This is not when they germinate! They actually started germinating when they were sown in the autumn.

This is a complicated explanation of what is in fact an even more complicated biological process. But from the gardener's point of view, it's actually quite simple: sow the seeds in autumn, don't expect them to emerge straight away, up they'll pop in the spring when they're ready to and conditions are right. It's really that easy. What is tricky is that this is not what we're used to when sowing vegetable seeds. Also while the seeds are lying in the ground over winter they are vulnerable to animal and insect predations, waterlogging and compaction of the soil surface by winter rains can hinder their emergence, they might be completely forgotten about and something else sown in their place instead, or they may get turned under by subsequent cultivations. To avoid all these problems it is better to sow them under a cloche or a cold frame. This keeps the worst of the winter rains off while still allowing the cold in to activate all the seeds' chemical triggers. The plants are never going to be very big, so sow in rows 15cm apart, any narrower and you won't be able to hoe between them. Space the seeds thinly if you can. I find sowing in early autumn to be a very leisurely pursuit and I take my time to space the seeds, which are quite easy to handle, at 5cm spacing. They can be sown thicker and thinned later. Cover them with a cloche or frame and leave them alone until late winter. Ensure that the soil is not too dry through the winter, maybe leaving the top off on some wet days to moisten the soil.

Emergence can be as early as February so you can start hunting for seedlings from then on. Once they're all up, you can take off the cover as they're quite hardy. The seedlings grow away very quickly with lengthening days. No particular attention is needed apart from the usual weed control by regular hoeing. Growth is always quite spindly and delicate, so be careful not to chop any off when cultivating near them. By the end of June, the foliage will have died off and the roots will be ready for harvest. This is not when you usually expect to be harvesting root

vegetables, so it is very easy to end up unwittingly clearing them out of the way to make way for another crop, forgetting that they are there. This early summer maturity is actually very convenient for following on with other crops. For example, they could be followed by winter Brassicas. I cannot stress too much how important it is to harvest the tubers as soon as they are ready because otherwise they will be eaten by mice. If there's a crop that mice simply cannot resist, it's Bulbous Chervil. While they're growing they can be vulnerable, too, so a net cloche or wire mesh cover helps keep them off. Store them somewhere cool and dark. The 'fridge rather than the shed, which can tend to overheat in the summer.

Varieties

There are no known varieties of Bulbous Chervil. Many varieties may, at one time, have existed. There is scope for selection for an increase in the size of the roots. If a seed strain can be created which germinates without the need for vernalisation, that would be a major breakthrough.

Burdock, Gobo

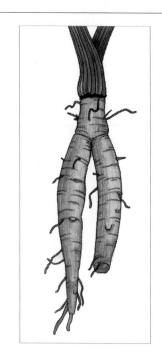

Latin Name – Arctium lappa
Family – Compositae
Type – Hardy Biennial
Hardiness – Zone 3
Height – 50cm
Rotation – Treat as Umbelliferous

The Burdock of hedgerows is valued in Japan as a root vegetable, and elsewhere as an ingredient in soft drinks. But be careful where you site this horticultural bully.

Origin & History

Burdock grows wild throughout Europe to the Caucasus, and it is unusual that a plant which is not native to the Orient is better known as an edible in Japan than it is in its place of origin. It is thought to have been introduced to Japan via China, where it was used as a medicine. Having escaped from gardens, it is now naturalised on Hokkaido and in North America.

Uses

The roots can be boiled until soft, or eaten raw if the root is very young. The Japanese favour pickling lengths of root and serving them with a sweet brown sauce. In Britain,

extracts from the root are used as an ingredient in the once-popular fizzy drink Dandelion & Burdock. In the USA it is an ingredient in Root Beer.

Cultivation

Burdock root does have a reputation for becoming woody, and the roots can be small in comparison to the amount of leaf produced. This usually happens if Burdock is sown in the spring and harvested the same autumn. However, if the roots are sown in autumn and then harvested in the autumn of the next year a worthwhile crop can be produced. In mild climates this is practical, but in harsh winter areas they fare better from a spring sowing. Burdock is expansive and hungry for water and nutriment, so careful siting is necessary, away from plants which may be shaded by its broad foliage. Deep cultivation to incorporate plenty of organic matter will be rewarded.

Sowing – This is done direct into drills made 50cm apart. The seeds are quite large: sow two to a 40cm station, fill in the drills 2cm deep. If autumn sowing this should not be too early or the seedlings will become too large and therefore not as resilient to the ravages of winter weather as smaller seedlings are. Late September to early October is a good time, because it usually coincides with the onset of wetter weather, aiding germination and establishment. Spring sowing can take place as soon as the ground becomes workable.

Aftercare – No winter protection is needed for overwintering plants. They should be thinned to a single plant at each station as soon as the days start getting milder in late winter. Regular hoeing is necessary between the young plants, whether autumn or spring sown, but the canopy of foliage soon becomes dense enough for all weeds to be smothered out. After then, very little attention is needed apart from applications of water during drought conditions.

Harvesting – This can start from early autumn onwards. Foliage will be cut down by frost but the roots are quite hardy and can be left in the ground all winter where they will remain unharmed. However, if the ground threatens to freeze hard, hindering harvesting, they can be dug and stored in damp sand, plastic bags or in a clamp. They grow down to a considerable depth and you can count yourself lucky if you manage to dig one out in one piece. If the bottom half of the root has to be abandoned to the soil, it will not be a nuisance the next year as pieces of broken root do not regrow.

Varieties

Cultivated Burdock differs from the wild type in that less foliage is produced in relation to the size of the root. Wild Burdock has been used in the past. However the root tends to be small and woody in plants which have flowered or are about to flower.

A variety, Gobo, commonly encountered in Western seed lists, is probably just a type rather a distinct variety, named as it is with the Japanese name for Burdock. It differs little from the wild type.
Takinogawa Long has relatively small leaves and good root production.
Watanabe Early is a better variety for spring sowing and quick developing.
Mitoya Shirohada has whiter roots than normal, smooth surfaced with a tender texture, growing to just 1m which is quite shallow for Burdock.

Chinese Artichoke, Crosnes

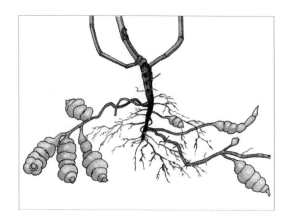

Latin Name – Stachys affinis
Family – Labiatae
Type – Hardy Perennial
Hardiness – Zone 6
Height – 50cm
Rotation – Treat as Permanent bed

Although the tubers are small, these are a real vegetable delicacy, favoured for French gourmet cooking. An excellent winter vegetable, very hardy & easy to grow.

Origin & History

Correctly attributed by its name as originating in China, Chinese Artichokes are also popular in Japan where they are regarded as an extra special vegetable. They're particularly esteemed there as they resemble jade when they are freshly dug. They are a relatively recent introduction to Europe, first presented in 1882 to the Société d'Acclimatisation in Paris, and grown in the garden of M. Pallieux, vice-president of the Société in his home in Crosne, hence the popular French name by which they are often called (pronounced crow–nay), a name under which they are sometimes listed in restaurants. For a long time, the French thought them to be of Japanese origin thus their full name, Crosnes du Japon.

Uses

Lightly steamed or boiled for 5 to 10 minutes, they can be tossed in butter, or eaten cold in a vinaigrette. They require no peeling, but should be thoroughly scrubbed to remove all earth, which tends to accumulate in the deep ridges of the tubers.

Cultivation

Chinese Artichokes are one of the easiest vegetables to grow. They are a very hardy perennial, so you will need to be careful about siting them as they tend to persist. It is probably better to give them a permanent bed rather than attempt to harvest all the tubers before following with a different crop. As they are not susceptible to pests and diseases it is quite safe to do so. A light soil is suggested, but I've grown them successfully in a heavy soil which has been elevated, for example in a raised bed, to ensure good drainage. If they get waterlogged in winter, the tubers will rot. It is also difficult to harvest the tubers in a heavy soil. They enjoy a rich soil and a position in full sun, although they seem to grow well in semi-shade. They are propagated entirely from tubers.

Planting – Space them equidistantly 15cm apart, plant 7cm deep. It is pointless growing them in rows as they tend to be far ranging and will soon break their bounds but putting them in in rows is a convenient way of planting a large area. Growth starts early in the year, so aim to finish planting before the end of March.

Aftercare – Chinese Artichokes require the minimum of care. They don't like to be dried out, and any weeds early in the year will be quickly smothered out by the dense foliage, but you should remove the worst of these if you are establishing a new bed. It is quite natural for them to flower, although the flowers are nothing to get excited about – they are small and pink. They do not need to be removed as they take nothing from the plant.

Harvesting – This begins as soon as the foliage is killed off by frost, usually after October. They are entirely hardy and should be left in the ground until needed. They easily shrivel if stored, so they're best lifted when needed, fresh. If the ground threatens to freeze hard, cover the bed with a thick mulch: this will freeze rather than the soil, and can be lifted off to reveal the tubers in workable soil underneath. I like to grow them through a thick organic layer. The tubers tend to grow near the surface, in this layer, making harvesting easier and the tubers much cleaner.

A permanent bed of Chinese Artichokes does not require harvesting every year for good yields. Unlike other hardy tubers (Jerusalem Artichokes, for instance) they do not dramatically deteriorate through overcrowding. They can be left to get on with it, benefiting only from an occasional mulch to maintain soil fertility and to retain moisture. The occasional thinning they receive as the result of harvesting will be all the thinning they require. I find that a good crop can be grown from the residual tubers left after attempting to harvest the crop completely. Most years I take up all the tubers I can find, but some will be left behind, no matter how diligently I have combed through the soil. These residual tubers grow away and produce a good crop, without the need to replant. By thinning them, slightly larger tubers result.

Varieties

There are no known varieties of Crosnes.
The plants do sometimes set seed, but they
are so easily grown from tubers that
seedlings are pointless, and show no
variation as a starting point for selection.

Will Chinese Artichokes become a nuisance?

If you are desperate to get rid of your artichokes and are not an
organic gardener, regrowth can be treated with a systemic herbicide.
Another way to get rid of them is to mulch the area with a light-
excluding layer to smother them out. A further method, if you are
patient and don't need the bed at the beginning of the season, is to
let them grow away as normal in the spring and through early
summer. Then when they are full size and coming into flower, dig
them all up. You don't have to be thorough as the plants will have yet
to produce any tubers. It is the tubers which are the nuisance as they
are the means for the plant to propagate itself, no tubers equals no
regrowth.

Chinese Yam

Latin Name – Dioscorea batatus
Family – Dioscoreaceae
Type – Hardy Perennial
Hardiness – Zone 6
Height – Climbing to 2m+
Rotation – Treat as Solanaceous

Normally regarded as a tropical crop, this hardy relative grows well in temperate gardens.

Origin & History

From China, Korea and Japan, this is one of 600 species of Yam. Out of that many, one of them is bound to be hardy, and this one is, in areas where winters are mild. Yams have been cultivated in the tropics since ancient times, and are an important staple in parts of Africa where they are grown on smallholdings rather than on any kind of field scale as a commercial crop. They are quite slow to mature, taking two or three years to produce a worthwhile tuber. Many yams are poisonous, and some are used for medicine. Chinese Yam was introduced to Europe, at first to France, by the French consul in Shanghai in 1848. It is naturalised in parts of the US.

Uses

Boiled or roasted, they are an important ingredient in West African cookery. They can be used in any dish which requires potatoes. They are floury when cooked, and are eaten in Japan combined with egg yolk and soy sauce.

Cultivation

Chinese Yam is very quick growing but slow to produce a tuber: from three to four years if grown from bulbils, two years if grown from a section of root. It needs support and although it is hardy it is best started off under glass and then planted out. To extend the season it should be grown entirely under protection. Chinese Yams have never been known to set seed, although they often flower profusely towards the end of the season. The flowers are insignificant, although highly scented of cinnamon, hence its other name of Cinnamon Vine.

Chinese Yam requires a rich soil, and some references insist on a well-drained one although I have been successful growing it in a heavy, even a waterlogged soil. Harvesting the long, club-like roots requires digging down to a considerable depth and I suspect that a light soil is of more benefit to the grower than it is to the plant. Instead of seed, the vines set bulbils in the axils of their leaves, near the end of the shoots. The plant can be propagated from these bulbils or a section of tuber can be planted. They can also be grown from cuttings taken from the shoots as they first develop in the spring.

Growing from bulbils – These are black, almost spherical, and drop off easily from the vine as the leaves start to colour at the end of the growing season. Care has to be taken that these do not become prematurely dislodged when gathering them as they are very easily disguised against bare soil and amongst undergrowth. They can be planted in early spring, individually in 9cm pots of potting medium to start with. They climb immediately they emerge (emergence can be erratic) and should be provided with a short split cane or similar support. They will make little progress in their first year and should be potted on as they develop. Ideally, they succeed best in a "long-tom" pot, the type commonly favoured for growing containerised rose bushes, to accommodate their long root.

Growing from tubers – Small tubers, perhaps tubers raised from bulbils the previous year, can be lined out at 30cm spacing and provided with support. It is better to pot these tubers on at first, to bring them on under gentle heat before planting them out after the danger of the last spring frost has passed.

Growing from sections of tubers – The top section of a large tuber can be cut off and grown on in the same way as growing from small tubers. The bottom section can, of course, be eaten.

Growing from cuttings – The shoots which rapidly emerge in the spring can be detached and rooted. If they are severed from the parent tuber with a piece of the root attached, they grow away readily once they have settled down and will form a new tuber, albeit a small one, by the end of the season.

Harvesting – Roots are fully formed when the top growth starts to die off. The foliage turns a very beautiful golden yellow in the autumn. The tip of Yam tubers usually starts at about 20cm below the soil surface, and the tuber can extend to 1m long. This root is very difficult to dig up in one piece! And to complicate matters, it is very brittle. It is best to dig a trench as deep as possible next to the root, then pull the root away sideways into it. I favour growing my plants in large containers. Although they grow in a spiral around the bottom of the pot and require watering and feeding, I can be sure of harvesting everything.

Varieties

There are no known varieties.

Chufa, Tiger Nut

Latin Name – Cyperus esculentus
Family – Cyperaceae
Type – Hardy Perennial
Hardiness – Zone 8
Height – 60cm
Rotation – Treat as Onion family

Related to Papyrus, this rush-like plant yields small tubers of exquisite flavour. Not productive, but worth attempting as a gourmet veg.

Origin & History

Originating from Southern Europe eastwards to India, and into North Africa. It has been found in ancient Egyptian tombs dating 2000BC. The Tiger Nut has been cultivated for a long time, but is rarely eaten. It is hardier than most other members of the Papyrus genus and though not grown for its tubers necessarily, it is a fine ornamental for pond margins.

Uses

The tubers are aptly named as they are very like nuts, in appearance and flavour, and banded with stripes. The flesh is yellow, sweet and with a nutty flavour. They are delightful eaten raw, seldom are enough produced to warrant cooking them, but they can be lightly boiled or steamed. In Fearing Burr's 'Field & Garden Vegetables of America,' he says that "when dried and pulverised, they are said to impart to water the colour and richness of milk".

The ancient Egyptians cooked them in barley juice, and ate them as a sweet meat. The Spanish, too, either eat them sweet, and make a drink, horchata de chufa, from them with water, cinnamon, sugar, vanilla and ice, or eat them savoury roasted as tapas. Roasted tubers can also be used as a coffee substitute. They yield a high quality oil, comparable to olive oil.

Cultivation

Tiger Nuts are quite hardy but they yield better where summers are good, or if they are given a head start under glass or with cloche protection in colder temperate areas. They enjoy wet conditions and grow naturally at water margins but take to being grown "terrestrially" if they are provided with lots of moisture. Suffice to say, they enjoy a well cultivated soil which has been enriched with organic matter, and mulching is also beneficial. They lend themselves to being containerised, the base of the container immersed in water, cultivated in a similar way to Wapato (see page 143).

Plant the tubers in spring. Outdoors they can be planted into drills made 5cm deep, 60cm apart and the tubers spaced 15cm in the drill. To bring them on indoors, pot them one tuber per 9cm pot, buried 1cm below the surface. Keep in gentle warmth and grow them on until they are ready to be planted out, into a warm soil when all danger of frost has passed, at the end of May or the beginning of June at the same time spacing as tubers planted direct.

Aftercare – They require no particular attention apart from weeding. They're very robust and can withstand quite a dense weed infestation. In a dry season they will need extra watering if they are grown in open ground.

Harvesting – The tubers are ready when the plants have been cut down by frost, or when they are starting to yellow. Dig up the clumps with a fork and work the tubers out from the dense roots. They do not shrivel when dried and can be stored for a considerable length of time. Even tubers which have been in storage for over a year remain viable for growing from.

Varieties

There are no known varieties of Chufa. The subspecies var. sativa has larger, banded tubers which are better for growing for eating than the type species.

Egyptian or Tree Onion

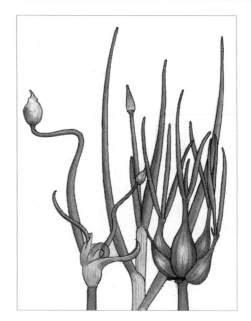

Latin Name – Allium cepa var. proliferum
Family – Liliaceae
Type – Hardy Bulb
Hardiness – Zone 6
Height – 40cm
Rotation – Treat as permanent bed

Rather than seeds, this curious perennial onion produces plantlets at the end of its flower stalks. These arch over and root, giving this onion its other name of Walking Onion.

Origin & History

The origin of this type of onion is unknown. It is derived from the cultivated onion which is known to have been first grown by the Egyptians in 3200BC but may have been in cultivation for long before then. Onions are unknown in the wild, several species with similar characteristics exist in Central Asia to China although none of them are compatible with the cultivated onion. Any attempts to hybridise with them have resulted in sterile plants.

Uses

Through the summer, the stems and stem bases can be used in place of scallions or spring onions, or eaten like Chinese Chives. In winter, they're used in place of shallots. It is a useful onion for bridging the "hungry gap", the period when onions in store are starting to sprout and just before the new crop is mature.

Cultivation

Tree Onion is particularly hardy and long lived. It is evergreen and will grow continuously: it is possible to harvest it in winter although growth is, of course, much slower at that time of the year. It responds well to a rich soil and good cultivation, full sun and no waterlogging. It can occupy the ground for many years so be careful about siting if it is to remain undisturbed. Having said that, it does transplant readily and is easy to propagate.

Plant the bulbs in spring or autumn, pressing them into the ground at 25cm spacing. They require no particular aftercare apart from regular weeding. By midsummer they send up flowering stalks which give rise to the clusters of bulbs at their apex, each with a leaf. Some flowers are also produced. On vigorous plants these bulbs may in turn give rise to further subclusters of bulbs on their own flower stems. Left to their own devices, the stems arch over and the bulbs root into the ground, hence Walking Onion. The plants are clump-forming and can become quite congested in time, so after a couple of seasons it may be necessary to thin clumps a little to re-invigorate them.

Harvest the bulbs from the flower stalks when they are ready and use them like spring onions (scallions), or they can be left through the season right into the winter and used when needed. The basal growths can also be detached from the main clump and eaten like green onions. By winter the bulbs "tunicate" (become clothed in a skin of dead leaf scales) and they can be used in place of shallots.

Varieties

There are no named varieties of Egyptian Onion. There do appear to be two types, though: one with brown skin, the other red.

Since it is a form of the common onion, Tree Onions are susceptible to the same pests and diseases that attack onions. It is not wise, for instance, to plant them in ground which has become infected with Onion White Rot as Egyptian Onion is equally susceptible, and therefore just as likely to perpetuate this insidious disease.

Hamburg Parsley

Latin Name – Petroselinum crispum var. tuberosum
Family – Umbelliferae
Type – Hardy Biennial
Hardiness – Zone 7
Height – 40cm
Rotation – Treat as Umbelliferous

This is a parsley that has been selected for its thick, parsnip-like root.
The tops are aromatic and can also be used.

Origin & History

Parsley is common throughout most of
Europe, having been dispersed from
Southern Europe by the Romans. It is not
known as a wild plant, and any that are
encountered in the wild are thought to be
escapees. It was also grown by the ancient
Greeks; Theophrastus wrote about it in
320BC. Parsley is now naturalised
throughout most temperate countries in
the world. The "herb" parsley, grown
principally for its leaves, is a common
commercial crop and garden plant, but the
tuberous form, Hamburg Parsley, still
remains relatively unknown. It is
occasionally seen in markets in Eastern
Europe and in Russian, where it is an
important ingredient of bortsch, but few
other places besides.

Uses

The roots can be peeled, then boiled,
roasted or added to stews and casseroles
where parsnips would be used. In Eastern
Europe it is used quite imaginatively. Jane
Grigson reports of them being used in hare
soup in Bulgaria, and in Croatia as an
ingredient in a pig's trotters soup. There's
also a traditional recipe for Hamburg eel
and beef soup, incorporating the parsley
root.

The leaves can of course be used in the
same way as other parsley. It is a flat-leaved

**GROWING
UNUSUAL VEGETABLES**

type, which many chefs consider to be superior to the curled-leaved sort.

Cultivation

Parsley is simple enough to grow once it has been persuaded to germinate, but for some gardeners that's the rub. It does have a certain reputation for being stubborn, and while some growers report great success using a particular technique, other gardeners may be met with complete failure following the same instructions. While I cannot suggest a panacea for getting parsley to germinate unfailingly, if you bear in mind the following pointers, success ought to follow:

Only fresh seed will germinate. It has a viability of only a year, and although it may germinate from two year old seed, taking a risk with sowing old seed considerably reduces the chance of success.

The seed is quite hard-shelled and can be soaked overnight. It is unclear whether any natural chemical inhibitors are present in the seeds, but rinsing the seeds once or twice, or running them under the tap for a few minutes in a fine sieve after soaking, at least eliminates that possibility by rinsing away any which might have been present.

Once germination has been initiated, that is, once the seeds have taken on water, they should not be allowed to dry out. So, keep the seed regularly and thoroughly watered until the seedlings have got well established.

The seed does not like high temperatures. Sowing in late spring into early summer, the temperature of the top two or three centimetres of soil can sometimes be excessive on clear days, and this can inhibit germination. Earlier sowings avoid this possibility. However, parsley can be sown in early spring or in early autumn to give a crop the following spring, in August and September when soil temperatures are often very high. In which case, cover the sown rows with sacking or similar to keep it shaded, but be sure to check regularly for germination. On the other hand, a very cold soil is inhibiting to the seeds and sowings made very early in the year straight into the ground usually meet with failure. Having explained all this, I have on many occasions sown parsley direct into the ground at various times of the year and it has come up like mustard and cress, and that's without me taking any sort of precautions against overheating, nor have I soaked the seed beforehand. There does seem to be a certain alchemy to it.

Even if parsley does germinate well, it always does so slowly and erratically. This usually means that it can readily become swamped with weeds. It is often a good bet to start plants off in cells or modules, to give them a head start.

Sowing in modules – Sow into cells, several seeds per cell, from late winter to late spring. Keep the cells moist, and cover with damp newspaper to ensure that they don't dry out excessively between waterings. Use a seed-sowing medium and barely cover the seeds. Once they begin to germinate, admit light and air and continue to keep the modules well-watered to help along those seeds which have still to emerge. If sowing very early in the year, germinate with gentle bottom heat if possible, around 12°C, but with later sowings the ambient temperature in a cold greenhouse is sufficient. Plant out the modules as soon as the roots have filled them, spacing each 10cm apart in rows 20cm apart. It is important to plant them out in good time so that their tap roots do not become restricted, which can lead to them becoming distorted.

Sowing direct – Sow into shallow drills, no more than 1cm deep and spaced 20cm apart. Sow thinly and don't sow direct until mid April, when the soil has warmed sufficiently. Keep constantly moist and thin the seedlings after they emerge to leave them 10cm apart.

Aftercare – Once it's got going, parsley needs little attention apart from weeding. It is quite slow growing and easily smothered. It is actually quite tolerant of drought once established, but will give a bigger and better quality crop if watered during dry spells.

Harvesting – Take the leaves when required, a few from each plant. The roots are ready by late autumn, and can be pulled when required. Parsley is quite hardy and can be left in the ground through all but the worst of winters, and will stay quite fresh. Stored roots tend to shrivel readily.

Varieties

There are many varieties, but most catalogues do not specify these when listing Hamburg parsley. Mostly it is a rather low-yielding, tapered-rooted sort which is sold. But specific varieties are well worth seeking out.

Bartowich is long narrow shouldered type with a particularly fine flavour, nutty. Best sort for autumn sowing for winter and spring harvests.
Berlin Half Long is short and stocky sort, with wide shoulders, root not tapering. Introduced 1908.
Early Sugar is small but particularly sweet flavoured. Best for heavy soils where other varieties may become misshapen.
Hamburg Half Long is half-long, wedge-shaped roots, like a short Chantenay carrot. Commonest variety in the US.
Hamburg Long – The commonest European form, with narrowly tapering root to 23-28cm long.
Omega is a variety with a flavour likened to celeriac. Thick roots, cylindrical.

Jerusalem Artichoke

Latin Name – Helianthus tuberosus
Family – Compositae
Type – Hardy Perennial
Hardiness – Zone 5
Height – 3m
Rotation – Treat as Umbelliferous

While not really within the definition of 'unusual', Jerusalem Artichokes deserve to be more widely grown. Many varieties exist which have a lot to offer. Eaten regularly, they give no ill effects.

Origin & History

Jerusalem Artichokes are not from Jerusalem (they're from North America, from Arkansas all the way up to Ontario) nor are they artichokes in the sense that globe artichokes are. It's the tubers that are eaten. They get their name from a corruption of the Italian 'Girosole', meaning sun root in allusion to their resemblance to sunflowers, which botanically they are. On the other hand, it might be that because they became a staple for the pilgrims to the New World, the "new Jerusalem". More recent dispute is over which came first, the Italian name or that of a 17th century gardener named Petrus Hondins of Ter-Heusen, Holland who was known to distribute his artichoke

apples throughout Europe. Like 'girasole', his name became corrupted to Jerusalem. The name Sunchoke is coming into regular use lately as a name that is less of a mouthful.

Uses

As a root vegetable they are underrated, and have a reputation for being difficult to prepare. Some varieties are much smoother than the types usually grown, and if they are cooked with their skins on and peeled afterwards, the skin is much easier to remove and less is wasted.

They are excellent for thickening soups, or as a soup ingredient in their own right, because they impart a unique smoothness and density. They have a flavour which is widely described as "smokey".

They are sometimes grown as a commercial crop for the production of a sugar that can be tolerated by diabetics. Fructose can also be synthesised from them, too.

Cultivation

Artichokes have a reputation for being one of the easiest vegetables to grow (and they are) but have ended up with a bad reputation because neglectful cultivation only leads to poor crops, and therefore disappointment. As with any crop, you get out what you put in, and good cultivation is rewarded with excellent yields of flavoursome, good quality tubers. They are mostly all very tall (3m) so make excellent windbreaks, but they do cast heavy shade so site them carefully. One variety, though, is dwarf and makes an excellent addition to the ornamental border. Dig the soil deeply and incorporate plenty of organic matter. It is usually recommended that root crops are not grown on freshly manured soil as it leads to forking and hairiness of the roots, but this is not the case with Jerusalem Artichokes as they love a rich soil and plenty of moisture.

Planting – Draw out a deep trench or put them in with a trowel, either equidistantly in a block in a deep bed at 30 cm apart, or in rows 40cm apart at 20cm spacing. Double or treble rows work best, or they can be grown in a deep bed equidistantly spaced at 30cm. They emerge quite late, and when 30cm tall they can be earthed up a little. Rabbits are keen on the emerging shoots, but their predations do no harm to the plants, which end up being more densely branched than they would otherwise be.

Aftercare – No other care is needed apart from weeding, but being tall they tolerate, and indeed smother out, a fair amount of weed infestation. In extreme drought, they should be watered to avoid the tubers becoming too knobbly.

Harvesting – They are frost hardy, and the leaves do not so much get frosted off as turn naturally yellow with the increasingly colder and darker weather at about the end of October, when the tubers have matured. Cut the stems down when they've turned yellow so that they don't rock the tubers out of the ground in winter storms. The tubers are best left in the ground as they shrivel if stored in paper sacks. They can, though, be lifted if you like and stored in plastic sacks with a few holes cut in them, but you're likely to experience a few rotten tubers this way however it means you can have fresh tubers when the ground's too frozen to dig.

Because they're so hardy, they do tend to persist and the next year it's highly likely you'll have a few stray tubers come up on the site where they were grown. Wait until they are a fair size and then fork them out

– they can all be got rid of easily this way. If you don't get round to eating or lifting all your tubers, it's important that they are all lifted and replanted into improved soil. While they can be left on the same piece of ground undisturbed year after year, they quickly become crowded and the soil impoverished, with tiny, overcrowded tubers which are quite useless. They don't accumulate viruses (like potatoes might, for instance) so it is easy, if a bed has become overcrowded and seemingly useless, to refresh old stock by lifting and replanting.

They will generally flower in the United Kingdom about one year in five or during an Indian summer. In most parts of the United States they will flower regularly.

Dwarf Sunray tuber

Varieties

Dave's Shrine was first collected by Dave Briars of Vermont. Plants grow to 2.2m in the UK, maybe more where the climate suits them better. The long, fat tubers are higher in dry matter than most other varieties, and are red skinned. It is actually possible to make fries from them – if you haven't tried artichoke chips, this variety is a good starting point.

Dwarf Sunray is a short variety suited to exposed gardens, growing to no more than 2m. The tubers are knobbly but very high yielding, and cluster around the plant's main stem – this results in fewer stray tubers after harvest. It flowers unfailingly in even the shortest summer and most northerly climate, coming into flower in September in most years.

Fuseau is the one most recommended as the easiest to prepare and most flavoursome, and also (at the time of writing) most widely available named variety. The tubers are quite long and smoother than others, making peeling easier. Growing to over 3m. I've not known it flower in the UK, but I'm sure it will on its native patch.

Garnet is the other one of the two red skinned varieties. Very high yielding, it grows to over 3m. Red skinned varieties produce very long, easy to prepare tubers. Fuseau has the reputation for being the easiest to prepare, but I would argue that it is this variety or Dave's Shrine which are easier, being smoother and more elongated. Stampede is a particularly early maturing variety, popular in the United States, maturing in 90 days.

Sugarball is sweeter than the other varieties (hence its popularity for commercial diabetic sugar production). It produces huge quantities of knobbly tubers on plants just 1.7m tall. Like Dwarf Sunray, it is a good bet for an exposed garden, but does

not flower reliably in short summers. Wilton Rose is a tall variety (2.7m) that arose as a distinct seedling in a renowned collection. It has elongated rose and cream tubers, mottled; the colouration remains on cooking if they are not peeled.

Flatulence

Eating Jerusalem Artichokes has a reputation for anti-social after-effects. The first time they are eaten this can, alas, be the result, but if they are eaten regularly you will find that ill effects will abate after a while.

They contain a sugar called levulose (a sugar useful to the production of sweeteners for diabetics and for which purpose they are grown commercially). We cannot digest this sugar, but the flora and fauna in our stomachs can. When we eat them, all the sugar in the roots is made available to the micro-organisms naturally inhabiting our digestive tracts. They have a party on all this sugar, the result being that they produce a lot of gas, which we are then, to avoid discomfort, forced to vent. But if they're eaten regularly, the microbes calm down somewhat when faced with a regular feast of levulose, and consequently things calm down for us, too. Used in soups or as a thickener, any ill effects are further lessened.

Jerusalem Artichoke - Plant Habit

Jicama, Yam Bean

Latin Name – Pachyrhizus erosus
Family – Leguminosae
Type – Half Hardy Perennial
Hardiness – Zone 10
Height – Climbing to 3m+
Rotation – Treat as Legumes

A climbing bean which is grown principally for its tuber, but the young pods are also edible.

Origin & History

Originating in Tropical America, Yam Bean is grown mainly for its root, but also for the immature seed pods. It is capable of growing tubers 2m in length and weighing as much as 20kg. However, it is the immature roots which are eaten; older tubers become woody and unpalatable. It is naturalised throughout much of Florida.

Uses

Roots are crisp, juicy and sweet, hence its other popular names of Potato Bean and Mexican Water Chestnut. They can be eaten raw, stir-fried, added to stews and casseroles, or braised or boiled. Their crunchiness is retained after cooking, and they're good sprinkled with salt, chilli pepper and lemon juice after being thinly sliced.

The pods can be picked when very young and must be boiled thoroughly. Mature pods contain the toxic principal rotenone, a natural pesticide.

Cultivation

Although Jicama is easy to grow in temperate regions, it is very sensitive to day length. Tubers are not formed in day lengths over 14-15 hours. For this reason, the tubers are only produced in late autumn, as a response to shortening days. Outdoors, this often coincides with the first frosts. Indoors the vines should be encouraged to grow large. They will then have enough energy to put into producing sizable tubers before the onset of cold weather and low light levels. The further south it is grown, the better the chance there is of growing big tubers. Even if it does perform below expectations some years, Yam Bean is highly ornamental and is worth growing for its long rhizomes of violet and purple flowers.

Sowing – Two to a 9cm pot, then thinned to the most vigorous seedling if both seeds germinate. A seed-sowing medium should be used, and the seeds germinated at 20°C. They grow quickly and will need moving on to larger pots after a short time, each provided with a short stick for support. Sowing time depends on the time of the last frost in your area and how big you are prepared to allow the plants to grow before they are planted out. Although they are dependent on shorter days for the tubers to be formed they won't produce even the skinniest of tubers all summer. However, the more top growth is produced the better set up they are for tubers to be formed when the days shorten. So, if you can pot them on and keep them frost-protected until they can be planted out, a sowing time of about the end of April will ensure large plants.

Aftercare – If they're to be planted out, space them 20cm apart and grow them as you might grow runner beans. The vines are actually very similar, and conditions have to be the same for them before considering planting them out. The soil needs to have warmed and all danger of frost passed. A support consisting of a wigwam or row of bamboo canes is needed to support the twining stems. I incorporate them with my runner beans, a few snuck in at the end of the row. Growth is as vigorous as that of other climbing beans when they're at full spate, and they're quite capable of reaching 7m in their native habitat, but they stay smaller grown in temperate areas. If they do get a bit too big for their station, their tops can be pinched out This is supposed also to encourage their tubers.

Under glass, they should be potted on until they are in large tubs, or they can be grown in the greenhouse border soil. Wherever they are grown, they appreciate liberal watering and they're heavy feeders, so a deep, rich soil is beneficial, as is a position in full sun.

Harvesting – This should be as late as possible in the season. Once the top growth has got frosted off the tubers can be dug. Pods can be picked as soon as they are large enough, if you are adventurous enough to try them, but pods which are mature should be avoided.

Varieties

There are no known varieties. If a really good individual is discovered which shows good potential to produce usable tubers in temperate areas, it can be propagated by reserving its tubers for replanting the next year, splitting it into individual shoots once it has sprouted.

Holey seeds

The seeds of Jicama are sometimes riddled with holes. This is caused by Bean Seed Weevil, an insect pest which infests the seeds where they are produced. If the beans are kept stored for long enough, the grubs inside the seeds hatch into adults. However, if seeds with holes in are sown, you might be surprised to find that they germinate perfectly well. It appears that the weevils selectively eat away at the seed. They tunnel through most of the food store part of the seed while leaving the vital parts (the embryo, the bit that actually grows into a plant) completely intact.

If you think that the weevils may increase and become a nuisance, they can be killed off by deep freezing the seeds (ensuring that they are completely dried beforehand using silica gel) for a few days.

Madeira Vine

Latin Name – Anredera cordifolia
Family – Basellaceae
Type – Half Hardy Perennial
Hardiness – Zone 9
Height – Climbing to 6m
Rotation – Treat as Permanent bed

A perennial vining plant for greenhouse or conservatory. The leaves
and the knobbly tubers can be eaten.

Origin & History

Madeira Vine is not from Madeira, but has
become naturalised there, as it has in many
subtropical parts of the world. It was
introduced there from its native South
America where it grows from southern
Brazil to northern Argentina. It has been
grown for a long time in Europe as a
curiosity, and for its scented flowers (similar
in scent to Mignonette) but all parts of the
plant can be eaten.

Uses

Leaves can be eaten raw. They are succulent
and mucilaginous. They do not stand being
cooked, turning to useless mush. The
tubers are very knobbly and difficult to
prepare, but can be eaten like potatoes.

Cultivation

Madeira Vine is a very resilient plant, and
although it is classed as half-hardy I have
found it able to withstand very low
temperatures while dormant, as long as it is
kept quite dry. It is tolerant of drought and
poor soils. Where hot, dry weather is
experienced, it thrives. Although it grows
well outdoors in most summers, it is best
accommodated in a greenhouse or
polytunnel as long as space is not limited, it
does tend to rampage once it has got
going. It is grown from sets.

Planting – Plant sections of tuber spaced about 30cm apart. Provide a support of canes, string or netting – it climbs by twining. You can take your cue for planting from the emergence of new growth.

Aftercare – Very little attention needs to be given, and it is very forgiving of shortfalls in watering or feeding. The vine may need to be pruned back occasionally if it is becoming a nuisance to its neighbours, or if it is excluding too much light.

Harvest the leaves when needed. The tubers are ready when the plant goes dormant in late autumn, when all the top-growth dies back to the rootstock. Dig the tubers up and store them somewhere dry and frost-free, but not somewhere warm where they may shrivel. I have, however, left the tubers in the ground over winter and as long as they remained dry enough, they've grown away vigorously the next spring.

Varieties

There are no known varieties.

Madeira Vine Tuber

Mashua

Latin Name – Tropaeolum tuberosum
Family – Tropaeolaceae
Type – Half Hardy Perennial
Hardiness – Zone 8
Height – Climbing to 2m
Rotation – Treat as Solanaceous

The Tuberous Nasturtium has been grown for thousands of years in the Andes. Easy to grow and productive, it can be stored through the winter like potatoes.

Origin & History

Mashua originates in the high Andes and is an ancient crop in Peru growing alongside potatoes, oca and ulluco where it was first cultivated by the Incas. It is a relative of the common garden Nasturtium, which it closely resembles and which originates from the same part of the world. It has been in cultivation for so long that its ancestry is unclear, but the modern Mashua is a triploid, similar in characteristics to the wild subsp. sylvestre.

Its introduction to the West is obscure, but experimental crops are now grown in New Zealand where, like other tuberous crops from the Andes, it is proving to thrive.

Mashua is known to have nematocidal, bactericidal and insecticidal properties and is considered by the Andeans to be an anti-aphrodisiac.

Uses

The raw flavour of Mashua is quite sharp, but it is mellowed by cooking. The flavour is fragrant, with a slightly vanilla taste. Traditionally they are a component of stews in the Andes, or baked or fried with eggs and onions. There are reports of the tubers being soaked in molasses and eaten as sweets. Young tubers can be eaten whole but older, larger roots should be peeled. The flowers and leaves can be eaten: they have a sharp flavour like that of Nasturtium.

Cultivation

Mashua is a climber and needs some support, but otherwise it is grown in the same way as potatoes, in a rich soil with plenty of organic matter added, and in full sun. It prefers warm rather than hot weather and it is frost tender, so a maritime climate suits it better than the a hot continental summer. For the same reason, it does not particularly enjoy glasshouse conditions. It has a reputation for being daylength-sensitive, forming tubers when days are twelve hours or less. In areas where early autumn frosts threaten, this may hamper tuber production. However, if the daylength-neutral cultivar Ken Aslet is grown this should not be a problem. It is grown from tubers.

Planting – Tubers can be started off in pots under glass or on a windowsill, planted individually in 12cm pots of potting medium. However, progress is slow at this early part of the year and I have found little advantage in raising them early. Instead, I plant the tubers direct where they are to grow, at 30cm stations in a position in full sun, although they will tolerate some shade. They should be planted 3cm deep and given some protection from slugs. A little cloche protection may be needed in colder areas to bring them on a little, but if they are planted from late May this should not be necessary.

Aftercare – They are slow to appear and it is possible to raise a quick crop between the plants while they are developing. They should be kept free of weeds at first, but once they get going the foliage is dense enough to smother any further seedlings. Provide a support of netting, and I have also found rings of fencing wire to be effective. Although they can climb to 2m, in most years they make about 1.5m and they can be allowed to sprawl. Growth is dense and bushy and they do not climb well up individual canes. They require constant water and will go dormant if they are allowed to stay dry for long periods, often before the tubers have reached full size. A good thick organic mulch helps retain moisture.

Harvesting – The plants can be allowed to be cut down by frost before an attempt is made to dig the tubers, to allow them maximum time to develop. Dig the tubers and allow them to air dry before putting them into paper sacks for storage in a dry, frost-free place.

Pests and disease – Mashua is not subject to any specific pests, but it does have a propensity to accumulate viruses, including those which affect potatoes. The same precautions used to isolate potatoes from the spread of virus should be applied.

Varieties

Ken Aslett is the only variety worth attempting in cold temperate regions. It appears to yield the largest tubers.

There are other forms which can be attempted in warm areas (but which will probably not fare well under glass, unless summer temperatures can be kept low).

Subsp. pilifera is grown in Colombia. It has slender white tubers with a purple apex. Subsp. tuberosum has bright red flowers and deeply cut small leaves, small tubers.

Who was Ken Aslett?

He was the supervisor of the rock garden at the Royal Horticultural Society's garden at Wisley, Surrey, and was instrumental in bringing the daylength-neutral form of Mashua into cultivation.

Mashua tubers

Oca, New Zealand Yam

Latin Name – Oxalis tuberosa
Family – Oxalidaceae
Type – Half Hardy Perennial
Hardiness – Zone 7
Height – 30cm
Rotation – Treat as Solanaceous

This Andean tuber has a similar flavour and texture to potatoes but is not troubled by the same pests and diseases; a useful alternative.

Origin & History

Oca is a very popular crop in Peru and Bolivia, where it has been cultivated alongside potatoes for thousands of years, and in New Zealand, where it was introduced from the Andes in 1869. It is unknown as a wild plant. In Europe it has enjoyed varying popularity over the years, and if it had been persistently selected in the same way as potatoes it might today be enjoying the same popularity. It has been grown and eaten in Britain since its introduction in the 1600s.

Uses

Anywhere that potatoes are used, Oca can be used instead. As a salad tuber it is particularly fine, having a similar texture and firmness as a salad potato; they are a little too waxy to be successfully mashed, but they deep fry superbly. In their native Andes they are left in the sun for a few days after harvesting to shrivel and reduce their acidity – they have an oxalic acid content which some people find unpleasant, similar to that found in unforced rhubarb or in spinach. However, I have found that, grown in Northern Europe at least, they develop none of this and are quite without sour undertones. They're delicious eaten raw, too: very crunchy and refreshing.

Cultivation

New Zealand Yam is day length dependent, tubers are not formed if the day length is over 12 hours. In practical terms this means that they form at a time of year when, in most cold temperate regions, the first frosts start to threaten. It is therefore important to encourage them late in the year, rather than aim for a very early planting.

Propagation is by tubers: no seed strains are known. Start them off as you would seed potatoes. Chit them (that is, encourage the tubers to sprout) in a cool and light place such as a shed or garage, keeping them frost-free. A windowsill is good. If chitting is delayed or is not possible, it is not absolutely vital that they have been encouraged to form sprouts as their main growth is made after mid-summer. Plant the tubers out when all risk of frost has passed. There is little to be gained by planting very early, and I have found no benefit in early planting under cloche protection. Space about 30cm apart in rows 60cm apart, or equidistantly at 40cm. I like to grow them at this latter spacing in deep beds, and they are particularly suited to this method. This spacing might seem excessive compared to the size of the tubers, but the foliage does become quite extensive.

Aftercare – As the plants develop, they soon begin to look like giant Wood Sorrel, to which they are related. It is unnecessary to earth them up as one would potatoes as they do not become poisonous if they turn green, and the density of the foliage tends to blanch any which appear on the surface. The plants are quite neat and tidy in habit. I have found that only one weeding is necessary, after then, the foliage becomes so dense that further annual weeds get smothered out. Some yellow flowers are sometimes produced later in the year, but fruits are rarely set.

Harvesting – It is important to wait for as long as possible. You cannot realistically expect tubers until the end of October at the earliest. You might be tempted to inspect the plants for tubers forming in late summer, but usually there is no sign; the tubers seem to grow right at the last minute, when a full canopy of foliage has been built up. A light frost will sometimes harm the tips of the foliage, but leave the top growth on for a little longer as further growth is often made if milder weather then follows. Only when the leaves have completely turned to mush should you dig them up. Insert a fork near the centre of the plants and lift – the tubers do not extend out very far so they are all easily gathered in. The colourful tubers are very easy to spot, and should be detached from the stout rhizomes. Sometimes the odd tuber or two forms where a stem has rested on the ground. Leave them to dry a little on the soil surface, then store in bags in a cool shed.

Pests and disease are almost unknown with Oca. Unlike potatoes, they do not suffer from blight or wireworm, scab or blackleg. They do accumulate viruses, but not outside their native haunts. In Peru and Bolivia, Oca Weevil is a major problem which has fortunately not migrated. That they do not accumulate virus is a great advantage to gardeners in cold temperate regions. It means that tubers can be saved from year to year for replanting without any loss of vigour.

Varieties

There are several different forms, differing in the shape and colour of their tubers. None have specific variety names, only Spanish or Andean names descriptive of them: there are purple, yellow, red and very dark, almost black, tubers; some that are short and others that are long, some that are a shape in between. The form most commonly grown in New Zealand is long (about 10cm) and red, and is the sort best suited to growing in cold temperate regions.

Is Oca the next Potato?

It's been a rocky ride for many plants which have now become staples the world over. The potato, for instance, didn't at first seem to be a strong contender to become the West's most important form of storable starch. When they were first introduced to Europe (and not, as is too often incorrectly reported by Sir Walter Raleigh, but by the Spanish conquistadors) potatoes grew well enough but gave poor yields; also, the tubers did not store for any length of time, sprouting soon after harvesting. But a few dedicated horticulturists saw potential in this plant, and grew thousands of seedlings. They saved seed from these (from the stronger and better yielding ones) and grew thousands more. They at first got the yields increased and, with further development, tubers which went dormant for a long time so that they were storable. As for tomatoes, they were at first thought to be poisonous and for decades they were grown only as an ornamental.

Oca might today be as successful and ubiquitous as potatoes if it had been worked on as hard as they were when first introduced. Of course, it would be an advantage if they set seed in most climates, so that seedlings could be obtained to work from.

Oca Tubers

Rampion

Latin Names – Campanula rapunculus,
               Phyteuma orbiculare campanulaceae
Family – Campanulaceae
Type – Hardy Biennial
Hardiness – Zone 7
Height – 10cm
Rotation – Treat as Umbelliferous

Two different plants with the same name and function, but both
edible members of the Canterbury Bells family. Roots are eaten like
radishes, raw in salads, along with the leaves.

Origin & History

Like Bulbous Rooted Chervil, this was
once a widely grown and eaten vegetable,
held in high esteem. It is a native of
Northern Europe, and Britain. The Grimm
fairy tale Rapunzel (another name for
rampion) revolves around the stealing of
rampion from the magician's garden. John
Evelyn in his Acetaria describes it as the
"esculent campanula, the tender roots eaten
in spring, like those of radishes, but much
more nourishing." In actual fact the roots
grow through the summer to mature in
the autumn, but they are hardy and can be
dug for use in the spring. Several different
varieties of Rampion existed before the
1820s which were selected, like carrots, for

different lengths and shapes of their roots.
They all appear to have died out since.

Uses

Eaten raw, they can be used like radishes in
a salad. They lack radishes' heat, but have
the same freshness and crispness which
makes them so pleasant. The leaves are
good raw, too, or briefly steamed.

Cultivation

Rampion is fairly quick growing and, like
radishes, can be sown between other crops
before they get too big.

Sowing – Rampion is not particularly
straightforward as the seeds are so tiny. It is

a hardy plant, but it is better to wait until late spring or even early summer before sowing as it is inclined to run to seed if it is sown earlier. Mix the dust-like seed with fine sand and sow this mixture into a very shallow drill, little more than a slight depression in the earth. Mixing the seed with the sand helps to distribute the seeds evenly and makes them less difficult to handle. Because the seeds are close to the surface, you will need to water the drill, if it looks like it is becoming dry, until the seedlings emerge. Drills can be close together, no more than 20cm, but not so narrow that you cannot then hoe between them. Once they start to show themselves, you can start thinning the seedlings. Larger thinnings can be used as salad leaves, aiming for a final thinning to a 10cm spacing.

Aftercare – This is simple enough: regular hoeing to keep down weeds, and watering in drought conditions. Rampion is always inclined to run to seed, although not as readily as radishes (with which it is difficult not to make a comparison), so it should be kept well watered during dry weather. The roots start maturing in late summer into autumn. Pull them as required. You can selectively pull leaves through the summer to use.

Varieties

There are no named varieties of Rampion remaining in existence. The fact that there were once many different forms proves that there is scope for selection for root shape and length, and for yield.

There are two different Latin names for Rampion listed in the heading. Why?

Campanula rapunculus is the one most commonly offered in catalogues as Rampion and is the one that I have grown and used as Rampion. The other, Phyteuma orbiculare, is so similar as to be easily interchangeable and in some parts of the world this is what is offered. If you look up Rampion in botanical references, both are usually listed. They are both grown and eaten the same way, and they're both in the same family. Phyteuma is well known as an alpine plant, and enjoys good drainage and full sun. It's very ornamental; indeed they both are when allowed to flower.

Rocambole, Serpent Garlic

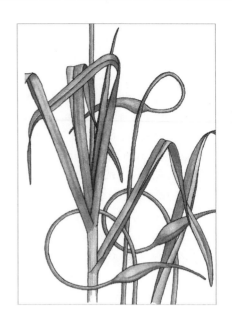

Latin Name – Allium sativum var. ophioscordon
Family – Alliaceae
Type – Hardy Bulb
Hardiness – Zone 6
Height – 60cm
Rotation – Treat as Onion family

A garlic with serpentine flowerheads that execute an elegant sinuous bend as they develop. Early and productive, it makes a striking feature in the ornamental kitchen garden.

Origin & History

Garlic has been in cultivation for so long that its true origins are blurred. It is perhaps derived from the wild Allium longiscuspis, and it was grown as long as 5000 years ago by the ancient Egyptians. The Rocambole Garlic of cultivation is derived in turn from garlic, and has been selected for its curving flower stems and ability to set bulbils rather than true seed. Another species, Allium scorodoprasum, is often called Rocambole and is usually known as the Sand Leek. It differs in having upright, rough-edged leaves and purple colouration; it is naturalised in sandy parts of Northern Europe, including the British Isles, but originates in Eastern Europe and the Caucasus. Milder than garlic, it was popular up to the 19th century but is now seldom cultivated.

Uses

Used wherever garlic is, Rocambole is one of the earliest types to mature for fresh use. As a cooked vegetable it is sublime roasted with meats, and a great aid to the digestion.

Cultivation

Both Rocamboles are grown the same way. Sand Leek, though, requires good drainage and should only be attempted on free-draining soils. Remember, too, that it will not produce a curly flower scape like that of the Serpent Garlic.

Planting – This should really be in the autumn for best results, in October, November and even into early December. They are a good follow-on crop after ground has been cleared of summer vegetables. They do not require heavy feeding and indeed do not like freshly manured ground. All garlics are summer flowering bulbs and should be treated thus; while a spring planting is successful, the best crops are obtained planted in the autumn. Garlic withstands more cold and waterlogging than it is generally given credit for, and Rocambole is one of the hardiest. However, if soil conditions really are atrocious for planting in late autumn, you can wait until no later than February and put them out, or they can be brought on in small pots or modules and planted out to the same depth as cloves in spring, just as soon as soil conditions allow.

Rocambole produces two types of bulbs from which it can be propagated: cloves, like a normal garlic (bottom set), and bulbils which are produced on the end of the flower scapes (top set). Bottom sets are not as numerous per plant as top sets. For a good yield in the first year, bottom sets should be used, but for increasing them quickly they can be propagated from top sets. The plants produced from top sets will be quite small the first year, but the bottom sets produced from them will yield heavily the next year. So, spacing should be done as follows:

Bottom sets – spaced 15cm apart in rows 30cm wide. In a deep bed (where they particularly enjoy the good drainage and deep root run) they should be spaced 18cm apart each way. Never plant cloves which are damaged or show signs of disease.

Top sets – spaced 8cm apart in rows 15cm wide. Or equidistantly in a deep bed 12cm all round.

It may be hard to determine which way up to plant the top sets, but don't worry too much if you think they might be the wrong way up as they are capable of righting themselves. Garlic should be planted quite deeply, as long as soil conditions allow. Larger bulbs are produced from a deeper planting, but there is a risk of rotting off if they are planted too deeply in a heavy soil. A good rule is to plant them to twice their own depth, but for optimum yields the biggest cloves should be planted 4cm deep.

Aftercare – This is minimal. Autumn planted bulbs may suffer from a compacted soil surface following winter weather and a shallow cultivation of the soil in early spring alleviates compaction and removes weeds at the same time. Other than that, regular weeding is all that's needed. But if you take your eye completely off the ball, you could miss the best bit! Come early June, Rocambole starts to flower. Unlike most other veg, garlic can be allowed to flower without it harming the plants or the crop, and Rocambole does so spectacularly.

As the flowering scapes form, they curl through 360°. As they develop, the stems straighten and harden until they are quite erect. Flowers form at the top of each, but mostly they produce a cluster of bulbils, tiny bulblets which, when detached (and they remain on the head quite firmly) can be planted and grown on. Rocambole has never been known to set seed.

Harvesting – The right time to harvest is determined by how good a season it has experienced, and in a poor season this might be quite late, into July or August. The leaves will turn yellow to indicate the right time to lift – when the six lower leaves have turned is said to be the optimum stage. Harvesting must be timely if the bulbs are to store properly; if they are left in the ground for too long after

ripening they will soon resprout. Leave the lifted plants out in the sun to dry until they are rustle-dry. It may be necessary to keep the rain off, or dry them under glass or under cloches for best results. Because Rocambole have a hard flower stem running through the middle of them, they cannot be plaited like other garlics, to be hung up for storing – the tops are best cut off, and the bulbs stored in net bags. They will keep for 10 months or more.

Varieties

There are no named varieties of Rocambole.

Salsify, Vegetable Oyster

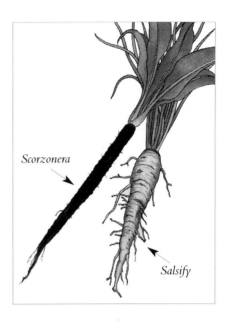

Scorzonera

Salsify

Latin Name – Tragapogon porrifolius
Family – Compositae
Type – Hardy Biennial
Hardiness – Zone 5
Height – 30cm
Rotation – Treat as Umbelliferous

This root vegetable is a popular delicacy in Continental Europe, but remains virtually unknown elsewhere. Easy to grow and productive.

Origin & History

Salsify (sols-í-fee) originates from the Mediterranean as a selection of Tragopogon pratensis, a plant of dry grassy meadows which has become naturalised through most of Europe, including Britain, and is often seen naturalised in roadsides in North America. It is sometimes known as Jack-go-to-Bed-at-Noon in reference to the flowers, which close after the sun has crossed its zenith. Cultivated Salsify is little different from the wild species, differing in its fatter root and slightly broader leaves (porrifolius = "leaves like a leek"). Superior selections of the wild plant probably originated in Renaissance Italy, arriving in England via France in about 1700. There are records of it having been grown in

John Tradescant the Younger's garden in 1656, but no mention is made of whether it was grown as an ornamental or as a vegetable. It remains a very popular vegetable in France and Italy, but is virtually unknown elsewhere.

Uses

The roots are delicious, boiled, braised or baked, or sautéed in butter, or eaten raw in a salad. They make excellent soup. The likeness of their flavour to oysters is fanciful; they're quite nutty. The flowers can be eaten, cooked and dressed like asparagus, or pickled, and the emerging shoots can be blanched in the spring and eaten like chicory.

Cultivation

Salsify is very easy to grow. It likes an open situation, in a well-cultivated soil, preferably one with few stones – the sort of soil which suits carrots is particularly good for Salsify. It must be well-drained, but not freshly manured, which may result in forked roots. Salsify has naturally quite whiskery roots.

Sowing – Direct sow the seed into drills 15cm apart, 1cm deep. The seeds are large and easy to handle, and can be space sown at 10cm, or thinned to this density after emergence.

Aftercare – Regularly weeding by hoeing between the rows, and watering during dry weather is beneficial, although not essential. Watering, though, will ensure good quality roots.

Harvesting – The roots are ready for lifting as soon as they are large enough, from late summer onwards. It is as a winter vegetable that the roots are their most useful, though, and they can be left in the ground through all but the worst weather. If they are threatened with deep freezing in the ground, they can be lifted and stored in boxes of damp sand in the same way as carrots.

Blanching – To produce chards similar to forced chicory, cover the plants in the autumn with a good layer of soil, about 15cm deep, after first cutting off the leaves at ground level. The shoots are blanched as they force their way through. For really clean chards, they can be covered in straw or bracken.

Varieties

Salsify has received little attention from plant breeders, with the result that Mammoth Sandwich Island is the main and, it appears, only variety of Salsify. There's an Improved Mammoth Sandwich Island purported to to be even better yielding, with larger roots.

Sandwich Island

Sandwich Island is a small island off the coast of British Colombia. It is reported that the native British Colombians made chewing gum from the milky latex extracted from Salsify roots.

Scorzonera

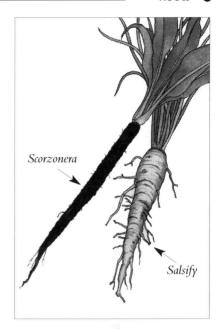

Latin Name – Scorzonera hispanica
Family – Compositae
Type – Hardy Perennial
Hardiness – Zone 6
Height – 60cm
Rotation – Treat as Umbelliferous

This perennial root vegetable is very similar to salsify, to which it related. It deserves to be more widely grown for its long, very hardy black roots. It is a useful winter vegetable.

Origin & History

Scorzonera (pronounced scortz-ó-NEER-a, with an Hispanic inflection) originates in southern Europe, from Portugal across to Russia, all the way to Siberia, but never in Spain. The 'hispanica' was earned due to its early popularity in Spain, from where it was distributed to the rest of Europe. It remains popular in all European countries except the United Kingdom. Like most deep, thick-rooted vegetables, it originates in dry soils in open woods and fields. In many respects it is a similar vegetable to Salsify, differing little in the flavour of its roots and use in the kitchen, and in the way it is cultivated. (The fact that they appear so close together in alphabetical listings in manuals and catalogues is coincidental, but very convenient.)

Uses

Boiled, braised or baked the roots make excellent eating, quite bland but an agreeable accompaniment to meats and fish, or served with a sauce. The roots bleed very easily and will do so if they are peeled before cooking. It is better to cook the roots first, then peel them – the skin then comes away very easily, often in one piece.

Cultivation

Scorzonera is as easy to grow as carrots; easier, some might say, given that the seeds are larger (and can therefore be readily sown thinly) and it is not bothered by the myriad pests which can afflict carrots, like carrot root fly. It does need a stone-free soil to give the roots opportunity to grow straight, and good drainage is required if the roots are to survive the winter outside. Organic matter is appreciated, but a freshly manured soil can result in the roots becoming excessively hairy.

Sowing – Sow direct into rows 15cm apart, 1cm deep. Soon after they emerge, thin the seedlings to 10cm apart.

Aftercare – Keep regularly weeded and water during dry weather. Like most root crops, it will tolerate drought, but better quality roots result if plentiful water is supplied.

Harvesting – It is very hardy (remember it originates in Siberia as well as Liberia) and the roots can be left in the ground all winter. It is perennial and the quality of the roots does not deteriorate with age. It is therefore possible, if the roots do seem to be a bit too small to be useful by the end of their first year from seed, to leave them to grow another year and get bigger. The

roots are ready from October and can be dug when required, or store them in damp sand if the ground threatens to freeze too hard and becomes impossible to dig. The emerging leaves can be blanched into chards in the spring by earthing up the plants in autumn.

Varieties

Black Giant Russian – The most popular variety for commercial production in Europe. Big shoulders, tapering roots up to 40cm long.
Duplex – Cylindrical roots 20–25cm long, blunt ended. Short roots are easy to dig up in one piece.
Flandria – Flavour is supposed to be somewhat reminiscent of coconut. Very uniform roots, cylindrical.
Long John – Uniform, smooth, thick roots.
Maxima – A top variety in Dutch trials. Heavy cropping, good-sized roots resistant to bolting.

Delicious Scorzonera

Anyone who regularly eats Scorzonera will tell you that it is, of course, delicious. But there's another species of Scorzonera, S. undulata ssp. deliciosa, which is commonly known as the Delicious Scorzonera. From the Mediterranean, it is widely used in Sicily for making various confections and sweetmeats: jam, sorbets, ice cream, and, combined with jasmine, a refreshing tea.

Skirret

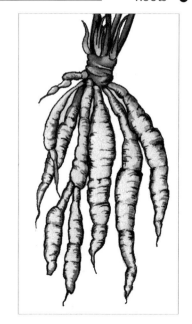

Latin Name – Sium sisarum var. sisarum
Family – Umbelliferae
Type – Hardy Perennial
Hardiness – Zone 6
Height – 1m
Rotation – Treat as Umbelliferous

An ancient vegetable once popular with the Romans. Perennial, it can be divided many times to yield its curious white forked roots. For ease of growing and unique flavour it deserves to be revived.

Origin & History

Skirret's true origins are unknown. In the wild it grows throughout Northern Europe to East Asia, in shallow fresh water. Wild Celery is found in similar places and, like celery, it is as accommodating in cultivation. The wild form, though (Sium sisarum var. lancifolium) does not produce a worthwhile root. The Emperor Tiberius liked Skirret so much that he demanded it as a tribute from the Germans, who reputedly introduced it from China. However some references still insist on its exclusively Oriental origins. The earliest reference to it in gardening literature was by John Worlidge in 1677 who praised Skirret as "the sweetest, whitest and most pleasant of roots ...". There are scant references to it over the last two centuries suggesting that, unlike for instance Bulbous Rooted Chervil, it has never achieved sustained popularity.

Uses

The roots have a reputation for being woody, which they can be if starved of water. It is true that the roots do have a central woody core, no matter how well they are cultivated and it might be this that detracts from them ever becoming popular. The core is easily accommodated if the roots are cooked whole and the outer flesh stripped off the core when eaten. It has a flavour like a combination of carrots and parsley, both close relatives.

Cultivation

Skirret likes a deep rich soil and a position in full sun or partial shade. Although it is a root vegetable, it does not matter if the soil has been freshly manured. I have achieved particularly good results with liberal applications of leaf mould. As it is perennial, Skirret can be propagated from seed or by division, at the end of March / beginning of April.

Sowing – Growing from seed is quite straightforward as long as you don't expect good germination. Since Skirret is basically a wild plant, it has not been selected – as have, say, carrots or beetroot – for rapid, even germination. Fresh seed is best, that saved from the previous year being ideal. It can be sown shallowly into a drill where it is to grow, as one would sow carrot seed, 13-20mm deep in rows 15cm apart. If germination is good (but don't expect any seedlings for at least two weeks), thin the seedlings to 6cm apart. Seedlings can continue appearing for about six weeks after sowing, so you may need to patrol the rows for some time afterwards, thinning and perhaps transplanting. Unlike other root vegetables of its kind – parsnips, for instance – the seedlings will transplant quite satisfactorily without running to seed or producing distorted roots. In fact, they are well suited to being started off in

modules. That way, any poor germination which you may experience is accounted for when they are planted out. Any which do not come up are simply not planted out, and no ground is wasted. There's a widely held belief that sowing in the autumn helps the seeds germinate more evenly after experiencing winter freezing and thawing, which is a technique commonly successfully applied to many tree and shrub seeds. I have not found this to be necessary, but autumn sowing under a cold frame can be attempted using the same technique described for Bulbous Rooted Chervil.

Division is quite easy to do and allows you complete control over which plants to propagate. Skirret is very variable from seed, some plants being higher yielding then others. So keep the best yielding individuals to divide from and discard (or eat) the others. What's lovely about growing from divisions is that you can still have roots for the cooking pot. The plants should not be divided until they have started to shoot. When they're uprooted, it can be seen that each crown has several shoots with fine new roots. These shoots are broken off and replanted, spaced 8cm apart in rows 15cm apart, leaving the roots for the kitchen. By the end of the season they will have made a whole new set of roots, and you know they'll be good ones.

Aftercare – Frequent hoeing to keep down weeds is helpful, especially when the seedlings are small and vulnerable to competition. They don't mind a bit of weediness around them when they are established as they are quite tall and capable of looking after themselves. They appreciate some extra watering to maintain their general health and to prevent the roots becoming woody, and higher yields will result if irrigation is applied during times of drought. Be warned, though: don't take the fact that they start to flower as a cue to start giving them extra water, or to remove any plants which start flowering. It is quite natural for them to flower and they will do so as a matter of course, not because of any shortcoming in their husbandry. If you leave the flowers on you will be able to collect seed from them later.

Harvesting – The roots are ready by the end of summer, just as soon as they are big enough, but it is as a winter vegetable they are most useful. They are quite hardy, and can be lifted for use when needed. Like other root vegetables, they can be lifted and stored in damp sand in a shed if heavy frost or snow threatens so that they don't need to be dug from a frozen soil.

Varieties

There are no specific varieties of Skirret, certainly there are no seed strains. If you do find a particularly good individual, increase it by division. There is a lot of scope for selection with Skirret, for bigger roots or better and more even germination from seed, or for less stringy core. Don't grow Skirret from the seed collected from wild plants as they do not produce a worthwhile root.

Germination

Nearly all modern vegetables germinate well. We can expect that if we sow, say, a packet of radish seeds, we'll see the seedlings all emerge at about the same time, usually within a few days. If they didn't, that would be very inconvenient. If the seeds are slow to emerge, weed seedlings get a hold and weeding them out later becomes complicated. If they are uneven, we cannot be sure about timing our harvest. Wild seeds, however, will nearly always germinate unevenly, which for them is a survival mechanism. Some might germinate early, catching a good spell of weather which may follow through to allow them to mature and set seed. But in a bad year, germinating early may not be so providential, and the seedlings which emerge later catch the better growing conditions and they are the ones which complete their life cycle. All sorts of eventualities have to be covered. Most of what we grow for eating now has been grown for many centuries, and over the years any tendency for the seeds to germinate erratically has been eliminated through selection. Wild Carrots, for instance, germinate over many months; those varieties we grow in our gardens do not.

So it is with some of the crops mentioned in this book. Skirret, Bulbous Rooted Chervil, Seakale – all of these are unselected plants which differ so little from their wild ancestors that they have not had their tendency to germinate erratically bred out of them. If they're grown for long enough and selected further by diligent gardeners, in time their seed will germinate as readily as mustard and cress.

Skirret – foliage

Sweet Potato

Latin Name – Ipomoea batatus
Family – Convolvulaceae
Type – Tender Perennial
Hardiness – Zone 9
Height – Trailing to 1.5m
Rotation – Treat as Solanaceous

A tender tropical crop, recent developments in breeding means that this popular staple can, with a little care and attention, be grown in temperate areas.

Origin & History

Sweet Potato was widely grown in South America by pre-Inca civilisations. Curiously, it was grown at the same time in eastern Asia, and in Polynesia, finding its way to New Zealand where it was growing before the arrival of Europeans. The Spanish introduced it long before the true potato, and early references to potatoes, including those by Shakespeare, were to this crop. Ubiquitous throughout the tropics, it has never been successful in more northerly or southerly climates (it was only ever grown in the most northern latitudes of New Zealand) until recently. They are now grown in the southeastern United States and Japan, and some of continental Europe. Varieties have now been developed which succeed in Britain.

Uses

Used in the same way as potatoes. The flavour is quite sweet and they are generally not considered to be an acceptable substitute for potatoes in European dishes. They are high in dry matter, suitable for chips and crisps, and for mashing.

Cultivation

While it is possible to grow a useful crop of Sweet Potatoes in cold temperate climates, they do need a little coaxing in order to do so. Recent trials have proved that although they will succeed grown outdoors for part of the year, a better chance of success is assured if they are afforded some protection throughout the growing season, in a polytunnel, under cloches or in a cold frame. They enjoy similar conditions to those enjoyed by melons: warmth, a rich soil with plenty of organic matter, and regular watering, but not a waterlogged soil. They are grown by planting tubers, or cuttings taken from tubers called 'slips'. In either case, the soil should be sufficiently warmed before planting, which should not be before the end of May. Soil temperature will dictate this, though, and in some areas planting should be delayed until the soil has reached 14-15°C, with a minimum of 12°C. Black polythene helps to warm the soil, but they cannot be planted through slits. The tubers are formed where the trailing stems make contact with the earth, and they cannot form tubers if they are prevented from doing so. Otherwise, put cloches in place to warm the soil about two weeks before the projected planting date.

Preparing slips – Healthy tubers should be started into growth in mid April. Pot them into any moist growing medium, the tubers do not need any sustenance at this stage. Place them into warmth (a propagating frame is ideal) and maintain a constant 18°C, admit lots of light. They will quickly sprout. The shoots should be left to grow to about 10-12cm long, at which size they are detached and treated as cuttings.

Place each 'slip' around the edge of a 15cm pot (about six will go around the edge of each pot) of seed-sowing medium, or a simple 50/50 mix of sharp sand and organic material. Keep them warm and they soon root. Then they should be separated out and potted on into potting medium and grown on in preparation for planting out. One or two shoots should be left on each tuber, which then can be planted.

Plant out when the soil temperature is high enough and is stable, spacing each plant 25-30cm apart on ridges made 30-40cm wide. The ridges encourage the development of tubers (see diagram p.139), and the plants should be planted deeply, 10-12cm, to leave at least half of the plant buried. Although sweet potatoes are trailing, they should not be given a support up which to climb or fewer tubers will be produced.

Aftercare – The plants need to be kept weed-free. Although they are rangy, they do not have particularly dense foliage and tend not to easily smother out weeds. They need to be kept regularly watered, particularly during hot weather when they can put on some extraordinary growth. In the tropics it is possible for sweet potatoes to crop within two months of planting, but in temperate regions they are much slower. Long spells of cold weather can seriously hinder progress, but once established they are fairly resilient to short drops in temperature.

Harvest – The tubers are ready as soon as they are large enough. They can be left to develop for as long as possible into the autumn, after the plants have been cut down by frost. It is important that tubers are lifted straight away to prevent damage from penetrating frosts. Before storing, they need to be 'cured', to build up their flavour and encourage the tubers to remain dormant. They need to experience a week at 25°C (in a warm kitchen or airing cupboard, say) and then stored at 14°C. They easily suffer from cold damage and must not be refrigerated.

Varieties

There are many different varieties, and lots of different colour forms, but only one which is suited to growing in the United Kingdom, Beauregard. It has orange skin and flesh, with sizable tubers, elongated. Trials by the National Institute of Agricultural Botany over several years have been very successful. It is not recommended that tubers bought from a grocers are attempted as they are most certain to have originated in the tropics, and consequently will be poorly equipped to yield in a cooler climate.

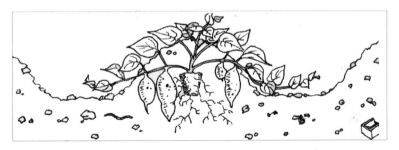

Cultivation of Sweet Potato

Ulluco

Latin Name – Ullucus tuberosus
Family – Basellaceae
Type – Half Hardy Perennial
Hardiness – Zone 7
Height – 30cm
Rotation – Treat as Solanaceous

A tuber from the Andes with flavour and use like potatoes. Worth attempting for its dense flesh.

Origin & History

Like Oca, Ulluco has been grown in Peru for thousands of years. It is grown amongst Potatoes, Oca and Mashua at altitudes of 3,000 to 4,000m. It has occasionally found its way into cultivation in the West as a curiosity. It has never become a staple in the rest of the world the way it has in South America. Much hardier than the other Andean tubers, it is cultivated as far south as Northern Argentina.

Uses

Lightly braised or boiled they are like potatoes, but with a slightly mucilaginous texture. They can be baked, but can become tough if they are cooked too long. They should not need peeling.

Cultivation

Ulluco is, to all intents and purposes, a tender crop; although it is reported to withstand temperatures down to –5°C in its Andean home, frosts this low are more damaging near to sea level. So they are best raised indoors and planted out when all danger of frost has passed. No seed is known to be produced, so propagation is always from tubers.

Planting – Start off the tubers in small pots on a windowsill or glasshouse, potted into 10cm pots of seed growing medium, planted 3cm deep. Give them gentle warmth and plenty of light and water to produce strong plants. Harden them off for a couple of weeks before planting them out by placing them outside during the day and back indoors again at night.

Aftercare – Plant them out when the soil has warmed and no more frosts are likely to be experienced. Space them 20cm equidistantly in a deep bed, or 15cm apart in rows spaced 30cm wide. They should be buried slightly when planted, deeper than when they were growing in their pots – about 5cm lower. Keep them well watered and weeded at first, but the canopy of foliage gets quite dense and most weeds are smothered later in the season. The stems seldom grow longer than 30cm and will arch over as they develop. Where they touch the ground, tubers are sometimes formed. To encourage this, they can be further earthed up once they are well established, and a thick application of leaf mould is reported to be beneficial. Certainly a deep rich soil suits them, as does an occasional feed. Some yellowing of the leaf margins is common and does not necessarily indicate a shortcoming in their husbandry, so be cautious about over-applying fertiliser or water as they will not withstand waterlogging.

Tubers are only formed after the day length drops below 13 hours, which usually coincides with a drop in general temperatures, particularly at night when there is a risk of frost which can bring the development of the crop to a rapid halt. Unlike potatoes, green tubers (which have been exposed to light) are edible, but they are more palatable if they are blanched by earthing up which usually happens from about the beginning of September. The tubers nestle around the base of the plants and have a rather endearing habit of pointing upwards, so care has to be taken that the tips are buried to blanch them.

Harvest the tubers when the foliage has been cut down by frost. The tubers cluster tightly round the base of the plants, so little excavating is necessary to get the tubers up, less than is required with potatoes. Tubers do tend to be small and can be a bit fiddly to harvest. Store in sacks, somewhere cool and dry and in the dark.

Tip: the tubers store for a very long time, and can be kept for over 12 months without them deteriorating. It is possible to use year-old tubers for replanting as they will sprout vigorously when planted. This is particularly useful if you don't want to grow Ulluco every year.

Pests and disease specific to Ulluco are uncommon outside their native South America. They do, though, easily accumulate virus, especially those, alas, which affect potatoes. To maintain vigorous stocks it is important to isolate them from potatoes, and not just physically as non-specific insect pests like aphids are quite capable of transferring viruses from nearby potato crops. Recent attempts to clear many old strains of Ulluco of virus using micro-propagation techniques have been very encouraging.

Varieties

There are many different colour forms of Ulluco: yellow, red, white and purple. There is one which is mottled and variously speckled, named Pica di Pulga (flea bites). None of the different coloured types seem to differ in tuber shape and size, or yield.

Native Growth

In its native Andes, Ulluco is grown amongst potatoes and other tubers Oca, Mashua and Araccacha. By maintaining this diversity in their fields, the Peruvians have kept their crops protected from pests and disease for thousands of years, a technique which can be attributed to their Aztec ancestors. The technique does not rely on their fields being entirely pest free, nor does it have any bearing on companion planting. Instead, in any one year, one of their crops is bound to be affected by some pest or disease. It might get it badly, but chances are they will not be entirely wiped out. The other crops in the field, on the other hand, will thrive and it is from these that the main harvest is guaranteed. The next year, a different crop might be plagued, but the others not. It is excellent form of insurance, and is a technique that Western agriculture, which relies on monoculture and pesticides for its plant protection, could learn from.

Wapato, Duck Potato

Latin Name – Sagittaria latifolia
Family – Alismataceae
Type – Hardy Perennial
Hardiness – Zone 7
Height – 1m
Rotation – Treat as permanent bed

An aquatic plant, easy to grow and prolific, it once fed the North American Indians. Aquatic vegetables are very easy to grow – no weeding or watering required!

Origin & History

Wapato originates in North America where for centuries it was an important food for the native people. When the tubers are mature in autumn they were said to have been harvested by women by wading through the beds on the edges of waterways and loosening them with their toes. The tubers rise to the surface from where they were gathered. They are popular with waterfowl, hence the name Duck Potato.

Uses

The texture of Wapato is very like a potato but a bit more floury, and their flavour is slightly bitter, which is not altogether unpleasant. Yields are seldom huge so they can never be considered a viable potato substitute, but they make an interesting accompanying vegetable to meats, and particularly fish. The tubers are quite porous, and readily absorb a dressing or sauce. They need very little cooking – steaming or boiling for five minutes is sufficient.

Cultivation

Wapato are aquatic, but they don't require much of a depth of water. An inundated soil is all that is required, and it is possible to grow them in pots which are kept standing in a tray of water. I have had a lot of success, and a great deal of fun, growing them in a child's paddling pool. They'll also grow at pond margins, but in areas with cool summers they are better grown indoors where they respond to high temperatures. They can be grown from seed, which is seldom available, or more conveniently from their tubers, more correctly termed turions. However they are grown, and particularly if they are potted, it is important that they are not grown in a growing medium which contains large quantities of (or indeed consists entirely of) organic material. This will decompose rapidly if kept very wet and unpleasant decomposition products, such as methane and ethylene, will be given off. It is better to use a soil-based medium such as John Innes, or good garden soil.

Sowing – Seed can be sown thinly on the surface of wet soil. The seedlings should be pricked out when large enough and grown on in the same way as plants grown from turions.

Planting – The tubers should be planted as soon as they are starting into growth, usually around the middle of April, into dwarf pots, about 15cm diameter. Keep at least the base of the pots immersed in water, or put them into their aquatic homestead straight away, be that a paddling pool, old tank, Belfast sink or whatever. They do like a bit of warmth from the start, so you could start them off in pots and put them in an outdoor pool when the water has warmed, about the end of May.

Aftercare – The plants should be released from their pots once they have filled them, if they are being grown under shallow water, or potted on into larger containers if they are simply to be grown standing in water. Little attention is required from then on. Indeed, they are a model of easy maintenance. Keeping the water topped up is all that is required. They're a very useful crop to grow for anyone who is likely to be away for a while through the summer as ensuring that they are kept well-watered need not be a worry. Some yellowing of the foliage may occur. This may be because they are ripening if this is occurring late in the season, but it may because they are falling short of nutrients. A few drops of liquid feed added to the water will correct any shortfall.

Harvesting – The plants will rapidly die down once the turions are fully formed. You can simply rummage around in the sludge to release the tubers, or turn the plants out of their pots and pick the turions off. Don't forget to retain a few turions for replanting the next year. They can be immediately replanted, or stored in a little water in plastic bags in the fridge.

Varieties

There are no varieties of Duck Potato.

Founding Fathers Food Foul-up

Revisionists of history are lately taking a very different view of the success of the first European settlers to the United States. Many were ill-equipped and had scant, if any, knowledge of the local fauna and flora, or indeed of what was good or bad to eat. They became reliant on the native population, many of whom took pity on them and gave them food that they themselves were used to eating and which was local to them. One of these was Wapato, the other was American Groundnut, both life-savers for the early settlers.

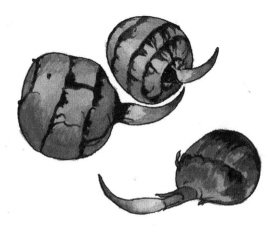

Wapato - root

Water Chestnut

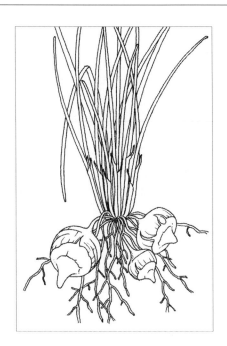

Latin Name – Eleocharis dulcis
Family – Cyperaceae
Type – Half Hardy Perennial
Hardiness – Zone 8
Height – 60cm
Rotation – Treat as permanent bed

This is one of two plants known as Water Chestnut. A familiar
ingredient in Chinese cooking, it is quite easy to grow as an aquatic,
in a greenhouse or polytunnel.

Origin & History

Water Chestnut has been grown for many
centuries in the Orient, in China and
Southeast Asia in shallow water, often
naturalised at the edges of paddy fields and
wet areas in these regions. It grows well in
parts of tropical Africa. It is a very similar
to plant to the European native Eleocharis
palustris, the Common Spike-Rush, a
coarse plant of wet places, but differs from
it in that it produces tubers, about 4cm in
diameter, by the end of the wet season.

Uses

A stalwart in Oriental cooking, Water
chestnuts are usually combined with other
vegetables, seasoned and stir-fried. Or,

unlike the other Water Chestnut, the Water
Caltrops, they can be eaten raw. The dried
tubers can be ground into flour, used for
thickening or for coating vegetables or
meat to give a crispy coating when deep
fried.

Cultivation

Water Chestnuts are not difficult to grow
provided they are given plenty of warmth,
lots of light and plenty of water at their
feet. In temperate areas, particularly in a
coastal climate such as the British Isles
where summers are unreliable, they are best
grown under glass or in a polytunnel. They
need to be partially submerged in some
sort of pond-like setup, be it a plastic pond
liner lining a shallow pit, an old sink or

even perhaps a child's paddling pool (a particularly cheap-and-cheerful container, and one which can be conveniently stored away when not in use). The best way to grow them is to copy their growing cycle in cultivation in China and southeast Asia. There they raise them first in a nursery bed and plant them out straight after the fields have been cleared of rice. They need a full 6 month growing season, after which the fields are drained and the tubers dug out.

Planting – The tubers need warmth to grow, and because they need a long growing season they are best started off with warmth by first planting them into pots, 13cm or thereabouts, and keeping the base of them submerged. They should ideally be started off about the end of March, so a heated propagator or warm windowsill is necessary to give them the warmth they require, about 26°C or above, which is quite high. As temperatures under glass start to increase naturally without artificial heat, the plants can be put out into their pool. A good layer of sediment is needed for them to grow in, and one which has been enriched. Large quantities of organic material are best avoided as they tend to ferment and can stagnate the water. A soil layer of at least 20cm thick is ideal. After planting the plants out at 60cm (or about 5 per paddling pool), water

should be topped up to 10cm above the soil level which should, if they are being grown in a paddling pool, bring the water up to just below the rim.

Aftercare – Water Chestnuts like really blistering temperatures, and a little reluctance to ventilate on clear mornings will pay dividends in increased growth, providing the health of the other greenhouse occupants is not compromised. Very little maintenance of these aquatic tubers is required, apart from keeping the water level topped up.

Harvesting – Conveniently, water chestnut enjoys lower temperatures as the turions start to form, in late summer. It is this which encourages them to form, on the ends of long rhizomes, and they are ready when the plants start to die down. Drain off the water and allow the soil to dry out, after which the tubers can be gathered. They must be stored damp, and in a frost-free place.

Varieties

There are no known varieties, but there do seem to be two different types, differing slightly in plant habit but with no difference in flavour or texture.

Water Chestnut, Water Caltrop

Latin Name – Trapa bicornis
Family – Trapaceae
Type – Tender Perennial
Hardiness – Zone 5
Height – 10cm
Rotation – Treat as permanent bed

The "other" Water Chestnut, Water Caltrop is a floating aquatic. It produces tuber-like nuts, rather than the nut-like tubers produced by the other kind.

Origin & History

Water caltrop is a floating aquatic that grows in southern Europe, across Asia to China and the Orient. It was formerly a native of Britain and evidence of it has been found in peat deposits in East Anglia. In parts of the world where it has been introduced it has become a pest, particularly in the southern US and Australia, and in the Caspian Sea where it threatens sturgeon feeding grounds. The wild species is Trapa natans, the true Water Caltrop. It has seeds with four horn–like protuberances. A caltrop was a four-spiked iron ball used to maim horses in battle, which is what these seeds are thought to resemble. The cultivated form, Trapa bicornis, has just two horns and the nuts are slightly larger, up to 6cm.

Uses

The nuts are poisonous eaten raw, and must be thoroughly boiled, for at least an hour, before they can be eaten. It is surprising that this is the most popular of the two Water Chestnuts, and it is grown in quantity in Southern Europe for export to the Orient. It also needs to be shelled before eating.

Cultivation

Water Caltrop is not difficult to grow, and like the other kind of Water Chestnut it can be grown in a shallow pool, in an old tank or a paddling pool. The plants do not root directly into substrate, but some source of nutriment needs to be given to the plants and this is best provided by a good layer of silt in the bottom of their container, one that has been enriched.

Planting – Float the Water Caltrop in the water once it has been set up and allowed to settle for a while. For the best growth and highest yields (even though it is quite a hardy plant) they are best grown in a greenhouse or polytunnel to keep the water warm. A temperature of about 20°C or above is optimal but drops in temperature are tolerated. It is certainly tougher than the other Water Chestnut, Eleocharis dulcis.

Aftercare – Keep the water topped up. Very low maintenance!

Harvesting – The shiny black nuts are produced at the base of the leaves, tucked into the centre of the plant. They are fully ripe when the plants start to die off in autumn. The seeds do not stand drying out and should be kept moist in polythene bags or in a damp substrate.

Varieties

There are no varieties. The two-horned type is better for growing for eating than the wild, four-horned type which is low yielding.

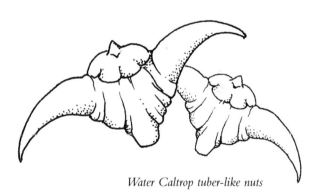

Water Caltrop tuber-like nuts

Yacon

Latin Name – Polymnia [Smallanthus] sonchifolia
Family – Compositae
Type – Half Hardy Perennial
Hardiness – Zone 7
Height – 2.5m
Rotation – Treat as Brassicas

This giant amongst vegetables is worth growing for its high yields alone. Related to the Dahlia, it is as easy and rewarding to grow.

Origin & History

Yacon originates in the Andes, at high altitude. Its history in the area is obscure but it is fair to assume, given the long history of agriculture in the Andean region, that it has been cultivated for a long time. Its introduction to the West has been slow, but wherever it has been introduced it has been found to be very adaptable, even to conditions at low altitude. And, unlike many plants from the Andes (such as Oca or Ulluco), it shows no sensitivity to day length so will produce tubers grown at high latitudes, which makes Yacon very versatile.

It is capable of remarkable yields. However, unlike most other tubers, its carbohydrates are not stored as starch (as is usual for potatoes, for instance) but as a complex sugar, inulin. Inulin cannot be hydrolysed by humans, and passes through the gut undigested. It therefore has great potential for the production of diabetic sugar (which is currently extracted from Jerusalem artichoke tubers, which also contain inulin but in lower concentrations). The inulin can be broken down by artificial hydrolysis using the enzyme inulase to produce fructose. Currently, fructose is extracted from corn syrup, but Yacon contains far higher potential yield of fructose than its counterpart. It is a plant of great potential which has yet to be realised as it is not grown commercially anywhere.

Uses

The tubers can be eaten raw, and they are pleasantly crunchy and quite sweet when uncooked, with a refreshing taste rather like watermelon. They make a very pleasant addition to a salad, sliced or diced. They should be peeled – the skin can have an unpleasant taste.

They remain quite crunchy even after prolonged cooking, very much like Water Chestnuts, and they can be used as a substitute for them in Chinese cooking. They contain a lot of sugar but (unlike in late stored potatoes, for instance) at a level which is very pleasant in savoury dishes. They are used in some parts of the world for alcohol production. Steaming or boiling the tubers for 30 minutes tenderises them nicely without removing their crunchiness, and they easily absorb liquid, be it a sauce, gravy or dressing. They should be peeled beforehand and usually diced. Some tubers can grow as big as a pound or over, so they need to be reduced in size a bit to be more manageable.

Cultivation

Yacon is grown in nearly the same way as Dahlias, and if you've ever grown them before you'll know how easy that is. Like Dahlias, they produce a huge rootstock mostly consisting of root tubers which are fat and succulent, and grow on stalks away from the main stem – it is these that are eaten. But they also produce stem tubers which are knobbly and cluster around the main stalk – it is these that are used for propagation. One Yacon rootstock will produce about 8-10 separate stem tubers which can be detached from the main stem to make as many plants.

Planting – In cold temperate areas, it is wise to start the tubers off in warmth and plant out after the risk of frost has passed. Start the tubers by potting into 15cm pots, planting them just below the surface. Choose tubers which are showing signs of growth and select the most vigorous-looking ones. They usually start into growth at the beginning of April. A little gentle warmth helps them into growth. However if you're patient they'll emerge without any extra heat in a cold greenhouse or on the windowsill in a cool room. It's important not to give extra heat without it being accompanied by high light levels, otherwise leggy plants will result which will never be satisfactory when planted out. Sometimes the young foliage emerges quite colourless at first, often yellow or white. Why this should be is not clearly understood, but the foliage does green up in time and the plants do not seem to get set back in any way.

They should be planted out when the last frost has passed, by which time the roots will have quite filled the pot. Ensure that they're given a little feed if they become rootbound before you can plant them out, for maximum yield. They grow huge, and lots of space needs to be given between them. 90cm is sufficient to allow the enormous leaves the room they need. They don't fill their space very quickly at first, so it's possible to raise a quick catch crop (lettuce, spinach or radish, for instance) between the plants before they reach full size. The stems are tall and may need staking in a windy site. Their ultimate height depends on how good a summer they experience – up to 2.5m is not unknown.

Aftercare – There's little in the way of aftercare needed. They do require quite a lot of water for a good yield of tubers, but will tolerate some drought. They do not suffer from any specific pests or disease, but take a lot from the soil so, even though they are not related to them, they are best treated in a rotation as a Brassica. They can be, though, a martyr to slugs and snails.

Harvest – The tubers do not fully develop until well into autumn, and the plants will keep growing quite vigorously until the first frosts. It is when the foliage is killed off by frost that the plants should be dug up and the stems cut off.. Lift carefully with a fork (or, in a light soil, by pulling). Care has to be taken not to damage the brittle tubers. Store them in a frost-free shed or garage. When tubers are needed, detach them from the stored rootstock. Remember to use the root tubers for eating only. The stem tubers are left for propagating. Unlike potatoes or Ulluco, for instance, they do not accumulate virus so the same stock can be propagated from over many years.

Varieties

There are no named varieties of Yacon in cultivation. There are, though, many numbered clones which have been selected for particular characteristics in programmes where it is being researched for sugar alcohol production.

Flowers

In a good season, or if Yacon is grown under glass or in a polytunnel, flowers are sometimes produced. These are not, however, anything to get excited about! They are very small, kind of dirty orange in colour and slightly resemble a Zinnia. Sometimes, though, it is at the beginning of the season rather than at the end when the flowers are produced – newly emerged shoots sometimes flower when still only very short. Any propagated plants which start to do this tend not to give very satisfactory yields, so are best discarded.

Fruits

These plants are all botanically fruits, but some are used (like tomatoes) as vegetables.

Tomatillos are the traditional ingredient in Mexican dishes in place of tomatoes, and are just as easy to grow. Also similar to tomatoes are tree tomato and litchi tomato, the last one a relatively new introduction.

There are many cucumber relatives which are great fun to grow with a little warmth and protection: snake gourd, achoccha, kiwano, bitter gourd, and the pumpkin-like chilacayote is one of the most exciting vines to grow, if you can spare the space.

Achoccha, Korila

Latin Name – Cyclanthera pedata &
C. brachystachya
Family – Cucurbitaceae
Type – Half Hardy Annual
Hardiness – Zone 9
Height – Climbing to 3ms+
Rotation – Treat as Brassicas

A relative of the Cucumber, Achoccha can be used in the same way, eaten fresh or pickled. Space-age looking fruits are fun for children to grow.

Origin & History

Native to Central and South America at high altitudes, Achoccha is also grown and used in Nepal and Taiwan.

Uses

Used in place of Cucumbers, for eating fresh or for pickling in brine and vinegar. Cooked, they can be fried in oil, or stuffed and braised. The fruits should be picked when quite young. If they are left to fully mature on the plant they will eventually burst open to reveal the black, woody seeds within.

Cultivation

Achoccha thrives at high altitudes in its native tropics, and in tropical areas where it is cultivated, where it experiences relatively cool day temperatures. In temperate areas, cool summers therefore suit it best. It can be grown under glass or in a polytunnel where late spring and early autumn frosts are a threat. However it grows better outdoors in areas with a long growing season, where its expansive growth is more easily incorporated. Because the vines are ranging, care has to be taken to give it a site where it can rampage unfettered, over a trellis, an unsightly wall or up pea and bean netting. Mostly the growth is fairly spindly and other crops experience little competition from the exploring shoots, so to an extent they can be left to roam. Achoccha is tolerant of semi-shade, especially in hot summer areas where it is susceptible to scorch from full summer sun.

Sow seeds in seed-sowing medium, two to a 9cm pot, and thin to the strongest seedling if both of them germinate. Germination is rapid at around 20°C and lots of light and good air circulation should be given as soon as they have emerged. As with most Cucumber family members, I don't usually sow until May, when the ambient heat and light levels are higher than they are earlier in the season, sufficient to sustain vigorous growth.

Aftercare – Plant them out after the last frost. Space each at least 1m apart, and provide some protection from high winds in their initial stages. Development is slow at first, but once established they will need to be coaxed onto their supports. The earlier this is done the better, to avoid having lots of misbehaving stems to rearrange. They enjoy lots of water, and a good mulch with organic material is very beneficial.

Harvest the pods as soon as they are of a good size. The more they are picked, the more are produced. Cropping does not usually begin until quite late in the season, from around August.

Varieties

There are no known varieties, but there are two different species, both of which are similar to one another and which are usually known under variety names, both as varieties of Cyclanthera pedata.

Cyclanthera pedata is known as 'Lady's Slipper'. Its pods are always borne in pairs, and the foliage is distinctly palmate, like a hand with fingers.

The variety 'Fat Baby' is actually a separate species, Cyclanthera brachystachya. It has simpler leaves, more like those of a cucumber, and the pods are borne singly. They are distinctive for being covered in little fleshy 'horns'.

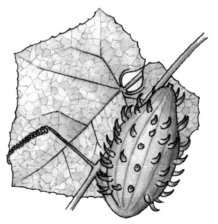

Achoccha Fat Baby

Bitter Gourd

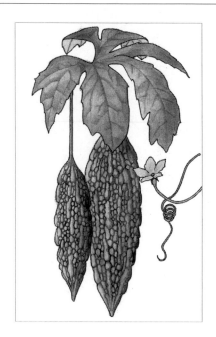

Latin Name – Momordica charantia
Family – Cucurbitaceae
Type – Half Hardy Annual
Hardiness – Zone 9
Height – Climbing to 3m
Rotation – Treat as Brassicas

Worth growing for its spectacularly unusual fruits, Bitter Gourd is a popular tropical fruit and one which is as easy to grow as cucumbers.

Origin & History

Bitter Gourd is a native of tropical Asia and has been cultivated there for many centuries. It has become naturalised in other tropical countries, particularly in India and Sri Lanka where it is an important ingredient in the local cuisine. In other parts of the world, the bitter flavour does not always appeal and it tends to be grown more as an ornamental. In Europe it has been known since the 17th century, but seldom grown.

Uses

The fruits are usually slit in two and the seeds and pulp removed, then soaked in salt to reduce their bitterness. They are added to stews, stuffed, fried, pickled or stir-fried. The immature fruits are also eaten. When the fruit ripens, it turns orange and splits into three along its length, revealing seeds covered in bright red pulp. The Chinese prepare Bitter Gourd with fermented black soya beans.

Cultivation

Bitter Gourd is simple to grow, as long as it receives lots of heat and humidity, and plenty of water. Like many members of its family detailed here, it enjoys conditions similar to those enjoyed by cucumbers. In cool temperate climates it does not succeed well outdoors, but will succeed outside in hot, continental summers. It can be grown in containers. A well-cultivated soil suits, with plenty of organic matter, and a position in full sun.

Sowing – Seedlings should be raised under glass, sown individually in 9cm pots. If there is enough seed to spare, sow two seeds per pot and remove the weaker of the two if both of them emerge. Sow into seed-sowing medium and germinate the seeds at 20°C or above. Keep the growing medium moist but not too wet, to avoid them rotting off. An early sowing, mid to late April, is wise in order for them to experience a long enough growing season to fully develop their fruits.

Aftercare – Keep potting the plants on if they are to be grown in containers. Otherwise, plant out to their final positions when their roots have filled their pots. Space the plants 40cm apart, and provide a support from the start. They climb by tendrils and growth is quite spindly, so are best supported with netting for them to intertwine with. Keep them regularly watered and fed.

Harvesting – The fruits are picked as soon as they are big enough.

Varieties

Coimbatore Long is the most popular variety in India. Ripens to pale green in colour.

Moonshine is a cream-fruited variety producing fruits 15cm long. Needs a long growing season.

Prodigy is a white skin and flesh, low bitterness, large fruits to 20cm.

Taiwan White is the dominant variety in Taiwan, another white-skinned, white-fleshed variety.

Another species of Momordica, M. cochinchinensis, is known as the Spiny Bitter Gourd. It is grown the same way, and used similarly in the kitchen. Its fruits ripen orange to red but are eaten when young. They are very small (7-9cm) but prolific.

Cape Gooseberry & Ground Cherry

Latin Name – Physalis peruviana & Physalis pruinosa
Family – Solanaceae
Type – Half Hardy Annual
Hardiness – Zone 8 & 5
Height – 1.2m & 80cm
Rotation – Treat as Solanaceous

The self-wrapped fruits of these two Chinese Lanterns are sweet and tangy, popular as canapés. Cape Gooseberry is not, as its name suggests, from the Cape but from tropical South America.

Origin & History

Cape Gooseberry can be a confusing name. It originates in South America, specifically Peru, but has become naturalised in other parts of the world, particularly South Africa, from where it was introduced to Britain by the Dutch in the 19th century. It was thought at the time that the plant was native to there, and the name has now stuck, but it was introduced to Spain long before then, and by the Dutch to the Cape in the 17th century.

Ground Cherry is a relative to the above with a lot of similarities, native to eastern and central North America. It has not become as widely accepted in cultivation as Cape Gooseberry, and its history of introduction to Europe is obscure. The two are so similar in appearance, and identical in use and flavour, that they have become interchangeable, with some references and catalogues directly interchanging the two. In terms of hardiness, though, there is an important distinction: Ground Cherry will withstand temperatures near to freezing, or even briefly below, whereas Cape Gooseberry is quite frost-sensitive. This may have a strong bearing when choosing which type to grow in marginal, cold temperate areas.

Uses

The fruits are quite sweet, but with a pleasant tanginess. They make attractive petit fours presented with their calyx turned inside out, to be eaten raw from the stalk. They can be cooked, made into jam or incorporated into desserts. Yields are seldom high so they are a treat rather than a main ingredient for a dessert.

Cultivation

Cultivation is very similar to that of Tomatillos. However, the plants are quite a lot larger and need to be given plenty of space to develop fully – 1m spacing between plants is still not always sufficient for Cape Gooseberry. Ground Cherries are slightly smaller (but only slightly) and can be given 75cm. They both need to be given a long season in cold temperate areas if they are to crop successfully, and it is seldom that a useful quantity is produced until late autumn. All the above, though, only applies to plants which are given the full range of an open field situation or grown in greenhouse border soil: anywhere where their roots are given a free run. If their roots are kept restricted in a container such as a large tub, they crop earlier and on smaller plants. While the total yield may be less from container-grown plants, a more useful crop is, in my experience, produced.

Sowing and Aftercare is exactly the same as it is for Tomatillo. When the fruits are ripe, they turn golden within their papery 'lantern' husk and drop from the plant. They are well protected within this husk, and can be left on the ground for several days before they deteriorate.

Varieties

Cape Gooseberry is Physalis peruviana. It has leaves which are basically heart-shaped and slightly asymmetrical, with one side of the leaf larger than the other, rather like an Elm leaf. The leaves have a grey underside and the plant is quite rangy and sparsely branched. It has papery calyxes which are quite a lot larger than the fruits they enclose. It is fairly frost-tender.
Gaillo Grosso has fruits which are larger than the typical species.
Golden Berry also has large, sweeter berries. Some catalogues only list this species under this name.
Ground Cherry is Physalis pruinosa. It has symmetrical leaves, its plant habit is slightly tidier, quite thick-stemmed and hairier. Its fruits are a bit smaller and their papery calyx tougher. There are no known varieties.

Chinese Lantern look alikes

I've seen another type of Chinese Lantern, a hardy perennial sort with an underground creeping stem. Can this be eaten?

This is botanically Physalis alkekengii and it most certainly cannot be eaten. The fruits are quite bitter and entirely unpalatable, apart from being extremely small and hard. They are excellent for decoration. Cut the stems when the lanterns have turned bright orange and hang them upside down in a warm, dry place having first removed all of their leaves. Unfortunately the edible sorts are no good for decoration as their 'lanterns' turn brown when ready, and the fruits within will eventually rot. Besides, they fall off the stems when they're ripe.

Chilacayote, Malabar Gourd

Latin Name – Cucurbita ficifolia
Family – Cucurbitaceae
Type – Half Hardy Annual
Hardiness – Zone 10
Height – Trailing to 6m+
Rotation – Treat as Brassicas

The Malabar Gourd is a spectacular scrambling vine good for covering fences and trellises. It produces enormous fruits used for making sweetmeats and a particular dessert, chilacayote.

Origin & History

Malabar Gourd is widely distributed in throughout South America, from Mexico all the way south to Chile. Archaeological finds in Peru date it as having been cultivated 4000 years ago. Despite it being in cultivation for such a long time, there do not appear to be any varieties. The wild form is identical to the cultivated type. In the wild it is perennial, forming a stout rootstock. It shows considerable resistance to the root diseases common in many other members of the cucumber family and is used commercially as a disease-resistant rootstock, particularly for cucumbers. It is also very cold tolerant, although frost-tender.

It has been grown in Europe since 1613 but appears to have only been grown as an ornamental or as a botanical curiosity. Except in France and South America, its edible potential seems to have been ignored.

Uses

The hard fruits contain a soft, white, fibrous flesh which is slightly sweet. It can be candied after first dicing and then processing with lime (the chemical calcium hydroxide, as opposed to the fruit). It is then boiled for several hours with sugar syrup and cinnamon, then dried: this is Chilacayote.

The French make a dessert, Cheveux d'Ange, which is similar to Chilacayote. The flesh is allowed to become fibrous, rather like spaghetti squash, and is mixed with honey, then bottled. It was once highly esteemed in Paris, and may have originated from an ancient Syrian recipe.

Cultivation

Malabar Gourd is fun to grow, especially for children. Most squashes and pumpkins are a great starter for juvenile gardeners, but the Fig Leaved Gourd (as it is also sometimes known and under which name it is occasionally listed in catalogues) makes particularly rapid growth. It will set fruits in even the most indifferent of summers. It does need to be given a lot of space to rampage, and even then don't be too surprised to find shoots of it growing in places many metres away from where they started, even up into trees. A deeply cultivated soil suits them, with lots of organic matter incorporated. It grows particularly well on top of the compost heap, as you would grow marrows. A particularly fine garden feature is a walk through, Malabar Gourd arch. It has to be strongly built, though, to take the weight of the fruits.

Sowing – Start the seeds off under glass, or on the windowsill. They should be started quite late in the spring or even into early summer, from mid May to the middle of June. Sow into large pots, about 12cm, and use a seed-sowing medium. Sow two seeds to a pot and remove the weaker of the two if both come up.

Aftercare – The seedlings should be planted out as soon as they have filled their pots with roots, which is about two weeks after sowing. The seed leaves of Malabar Gourd are huge and very beautiful. Plant them spaced about 2m apart, or even further apart if you can spare the space: it is not a vegetable for the small garden! Squashes like Chilacayote fare particularly well planted through a mulch of black polythene, ground cover mulch, cardboard or even through old carpet. Failing this, use a good deep layer of organic matter. All of these help to retain moisture and to keep the weeds down. Hoeing between a rapidly-growing Malabar Gourd is not a straightforward undertaking but as it grows quickly and forms a dense covering of foliage, so most annual weeds are smothered out before they get well established. They respond well to regular thorough waterings.

Harvesting – The immature fruits can be picked and used like courgettes, but don't overpick them at this stage if you want some to grow to maturity. The fruits are ready when they have fully grown and formed a hard shell. It is usual to let the vines get cut down by frost before the fruits are brought indoors. Cut them from the vine, leaving a short stem on each. Malabar Gourd stores extremely well, and would store indefinitely were it not for the fact that the flesh within eventually completely dries out. I have known fruits keep for over five years but the bright colours of the freshly-harvested fruits are lost, turning to uniform brown. If you shake them you can hear the seeds rattling inside the dried shell. The outer shell of the fruit is so hard that it is likely, given a bit of ingenuity, that they could be fashioned into musical instruments.

The best way to get into one is to simply smash it open with a hammer or, to preserve the shell, cut through it with a saw. Any attempts to open one with a kitchen knife will end in frustration or personal injury.

Varieties

There are no known varieties.

Garden Huckleberry

Latin Name – Solanum x burbankii
Family – Solanaceae
Type – Hardy Annual
Hardiness – Zone 8
Height – 1.2m
Rotation – Treat as Solanaceous

This productive relative of the potato has Nightshade-like berries
which are edible, giving colour and substance to jams and preserves.

Origin & History

Garden Huckleberry is an improved form
of the Common Nightshade, Solanum
nigrum, a weed throughout the world. Of
hybrid origin, the berries of Garden
Huckleberry are much larger and more
prolific, and entirely edible. The berries of
Nightshade are mildly poisonous and bitter
to taste, but the leaves are edible and are
gathered in some countries and eaten like
spinach.

Uses

The fruits have little if any flavour, but they
are highly coloured and nutritious, and
slightly sweet. Added to pies and jams they
eke out fruit where fruit may be scarce,
without tainting or interfering with the
main fruit component in any way. They
also enhance the fruit's colour and contain
pectin, helpful in making jam set.

Cultivation

Huckleberry is very easy to grow, and is
capable of self-seeding in mild winter
areas. It is better, though, in cold temperate
regions to start the seeds off indoors to
give them a head start for them to develop
a good crop of ripe berries. They grow
well in containers, and respond to a deep
root run outdoors in a well-cultivated
situation in full sun.

Sow seed in seed-sowing medium into
shallow pots, barely cover the seeds and

germinate them at 16-18°C. They are slow to emerge, about 2-3 weeks being usual and seedlings should be pricked out as soon as they're large enough to handle, at first into 9cm pots. Sowing indoors should be in spring, from mid March onwards. Seed can be sown later, outdoors in May, when the soil has warmed, sown into drills 30cm apart and later thinned to leave plants at 30cm stations.

Aftercare – They should not be allowed to get too hot or experience too much humidity or leggy plants will result, and the developing plants will need potting on as soon as they have filled their containers. Like a lot of plants in the potato and tomato family, though, they are responsive to pot size, and are capable of producing a crop (albeit a considerably diminished one) in a very small container. Indoor raised plants should be set out in May at a spacing of 50cm, and each provided with a stout stake. They need to be kept free of weeds, but they are tall and will grow above light infestations. The leaves are sparse and they do not shade out weeds or other plants growing nearby. They enjoy regular watering. Plants in containers need to be kept regularly fed and watered.

Harvesting – The berries are ready as soon as they have turned black. They keep for the whole season on the vine, so can be left on the plant until they are all ripe, and gathered all at once. This way they can be harvested at autumn jamming time, when they are most needed.

Varieties

Mrs B's Bitter-Free is the variety selected by Burbank from his first Huckleberry seedlings. It contains none of the alkaloid solanin which is the bitter component in Common Nightshade and green potatoes.

Luther Burbank, Father of the Potato

Although Huckleberry's parentage is obscure, what is known is that it was bred and introduced by Luther Burbank of Massachusetts, after whom the hybrid is named. Burbank was born in Lancaster, MA in 1849 where he was educated. In 1870 he bought a plot of land in Lunenburg, MA and within a year had produced the Burbank potato which he sold the rights to in 1875, the proceeds from which ($150) afforded him a move to Santa Rosa, California. Burbank's potato was exported to Ireland and was found to greatly reduce the incidence of blight. Russet Burbank is in cultivation today, and is a popular frying potato, low in dry matter.

Husk Cherry

Latin Name – Physalis pubescens
Family – Solanaceae
Type – Half Hardy Annual
Hardiness – Zone 7
Height – 90cm
Rotation – Treat as Solanaceous

Another Chinese Lantern-like plant, this is a very underrated
alternative, with smaller and more productive plants – smaller fruits,
but lots of them.

Origin & History

From Mexico and central North America,
the origins of this alternative to Cape
Gooseberry and Ground Cherry are
obscure. It occasionally appears in
catalogues, usually listed as its look alikes
Cape Gooseberry or Ground Cherry, but it
is a quite different plant.

Uses

The sweet fruits can be eaten raw or added
to jams, jellies, confectionery and pies.

Cultivation

Husk Cherry is grown in exactly the same
way as Tomatillos or Cape Gooseberry.

Unlike Cape Gooseberry, the plants are
very well behaved: they are smaller, bushy
and require no support for their stems
which are stout and erect. They can be left
to grow unfettered and they do not crop
any better for being constricted in a
container, as does Cape Gooseberry,
although they are easily accommodated in
a pot. A final spacing of 40cm allows them
plenty of space to develop.

Varieties

Cossack's Pineapple yields small fruits of a
distinctive pineapple flavour. Delicious and
productive.
Goldie is a good garden form with larger
fruits than the above on decorative, bushy
plants.

Kiwano, Jelly Melon

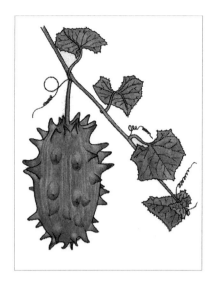

Latin Name – Cucumis metuliferus
Family – Cucurbitaceae
Type – Half Hardy Annual
Hardiness – Zone 10
Height – Climbing to 1.5m
Rotation – Treat as Brassicas

A common vegetable in the tropics, this curious horned fruit likes warmth and can be grown in the same way as cucumbers.

Origin & History

From tropical Africa, this novelty fruit has been slow to be accepted outside native haunts. It is occasionally encountered at Afro-Caribbean markets.

Uses

The immature fruits can be eaten like cucumbers, in salads, or pickled like gherkins. It matures when the skin turns bright orange, and the green, jelly-like, translucent flesh can be scooped out and eaten raw or cooked. It has a refreshing flavour somewhat resembling banana, and can be used as a component of sorbets, fruit cups and parfaits, or as an ingredient in cocktails. The French combine it into a unique and unusual seaweed sorbet.

Cultivation

Kiwano can be grown just like cucumbers. It enjoys hot and humid conditions to give of its best, but will tolerate quite low temperatures for short periods and will crop reasonably in a poor summer under glass without additional heat. To ensure a good crop of ripe fruits, though, it is best to raise plants quite early to give them a long growing season, and keep them growing quickly.

Sowing – Sow two seeds to a 9cm pot of seed-sowing medium, placed just below the surface, and maintain a minimum temperature of 22°C for strong germination – like nearly all Cucurbits (squashes, pumpkins, cucumbers and their like), poor development and consequently a poor crop will result if the right conditions are not provided at the initial stages. If both seedlings germinate, remove the weaker of the two. Give plenty of light and air, and high humidity.

Aftercare – Keep the plants growing rapidly, potting on if necessary to avoid any check in their growth. They enjoy lots of water and a soil rich in organic matter; they grow well in large tubs, or planted out into the greenhouse border soil. They can be grown in border soil where cucumbers have been grown previously without them contracting any of the soil-borne diseases to which many of the cucumber tribe are prone: Jelly Melon is very disease-resistant and is sometimes used as a rootstock for cucumbers. Plant the young plants out in May at 45cm apart and provide support.

They are tendril climbers so they are best supported with netting rather than trying to encourage them to twine around smooth stakes, to which they have trouble attaching.

Harvesting – You can start taking the fruits as soon as they are large enough if you want to use them green. Otherwise, leave them to fully ripen to orange. The fruits do not keep well and should be eaten fresh.

Varieties

The Cuke-Asaurus variety has a stronger flavour than the type species; when ripe, its flavour is likened to wild bananas.

Litchi Tomato

Latin Name – Solanum sisymbriifolium
Family – Solanaceae
Type – Half Hardy Perennial
Hardiness – Zone 8
Height – 1.2m
Rotation – Treat as Solanaceous

If only this fruit was less spiny it would be a very popular plant.
Highly ornamental flowers and foliage reward the brave gardener with
the sweetest, tastiest fruits.

Origin & History

What a pity it is that this is such a spiny
plant. Many fruits carry spines: gooseberries
and blackberries for instance (although
there are now thornless types). But
fortunately, although they can be a little
hazardous to pick, at least the fruits are not
then covered in spines. Alas, this is not the
case with Litchi Tomato. Although the
fruits themselves do not bear the thorns,
they are enclosed in a spiny calyx, very
similar to that enclosing the fruits of
Ground Cherry or Cape Gooseberry. But
what a treat there is in store for the
intrepid gardener: succulent, rich, sweet
fruits tasting rather like cherries, with an
aroma and piquancy to them which is
unique.

Litchi Tomato has no long history in
cultivation since it is a relatively new
discovery as an edible. It is native to the
Southern USA where it is widely
distributed, turning up on disturbed
ground as a weed in some urban areas.

Uses

Presently, Litchi Tomato has not been
sufficiently developed to yield very highly,
and the fruits can only be considered a
delicacy, one to be savoured on their own
as one would eat Cape Gooseberries,
perhaps accompanying petit fours.

Cultivation

Growing them is very like growing tomatoes. They're actually slightly hardier than tomatoes – I have known them to withstand a slight frost, certainly one hard enough to floor all the tomatoes. But unlike tomatoes they are not affected by blight, and they don't require heavy feeding.

Sowing – The plants should be raised under glass in cold temperate areas. Sow in early spring, around early April. Do not sow them too early or you will have plants which are too big before you can do anything about planting them out. They are so spiny I don't recommend potting them on. Also they will not withstand much frost while they are young and sappy. Sow the seeds into a small pot of sowing medium and lightly cover. Place in warmth, around 16°C is ideal and keep them moist. Germination is rapid and the seedlings should be pricked out once they are large enough to handle, when the seed leaves have fully expanded. I prick them into individual 6cm pots, but any medium-sized pot will do. The plants will grow quickly given lots of light and warmth and they often get quite leggy and will tend to lodge. This is quite normal, and if they are staked they will actually develop a stronger stem after a few weeks and will no longer need support. If you cannot plant your plants out once they have filled their pots, give them a light feed to stop the leaves going off colour, or pot them on if you are feeling brave. Once the last frost has passed, plant out at 30cm apart, water in well.

Sowing outdoors in warm areas is simple: take out a shallow drill and sow thinly, barely covering the seed. Water well if the soil is dry. Once the seedlings are evident, thin them to leave the plants at a 30cm spacing. They may need staking at first, like those raised indoors.

Aftercare in all instances is the same. Water them during drought (although they are more tolerant of dry conditions than normal tomatoes). No training is needed to encourage flowering and fruiting. Flowers should appear around June and will continue for the rest of the season.

Harvesting – The prickly calyxes turn yellow once the fruits inside them ripen; sometimes they split to reveal the red fruits. These should be diligently and carefully picked as they become ripe.

In cold areas, you may want to remove the plants when they have finished to make room for another crop, but it is worth experimenting with its hardiness. I have overwintered plants twice now over a mild winter and a little head start is gained the next year. However the plants usually get completely defoliated by the winter weather and have to do a lot of regrowing before they get to fruit again, by which time young plants grown from seed have nearly caught up.

Varieties

There are no named varieties of Litchi
Tomato at the time of writing.

Plant Breeding and Selection

I have been experimenting with selection for size of fruit, and there has been
a marked increase in fruit size since I started. The seed strain I was given was
from plants with larger fruits, and I have consistently saved seed from only the
largest-fruited plants. It is also worth looking for plants which are less spiny; a
spineless plant would be a significant breakthrough.

Not all fruit and vegetable varieties are arrived at through complex plant
breeding techniques; in fact very few are. Most are brought about by
selection. Over the years that crops are grown, diligent growers look for
changes in their crops which can be used to advantage, and save seed from
plants which show these characteristics. They make a good starting point for a
new variety. Take tomatoes for instance: seed saved from plants which show
fruits which are much larger than normal may, over the years of further
selection for the largest fruit out of each generation, create a beefsteak variety;
on the other hand, selecting and saving seed from plants with smaller but
more numerous fruits create a cherry type.

A new crop such as Litchi Tomato is at the start of its career in cultivation,
and its potential has yet to be realised. Although for now it is spiny and the
bushes are relatively low yielding, in the future there may arise forms which
produce larger fruits, possess less spines or are much hardier and sturdier. It is
by saving seed from these plants and furthering a particular breeding line that
new varieties arise.

Naranjilla, Lulo

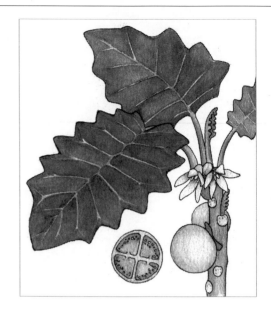

Latin Name – Solanum quitoense
Family – Solanaceae
Type – Tender Perennial
Hardiness – Zone 10
Height – 2m
Rotation – Treat as Solanaceous

An absolute gem from South America, grown since antiquity. It's not just grown for its fruit – the huge, fur-covered leaves are spectacular. "The Golden Fruit of the Andes."

Origin & History

Originating at high altitude in Colombia and Ecuador, this is a plant very specifically adapted to high altitude and has not been successfully introduced elsewhere. The juice and fruits do not preserve well, and the only way to appreciate this unique fruit is to eat it fresh. Lately, its productivity has seriously declined in Ecuador and Colombia, mainly due to intractible infestations of root eelworm.

Uses

The fruits are described as having a flavour combination of pineapple and strawberries. The pulp, and the juice expressed from the fruits, is green. It is said that the juice of

Naranjilla is one of "the most delicious beverages known". Attempts at canning the fruits have resulted in a complete loss of flavour; similarly the juice. Lately, progress with breeding is resulting in fruits with a better shelf-life and suitability for processing (see below).

Cultivation

I must admit that, despite having successfully grown this plant for several years now, I have never actually got any of my plants to fruit. And that's even by avoiding red spider mite (which normally make a feast of broad and hairy-leaved plants like this) and by having overwintered plants successfully, and by growing several unrelated individuals to ensure cross-pollination. It is a curious plant in that, even though it originates in the tropics, it is well adapted to growing at high altitudes where it experiences neither extreme heat nor extreme cold. It is quite frost-tender, but will drop its flowers if the temperature is too high. Given that Pepino succeeds well in a cool, maritime climate under glass, Naranjilla ought to also succeed in the United Kingdom and in coastal districts of the US.

Sowing – Raise the seedlings just like raising tomatoes. Sow several seeds thinly on the surface of seed-sowing medium in a 15cm dwarf pot. Barely cover the seeds and germinate at a steady 16-18°C. They germinate rapidly but seedlings are slow to progress. The seedlings should be pricked out as soon as they are large enough, at first into 9cm pots.

Aftercare – Naranjilla is unusual in that the plants don't mind being kept root bound. They will quite happily stay in whatever size pot they end up being grown in without displaying any ill effects. However it is important to keep the plants moving on by constantly potting on when they look like they've about filled the pot they are in. Unfortunately because they don't discolour or appear stunted in any way, the plants will give no clue as to when to do this. Just keep potting them on, is my advice! They require lots of water and a light liquid feed at regular intervals to ensure healthy growth. When they start to

flower, which they will start to do in their first year, it is important to keep the temperature low to avoid the flowers dropping. You can do this by moving the plants outside. The dappled shade created under trees suits them best, but be sure to get your plants under glass again in autumn before the first frost.

It is reckoned that plants are only capable of carrying fruits after their second year (they only live for three). To overwinter plants, keep them frost-free by moving them indoors or by using low-level artificial heat. It is important that they receive lots of light so that they don't lose too many of their leaves.

Varieties

Recently, cross-pollinating Naranjilla with another, closely-related fruit, the Cocona (Solanum sessiliflorum) has produced a productive and fertile hybrid, known as the Palora Hybrid. While this is not strictly a Naranjilla, it has similar characteristics in plant and fruit, but with the advantages a hybrid gives in better yields and adaptability. Further back-crosses to Naranjilla are showing great promise in producing seedlings which are adaptable to growing in other parts of the world, perhaps promising that this prized fruit, the "nectar of the Gods", may become more widely available.

Okra, Gumbo

Latin Name – Abelmoschus esculentus
Family – Malvaceae
Type – Tender Annual
Hardiness – Zone 9
Height – 1-4m
Rotation – Treat as Solanaceous

Lady's Fingers are a popular crop in the tropics, but can be coaxed into performing well in temperate areas. Even if not productive it is a very ornamental plant.

Origin & History

A native of tropical Africa or possibly India which is now widely grown in the tropics and subtropics, at least since the 19th century. Its true wild ancestry is unknown, but it is possibly of hybrid origin. Hybrids between Indian and Africa strains are usually sterile, suggesting that the two are not closely related. In India it is known as Bhindi, and in tropical Africa as Gumbo, from where it was introduced to America via the slave trade and where it is also known under the same name. Most of the Okra imported into the United Kingdom (where it is becoming an important ingredient) is grown in Cyprus, Greece and Spain.

Uses

The immature pods are picked and sliced or cooked whole. They are an important ingredient in Indian cookery, most especially in the savoury dish bhindi bhaji, and in American Cajun cooking.

Cultivation

Okra loves heat, and will barely grow when temperatures are low. But the plants develop quickly, and if they are sown in the warmest part of the year and grown away in the right conditions, a useful crop will soon follow. There is no benefit in attempting to sow too early in the year, at least not until after May, as conditions then are more difficult to maintain at that time of the year in cold temperate regions. Nor have I found it to succeed well outdoors: it is best to grow Gumbo under glass or in a tunnel.

Sow the seeds individually into 9cm pots. If you can spare the seeds, sow two to a pot and thin to the strongest seedling. The seeds have a hard seed coat and germination can be hastened by soaking them in warm water overnight. They are large and easy to sow individually. Germination is rapid if temperatures are maintained at 20°C or above. Seedlings will soon become leggy unless they are given lots of light immediately after they have emerged.

Aftercare – They should grow quickly if warm conditions are maintained, and they will rapidly become root-bound unless they are potted on. I've found that a check in growth is usually fairly final: if they are kept root-bound for more than a couple of weeks, the plants stand little chance of growing further if they are then belatedly potted on. That is, though, a good technique to keep plants dwarf, if that is what is required. Like all warm-weather crops, they enjoy heavy and frequent watering, and regular feeding, and high humidity to prevent the leaf tips scorching. Okra has a high potash requirement, which is conveniently applied by applications of Comfrey liquid.

Harvesting – The pods should be taken while they are still young and tender, 5-

12cm long. Older pods become unpleasantly stringy and are useless. Regular picking ensures regular cropping.

Pests & disease – There are no specific pests and diseases to Okra when grown in temperate gardens, but they do suffer from a "sudden collapse syndrome". This is simply due to cold, although the symptoms can often appear to be the same as those of a fungal infection.

Varieties

There are over 30 varieties, but few which are suitable for growing in temperate areas. Clemson's Spineless is the best known, bred in 1939 by the South Carolina Agricultural Experimental Station in Clemson. It will crop within 56 days, which is a good prospect for a short season. The Spineless reference is alluding to the pods, which in the landrace types tend to possess irritant hairs.
Pure Luck is a recent development, bred specifically for very short seasons and poor summers. It is the best sort for growing in marginal climates, and is low growing. It is an F1 hybrid.
There are several other fascinating types from the tropics, most of which are only worthwhile grown under heated glass: Burgundy has red leaf stalks and red fruits. Perkins Mammoth grows up to 4m. Vining Green is very tall and twining, requiring support.

Pepino, Melon Pear

Latin Name – Solanum muricatum
Family – Solanaceae
Type – Half Hardy Perennial
Hardiness – Zone 9
Height – 1m+
Rotation – Treat as Solanaceous

The Melon Pear is an underrated fruit, as easy to grow as tomatoes. Popular where it is grown, it is slowly gaining popularity in other parts of the world.

Origin & History

The Melon Pear is a native of the Andes: Peru, Chile and Colombia, where it is widely grown. Its wild origins are obscure, and no wild ancestors are known, but it is an ancient crop, represented in pre-Colombian pottery. Pepino is the Spanish name for cucumber, and it was so-named because of its cucumber-like flavour and resemblance. It is beginning to gain acceptance in parts of Australia, New Zealand, and California. It is particularly popular in Japan, where the highest prices for fruits are paid. They are popular as a gift, often wrapped, boxed and ribboned. The plants are shrubby in habit, slightly sprawling and loosely branched, giving the overall impression of a potato plant.

Uses

Usually eaten raw, out-of-hand, or as an addition to desserts and sweet meats. The skin is disagreeable and should be peeled. The fruit is very refreshing and is traditionally used by Andean herdsmen as refreshment on long treks. Mildly sweet, the flavour is similar to melon but with a pear-like undertone, hence its popular name. Cut in two, the fruit is densely fleshy with a small seed cavity.

In New Zealand, where its popularity is increasing greatly, it is attracting a lot of culinary experimentation and has been used in soups, sauces, served with prosciutto, fish and salads.

Cultivation

Pepino is in the potato and tomato family, and its requirements are similar to both. It is intolerant of heavy frosts but established plants will withstand temperatures down to -3°C, although they will lose most of their leaves. They are not daylength sensitive (unlike, for instance, maincrop onions which do not start bulbing until after the longest day). They will not usually produce fruits until early autumn, which coincides with a reduction in average temperatures. For this reason, they do not succeed well in hot, inland climates; maritime situations suit them best. The British climate suits them well, as long as they are given protection from late spring and early autumn frosts, and plants grown outside through the summer (where they experience cooler average temperatures) succeed better than those grown under glass. To summarise, plants perform best at around 18-20°C and suffer above 30°C.

Sowing Pepino can be grown from seed or from cuttings, which strike readily. Growing from seed produces very variable offspring, the result being that some of the plants may be of no merit, of poor flavour or low yield. However, most will be useful and it is the most practical method of propagation where vegetatively-grown cultivars are difficult to obtain, or where it proves difficult and expensive to overwinter plants. From cuttings, there is an increased chance of accumulating virus diseases and

nematodes, but with the advantage that plants will come into fruit earlier and results will be more predictable.

From seed

Sow seed like you would sow tomato seeds, onto the surface of seed-sowing medium and very lightly cover with sifted medium. I use a dwarf pot, 15cm, for sowing into and I space the seeds 1cm apart. If only a few seedlings are required, this method is more economical of space and materials than sowing into a seed tray. Gentle heat (around 20°C) will give rapid germination and the seedlings should be given lots of light and good air circulation once they have emerged; the latter is particularly important to avoid post-emergence diseases like 'damping off'.

Aftercare – Prick the seedlings out once they are large enough to be handled into 9cm pots, and into a potting medium. Growth is quite slow but steady, and they need to be potted on once they have filled their pots with roots.

From cuttings

Stem cuttings 7 to 10cm long should be trimmed of all but the topmost 4-5 leaves and inserted into a freely-draining, nutrient-free medium and kept in humid conditions. Rooting is rapid and there is not usually any need to apply rooting hormone. Indeed, the stems of established plants often root where they contact bare earth and these are a good starting point for propagation. Cuttings should be struck in autumn from selected cultivars, or from promising seedlings. Once rooted, pot them into potting medium, individually in 12cm pots and keep them frost-free through the winter, give good air circulation and admit plenty of light.

Aftercare – Seedlings and cuttings-grown plants can be planted out once the soil has warmed and the last frost has passed. They like full sun or semi-shade, and a rich soil into which lots of organic matter has been added. Space plants 50cm apart. Cloche protection is helpful to get them established, but should be removed once they have got going to lessen the risk of them overheating. Or they can be further potted on into large tubs and grown outside all summer, and moved in for frost protection at the end of the season. They enjoy frequent watering and feeding, with tomato feed: although they are tolerant of drought, fruit set and general health of the plants will be compromised if they are not regularly watered. Pepinos have a naturally sprawling habit, but if this is considered unsightly or results in neighbouring plants getting shaded out, the stems can be tied to short stakes. Young plants are intolerant of weeds, but established plants will outcompete them.

Harvest the fruits once they are ripe, indicated by them turning yellow to white with varying degrees of purple stripes. They should be left to ripen "on the vine" for as long as possible for maximum sweetness and flavour. Fruits will store for 3-4 weeks, but will lose their flavour if over-ripe.

Pests and disease – Pepinos are plagued by the same set of pests and diseases which affect other members of the potato tribe, including Potato Blight.

Varieties

There are many varieties, all of them grown from cuttings.

Colossal is the largest. Cream-coloured with light purple flecking. Free of soapiness. Ecuadorian Gold has pear-like fruits on self-fertile plants; fruits should be thinned if they are to full develop.

El Camino is the main cultivar in New Zealand, introduced there in 1982. Egg-shaped with bold purple stripes.

Miski Prolific originates in California. Sweet, rich and aromatic, early to mature.

New Yorker has oval fruit, originating in New York State. Good keeper.

Rio Bamba is a vining plant grown as a climber or in hanging baskets; purple veins and purple stems – very ornamental.

Suma is the most popular variety in New Zealand. Mild and sweet, globe-shaped with purple striping.

Temptation is a popular variety in Australia. Toma is prominently purple-striped. Main export variety in Chile.

Vista is a self-fertile, compact plant, seedling of Rio Bamba and is heavy yielding.

Radish Pods

Latin Name – Raphanus sativus & caudatus
Family – Cruciferae
Type – Hardy Annual
Hardiness – Zone 8
Height – 60cm
Rotation – Treat as Brassicas

The seed pods of all radishes are very good eating, and some are bred specifically for this purpose. The Rat's Tail Radish does not in fact produce any kind of taproot, only pods.

Origin & History

Radishes have been in cultivation for so long that their true origins are obscure. The ancient Egyptians grew and ate them as long ago as 2500 BC, as rations for workers on the Great Pyramids. The wild relative of the radish, R. raphanistrum, grows in many temperate parts of the world, in Northern Europe and Japan. It is unclear, though, whether the Oriental subspecies, R. r. subsp. raphanistroides is a true wild species or a degeneration from the cultivated form. Radishes have been grown in Japan since 700 AD, and in China since much earlier about 500 BC.

Uses

The succulent pods are best eaten raw, when they are juicy and crunchy with a slight pepperiness like the fresh root. They can be lightly steamed or blanched briefly to soften them for eating as a cooked vegetable. They combine well with other ingredients, in stews and curries, for instance, in place of Okra.

Cultivation

Growing radishes for pods is not much different from growing them for their roots, only in the case of summer radishes it is actually slightly easier. Normally radishes need to be thoroughly and regularly watered to stop them from running to seed. For growing pods, no such precautions need to be taken. However, they should not be starved entirely of water or the pods will be stringy and coarse. Grown for pods, they occupy the ground for much longer so site them carefully, accounting for their greater height and extensive growth, which can shade out neighbouring crops.

Sowing – Sow the seed as you would normally with radish, quite thinly direct into a shallow drill. Sow summer radish from early spring onwards in rows spaced 30cm apart; winter radish are sown in August and September. Keep the rows well watered. The first radishes to mature can be picked and eaten. By harvesting selectively, reduce the plants to one per 30cm of row. Normally, summer radishes can be sown from spring through summer into early autumn if they are grown only for their roots, but they will not mature in time to produce good pods from sowings made later than June. Winter radish can be left in the ground all winter in mild winter areas (with a covering of straw to protect against fierce weather) and allowed to run to seed the next spring. Winter varieties give the earliest harvest of radish pods.

Aftercare – For the best quality plants, and therefore the best quality pods, keep your rows regularly watered, especially in high summer when growth is at its most rapid. Regularly hoe to keep down weeds. Once they start to run to flower, it may be

necessary to stake the flowering shoots as they can become heavy when the pods form. On a windy site, this is essential.

Harvesting – Pick off the pods as soon as they are large enough. If they are left for too long the pods form an internal parchment, which is unpleasant to eat.

Varieties

Any radish can be grown for its pods, but some varieties are better suited than others. The sort to avoid are the round-rooted kind such as Cherry Belle or Prinz Rotin as they have very poor anchorage and the plants will need thorough staking.

Summer varieties
München Bier is a white-rooted variety favoured in southern Germany for eating with beer. This is one of the best varieties for summer pod production as it forms a large taproot which does not split and gives good anchorage.
Rat's Tail or Raphanus caudatus is a species from Java and India grows well in temperate regions. It forms no swollen root, instead it runs straight to seed, producing narrow pods up to 30cm long.

Winter varieties
Black Spanish Long is hardy and versatile. Black Spanish Round is similar to the above but with cylindrical root.
China Rose Red skin and white flesh.
Minowase Long is a white radish of the Mooli type, a very hardy Oriental sort.

Snake Gourd

Latin Name – Trichosanthes cucumerina
var. anguina
Family – Cucurbitaceae
Type – Tender Annual
Hardiness – Zone 10
Height – Climbing to 2m
Rotation – Treat as Brassicas

This cucumber relative can produce fruits of remarkable length – up
to 2 metres long. They're smaller grown in temperate regions, but
nevertheless very exciting to grow.

Origin & History

From India and Pakistan, where it is a
popular vegetable picked young. The young
fruits look particularly snake-like when
they're developing, twisting along their
length. They can grow very long, and
where they are grown in India a small
stone or similar weight is tied to the end of
the fruit to encourage them to grow
straight.

Uses

The young fruits are most used, pealed
along their length or sliced and eaten like
green beans, which they resemble in
flavour, or used in curries, sambals and
stews. The fruits turn bright orange when
ripe, and the pulp surrounding the seeds is
used in cooking in the same way as
tomatoes, hence its alternative name Snake
Tomato.

Cultivation

Snake Gourd is a tropical climber, and for
best results it should be grown under glass
everywhere but where the hottest summers
are experienced. It grows particularly well
in a polytunnel where it enjoys the higher
humidity. It particularly enjoys the soaring
summer temperatures. A deep rich soil is
appreciated, lots of water and organic
matter. It does not require full sun, and I
have grown lovely specimens at the end of
of a glasshouse overhung by trees.

Sowing Sow two seeds per 9cm pot, into seed-sowing medium, and thin to the strongest of the two if both germinate. They need high temperatures from the start, and they do not need a particularly long growing season so can be started off quite late into the spring, in early May. At that time of the year it is more feasible to maintain the high temperatures needed for germination (22°C minimum) and take advantage of the warmth of the sun rather than attempting to maintain temperatures artificially.

Aftercare The seedlings grow on quickly and will need to be potted on, into potting medium, and then finally into large tubs of potting medium, or into glasshouse border soil. A mulch of organic matter and/or black plastic keeps the soil warm locally and helps retain moisture. Plants need watering liberally and frequently. They also need support. A trellis of wire or netting is best, rather than canes which they tend to struggle to climb up; if they do, they tend to slide down them again when fruits have set! When the plants start fruiting, try to keep the fruits off the ground if possible to get them to grow straight, and to prevent the ends of the developing fruits from rotting.

Harvesting – As far as harvesting is concerned, treat them rather like you would treat courgettes. That is, take the fruits while they are small but at a useful size. Further fruits are encouraged through frequent picking, and a few should be left on the plants at the end of the season to fully ripen. They should be used as soon as they have turned orange: they rapidly turn to mush if left too long.

Varieties

Deccan Queen Long, has narrow fruits, usually green throughout but occasionally showing white striping.

Extra Long is a particularly long selection, for that record attempt. Also known as Extra Long Special.

Strawberry Spinach, Beetberry

Latin Name – Chenopodium capitatum
Family – Chenopodiaceae
Type – Hardy annual
Hardiness – Zone 5
Height – 40cm
Rotation – Treat as Brassicas

The leaves and the fruits of this curious Fat Hen relative can be eaten.
It is very ornamental, and great fun and easy to grow for children.

Origin & History

Native to Europe and naturalised in the US, this adaptable annual has become popular primarily as an ornamental, but all parts of the plant can be eaten.

Uses

The leaves and shoots can be picked as required and eaten like spinach, lightly steamed or boiled. The strawberry-like fruits can be picked and eaten raw when they are ripe in late summer. Although likened to strawberries, they're more like raspberries to eat – quite seedy, but without their sweetness.

Cultivation

A very easy and accommodating annual, it is indifferent to soil conditions and can be grown in sun or partial shade.

Sowing – Sow the seed direct in late spring, after the soil has warmed. Although it is quite hardy, early sowings tend to stagnate, only germinating when they feel conditions are just right for them, which can be frustrating. The first time I grew it I had nothing come up, and sowed something else in their place; I later had both crops to contend with growing in the same place. Drills for sowing should be 20cm apart, and seed is very fine and should be sown very shallowly, no deeper than 1cm, or it can be broadcast and lightly raked in.

Aftercare – Thin the seedlings when they're large enough to be easily pulled. Development is initially slow and they may be swamped by weeds unless regularly hoed. No extra irrigation is required, apart from in conditions of drought – growth can be stunted in a dry year.

Harvest the leaves when they are large enough, taking a few from each plant at a time. They are quite small and a lot need to be picked to make a decent meal. In late summer, the curious fruits formed in the axils of the leaves turn red as they ripen to indicate their readiness for picking. It is best to remove all the fruits before the end of the season to avoid being swamped with seedlings the next year.

Varieties

There are no known varieties of Beetberry.

Tomatillo

Latin Name – Physalis ixocarpa & philadelphica
Family – Solanaceae
Type – Half Hardy Annual
Hardiness – Zone 8
Height – 1m
Rotation – Treat as Solanaceous

The correct ingredient for Salsa, this tomato-like fruit is tangy and productive. Deserves to be more widely grown.

Origin & History

A native of Mexico, Tomatillo has for a long time been cultivated there but has never really caught on elsewhere. For a plant which is so rich in flavour, productive and easy to grow, this is surprising. In Mexican cookery it is important, replacing tomatoes which have come to be used in their place in other countries, particularly in salsa or other sauces for meat where they impart a unique tanginess which tomatoes never quite attain.

Uses

Traditional salsa is made from the purée of the fruits combined with other ingredients, usually onion and coriander. The purple form is quite tangy and sharp, useful only in cooking, but the green form is sweeter and can be eaten raw.

Cultivation

Tomatillos are grown in almost exactly the same way as tomatoes. They are always grown as a bush and do not require any pinching out or training, but they do need a stout stake for support as the fruits can be heavy.

Sowing – They are raised in gentle heat, sown shallowly in pots and covered, then pricked out into individual pots when large enough to handle. Growth is very rapid and they may need potting on before planting out after the last frost in cold temperate regions. They should be given a short stake while they are developing in their pots, and a longer, stouter one when planted out. The plants are extensive and at least half a metre spacing is needed. Unlike Cape Gooseberries, they do not fruit any better for being grown in containers, nor do they make significantly smaller plants. But they do lend themselves to being grown in pots, and will ripen sooner and for longer if they are grown under glass or in a polytunnel.

Aftercare – Water and feed thoroughly while fruits are forming. Where tomatoes would normally be pinched out and trained, especially in short season areas to promote the fruit to ripen, they require no training. A single fruit is formed in the crotch of each branch, and pinching and training is unnecessary.

Harvesting – The fruits are gathered as soon as they are large enough to be useful. When fully ripe they fall off, but are kept clean by their all-enclosing papery calyx; in fact they don't so much ripen as merely fully develop – they gain no sweetness when full size. Fruits can be gathered from June onwards if sowing is early, usually in early April. Plants will go on cropping until the first frost.

They suffer few of the diseases which affect tomatoes: certainly not Potato Blight, which can be destructive in late summer in humid climates. A close eye does have to kept for Pepino Mosaic Virus, which shows

as small perforations in developing leaves, and is seed borne. Any affected plants, and infected seeds, must be destroyed by burning.

Varieties

Physalis ixocarpa is the principal Tomatillo species. There are several varieties.
Golden Nugget has fruits are large and yellow.
With Large Green, the fruits stay green when ripe, calyx not veined.
Purple Husk has small fruits enclosed in all-purple husk.
Rendidore has fruits that are large, yellowish-green.
Verde Puebla has large fruits, yellow.
The Physalis Philadelphica is considered to be the Wild Tomatillo or Miltomate, and to some people it has a superior flavour, although the fruits are smaller. With their husks pulled back they can be stored for months threaded on strings. It's native to Central America, despite what its name might suggest.
Purple de Milpa fruits are small, purple-tinged with sharp flavour. It is this variety which is most favoured for sauces.

Tomatillo fruit

Tree Tomato, Tamarillo

Latin Name – Cyphomandra crassicaulis
Family – Solanaceae
Type – Tender Perennial
Hardiness – Zone 9
Height – 6m
Rotation – Treat as Permanent bed

Not really a tomato, but a sub-tropical tree related to the tomato, producing round red or yellow fruits in abundance.

Origin & History

A native of Peru, it has been introduced to other countries where similar conditions to its high-altitude habitat prevail, most notably to New Zealand where it has become a major commercial success. In South America is is a popular domestic tree, particularly in urban gardens where its umbrella-like canopy of leaves casts a welcome shade as well as providing fruit. Nowhere else outside New Zealand, though, is it grown commercially, but it is grown in Southern Europe outdoors, round the Mediterranean, but only succeeds with conservatory protection in Northern Europe.

Uses

The fruit is mostly eaten raw, out of hand, with the addition of a little sugar – they are quite tart. Or they can be stewed, and make excellent pickles and jams. The fruits are high in pectin.

Cultivation

Although it will normally grow into a small tree, it is possible to grow Tree Tomato in a container where it will fruit after the second year from seed. With judicious pruning and regular feeding it is possible to keep it as a small bush. Left unfettered, it quickly makes a small tree which is rather unmanageable for the average garden, and in such a state will be difficult for the gardener of modest resources to overwinter successfully.

Sowing – Sow and raise the seedlings like tomatoes. They should be sown into dwarf pots, 15cm, onto the surface of seed-sowing medium, and barely covered. Germination is fairly rapid between 22-25°C. It is better to sow seeds in mid spring, when temperatures are easier to maintain.

Aftercare – Prick the seedlings out into individual 9cm pots soon as they are large enough. With lots of light and air, and plenty of warmth, they progress very rapidly and by the end of their first year will have made large and very handsome plants, about 1m tall and with a single stem. The seedlings will need potting on regularly to keep them growing rapidly, and regular feeding keeps them in good health. Being originally from high altitudes, hot summers do not suit tree tomato and they are best stood outside through the summer months to avoid them overheating under glass – in areas experiencing day temperatures above 22°C for long periods, they do not fair well.

Overwintering – No matter how large a Tree Tomato eventually becomes by the end of its first season, it will not fruit in its first year. Plants need to be overwintered somewhere frost-free – on a windowsill in a frost-free room, in a porch or conservatory is fine. They must receive plenty of light but not too much warmth.

This encourages growth which the plants are unable to support. Most of the leaves will fall off by the end of the winter. To keep the plants bushy and manageable, in the spring cut the stems to half their length to encourage side-shoots to form. It is these which, the following summer, will flower and set fruit. Keep them restricted in a small container, but be sure to keep watering and feeding the plants regularly through the summer, but water very sparingly through winter. Sometimes roots will grow out of the bottom of the container which can be pruned off, to encourage fine feeding roots.

Varieties

There are two different types, red and yellow fruited. Lately, breeding work has been carried out, mostly in New Zealand, to improve on the standard red and yellow sorts which had, previously, been very variable.

Ecuadorian Orange is much sweeter than other varieties, and of course orange, with a creamy texture.

Goldmine is from New Zealand, a very superior sort, large fruited, golden-yellow.

Oratia Red & Oratia Yellow are two of the most promising recent commercial varieties, the basis for tamarillo production in NZ.

Rothamer is the largest-fruited variety, bright red skin, yellow flesh. Originated in California.

Wax Gourd, Hairy Melon

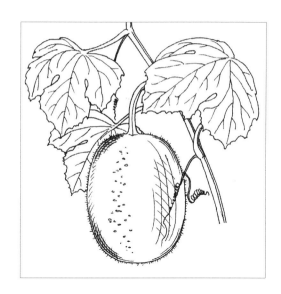

Latin Name – Benincasa hispida
Family – Cucurbitaceae
Type – Half Hardy Annual
Hardiness – Zone 10
Height – Climbing to 3m+
Rotation – Treat as Brassicas

The name of this plant depends on how big the fruits are when they are picked.

Origin & History

The two names for this vegetable are given according to its state of maturity: it is called Wax Gourd when the fruits are fully mature, or Hairy Melon if the fruits are immature and still hairy. It is an important crop in China, although it is thought to have originated in Java or Japan. It has been grown in China for over a thousand years and is now grown throughout southeast Asia. It is regularly imported into the West, where it is becoming better known.

Uses

The large Wax Gourds can grow up to 14kgs. They are eaten as the main component of a traditional dish, tong gwa, or Winter Melon Pond Soup. After scrubbing off the waxy outer coat, they are beautifully carved and then filled with several ingredients and then steamed for 3-4 hours. The soup is then served in the steamed gourd. The flesh is also cut into chunks and stir-fried, and a dessert can be made from the flesh, candied (presumably similar to candied chilacayote). The seeds can be roasted and eaten, like pumpkin nuts.

Hairy Melons are similar to courgettes, and can be used the same way. Traditionally, they are cooked in stir fries, as in Taiwan, thinly sliced and fried with chillies. The hairs can be rubbed off, but they disappear when cooked.

Cultivation

Wax Gourd needs a fair amount of heat to crop well, especially if the gourds are to fully mature, and a long season. If it is only Hairy Melons which are required, they can be sown a bit later when less artificial heat is needed. Indeed, for Hairy Melons they can be risked outside in most summers, especially where a continental summer is experienced. They enjoy a rich soil with lots of organic matter added. They are demanding of plentiful water, too, and are traditionally grown on the water's margin.

Sowing – Sow indoors in mid to late April, or perhaps into May, depending on the size of fruits you are hoping to achieve (the earlier the sowing, of course, the greater the chance there is of the fruits growing really big). Sow two seeds to a pot of seed-sowing medium and thin to the strongest of the two if they both emerge. A pot about 9cm diameter is large enough. They need plenty of warmth to germinate and for growing on: 16°C is about the minimum for healthy growth. Sowing outdoors is possible as long as the soil has warmed up and the danger of the last frost has passed. Sow several seeds to each station, at the spacings given below, and thin to one after they have emerged. Cloche protection in the seedlings' early stages will help them along.

Aftercare – Plant out to their final positions when the roots have filled their pots. Try not to delay planting when they have reached this stage or they may become stunted. The spacing depends on how they are to be grown: if they are being allowed to trail, give them lots of space, around 3m, but if they are to be grown up a support they can be spaced very closely, at 60cm. The latter method is best where space is limited, but they must be provided with a very strong support such as a substantial trellis or pergola. Keep them well watered and it is wise to mulch the plants with organic matter, or with some sort of plastic or weave mulch to keep down weeds and retain moisture.

Harvesting – The youngest fruits, the Hairy Melons, can be cut for use as soon as they are large enough. Wax Gourds should be left for as long as possible to mature, until the vines are killed off by frost. Make sure that the fruits are brought in as soon as a hard frost threatens or they may be damaged. A fully ripened Wax Gourd will store for over a year.

Varieties

Some varieties are good for growing for Wax Gourds, while other varieties are better for the production of Hairy Melons. There are two basic types: round fruited, popular in Japan, and blocky-fruited, popular in Taiwan and southeast Asia. Large Round has huge fruits of the round type.
Oblong has very long cylindrical fruits. Small fruits weight around 2kg and mature

quickly. The best sort to grow in temperate areas.

Edibility

Are there any other edible gourds? What about those little warty sort that you see in catalogues, the ornamental kind?

Most ornamental gourds you seed as seed mixtures are all derived from the pumpkins, Cucurbita pepo, and are quite edible but are not worth eating – they have been bred for their particularly thick skin, and they are full of seeds, leaving very little space for flesh. They don't constitute much of a meal!

The Bottle Gourd (Lagenaria siceraria) can be eaten at the very young stage, like Hairy Melon. They are also quite hairy when young, but the fruits are very hard when mature, with little flesh. It is for their hard shells that they are grown, for fashioning into musical instruments, ladles, drinking vessels and so on. Bottle Gourds are straightforward to grown like Wax Gourd, given warmth and lots of space.

Luffa is also edible. Everyone knows by now that the luffa of bathrooms is not a sea-creature, but is the skeletonised interior of the mature fruit from the luffa vine, Luffa cylindrica. Its fruits can be eaten when they are immature, but better to eat are those of its close relative, the angled luffa, Luffa angulata. Its fruits are similar but they do not produce such a fibrous skeleton and so can be eaten when they are more mature.

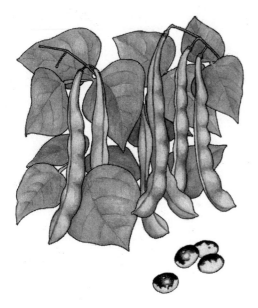

Seeds

Plants grown for their seeds or pods, eaten fresh or from dried.

Sunflowers are a familiar ornamental, but well worth growing for their flavoursome seeds.

Soya Bean and Yard Long Bean are more tender than other types of bean but with a little effort can be persuaded to crop. Soya Beans are becoming an increasingly viable crop in cold temperate areas through the efforts of plant breeders. And Chickpeas, too, are becoming increasingly popular.

The whole pods of Asparagus Pea are eaten. And you may have heard of Pea Bean, but just what is it?

Asparagus Pea, Winged Pea

Latin Name – Tetragonolobus purpureus
Family – Leguminosae
Type – Half Hardy Perennial
Hardiness – Zone 7
Height – 20cm
Rotation – Treat as Legumes

With the flavour of asparagus, it is the young pods of this attractive annual which are eaten whole. A flavoursome vegetable delicacy.

Origin & History

Asparagus Pea is a native of Southern Europe where it often finds its way into mixed forage as an agricultural crop, or used as a green manure. In Northern Europe it is better appreciated as a vegetable delicacy, only occasionally grown on any sort of scale as an edible crop because of the difficulties in harvesting. It has become naturalised in some southern counties of the United Kingdom.

Uses

The young pods are particularly fine lightly boiled or steamed and eaten as a vegetable accompaniment to other dishes, or lightly buttered and eaten as a dish in their own right.

Cultivation

Although they are quite a hardy crop, like many crops which are hardy but require a long growing season (like Celery, for instance) they should be raised under glass or cloches if you want a full season's harvest. They can be sown direct late in the season but their period of usefulness will be very short.

Sowing under glass – Sow two seeds per 7cm pot, placing the seeds just under the surface in seed sowing medium in April to early May. Gentle warmth is needed and germination can be slow and a little erratic, with seeds taking about three weeks to germinate. Once they are up, each pot should be thinned to a single plant by taking out the weaker of the two seedlings. The plants are initially quite slow to develop. They have a tendency to rot off so it is important that they are not overwatered, and that they benefit from lots of light and good air circulation.

Sowing direct – Direct sowing can take place from mid-May, once the soil has warmed. In drills 20cm apart, sow seeds 2cm deep, stationed in pairs spaced 15cm in the row. Because they are slow to germinate, a crop of radishes can be sown within the row to mark them.

Planting out – Raised plants can be planted out at the same spacing between and within rows as seeds direct sown, or in a block at an equidistant spacing of 15cm.

Aftercare is straightforward. Weeds should be kept down with regular hoeing. They're quite tolerant of heavy weed competition (they are used, after all, in mixed forage in some parts of the world), but a bad infestation can hinder harvesting.

Harvesting should be frequent, daily if possible. The winged pods soon follow their attractive red flowers and should be picked as soon as they are large enough, but before they are over-mature and have started to develop a harsh and unpalatable internal parchment. A method I like to use is to pick the pods daily, pinching them off their stalks (they're quite firmly attached) and them store them in an air-tight container in the 'fridge. Only once I've accumulated a really worthwhile quantity for a good meal do I cook them. Alas, Asparagus Peas are quite delicious, but not high yielding.

Varieties

There are no specific varieties of Asparagus Pea. There's scope for selection for plants which are less apt to produce parchment in their pods when they are fully mature.

Stringy

I've tried Asparagus Peas before and I've found them to be too stringy. Where am I going wrong?

Despite many recommendations that the pods are picked small (no larger than 2.5-3cm long) I have found that it is not the size of the pods which matters so much as how old they are. There's no denying that immature pods are ideal, but I've found that larger pods are really good to eat as long as they haven't been allowed to sit on the plant for any length of time. If they're allowed to fully mature, they develop an internal parchment, and it is this which can be unpleasant to eat. However, if they are picked as soon as they are fully developed, but only as soon as, then I've found them to still be really good eating, and you get a bigger total yield as a consequence. Like a lot of vegetables from which the youngest pods are eaten (runner beans, for instance), the more you pick them, the more are produced.

Breadseed Poppy

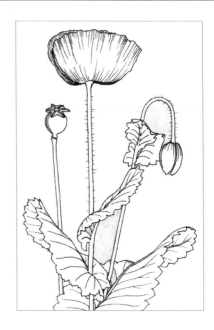

Latin Name – Papaver somniferum
Family – Papaveraceae
Type – Hardy Annual
Hardiness – Zone 7
Height – 40cm
Rotation – Treat as Onion family

As a flavoursome addition to breads and baking, poppy seeds are easy
to grow, and ornamental. Can be sown in spring or autumn.

Origin & History

Poppies have been cultivated for many
centuries, originally by the ancient Greeks
who knew their narcotic and
pharmaceutical properties. From Europe it
has spread to the Far East where it is
mostly grown illegally for opium. Until the
beginning of the 20th century it was
grown in Central Europe for
pharmaceutical use, for the production of
morphine and codeine for anaesthetic.

Papaver somniferum is a cultivated
derivative of Papaver setigerum, a much
hairier plant. The form grown for its seed is
distinct in that the seed pods do not open
to disperse the seeds when they are ripe; all
the seeds are retained until they can be
threshed.

Uses

The seeds are sometimes scattered on top
of breads to add a distinctive flavour. A
clear edible oil can be expressed from the
seeds, known as olivette. A second pressing
under heat produces further oil of an
inferior quality, used in paints and in
industry.

Cultivation

Poppies will fare well from a spring
sowing, but make stronger plants if sown in
autumn if the local winters are mild and
dry enough for them. Seed is very fine and
can be difficult to sow thinly. They will
grow even if severely overcrowded,
although small pods containing only small

quantities of seeds will result, albeit fully formed ones. It all depends on what you want to have to deal with: large pods are easier to thresh the seeds from, but in any instance the yield per square metre of ground will be the same.

Sowing – The seeds need light to germinate, so sow them very shallowly. Light will penetrate through a thin layer of soil so they can be lightly covered to prevent them drying out too readily. Poppies should always be sown direct as they cannot stand to be transplanted. Sowing should be in early spring to early summer in hard winter areas, and they can be sown in early autumn where winters are mild. Space the rows about 20cm apart and sow the seeds thinly. They can be broadcast, and it is often recommended as a technique for sowing the ornamental kinds to give informal drifts of flowers. However rows make life much easier.

Aftercare – Little maintenance is required apart from an occasional hoeing to keep down weeds. No irrigation is required – they're quite well adapted to a hot, dry climate but are accommodating of a cool, wet one too. If you think you have sown them too thickly, the seedlings can be thinned once established.

Harvesting – This is when the pods have become quite dry. The pods develop rapidly following flowering and will dry quite naturally, the plants turning straw coloured when ready. Pull them up and hang them in a dry place such as a shed or garage if wet weather threatens to turn the pods mouldy. The pods need to be lightly crushed to extract the seeds, and the debris is easily sieved and winnowed away. Seeds should be stored dry in paper bags or screw-topped jars.

Note: Ornamental varieties of Poppy tend to self-sow readily. Breadseed Poppy does not shed its seeds so will not do this. If you want to continue growing them each year you will have to deliberately resow them.

Varieties

There are no specific varieties of Breadseed Poppy. There are many varieties of Papaver somniferum, but they are only useful as ornamentals: they readily disperse their seeds when ripe so are useless if their seed is to be retained.

There's no denying the fact that the Breadseed Poppy is the same as the Opium Poppy. Grown in cool temperate climates, little if any of the narcotic alkaloids which this plant is notorious for are produced, and then they are only produced in the pods – the seeds contain no traces. There are some parts of the United States where it is illegal to grow Papaver somniferum without a license – for whatever reason, as an ornamental or for the seeds – so be sure to check before attempting to grow them there.

Chickpea

Latin Name – Cicer arietanum
Family – Leguminosae
Type – Half Hardy Annual
Hardiness – Zone 8
Height – 60cm
Rotation – Treat as Legumes

Much hardier than is generally supposed, Chickpeas are a versatile and flavoursome food deserving to be more widely grown.

Origin & History

Chickpeas have been grown for several millenia. Archeological finds around the Mediterranean, Ethiopia and India date from 5000 to 2000BC. It is a plant of arid climates, growing through the wet season, usually through the winter, to ripen the following spring – in India (where it is most commonly grown) this is just before the monsoon arrives. It is now most widely grown in Mexico at high altitudes, sown in spring, grown through a wet summer and harvested in autumn.

There are two types: a wrinkled-seeded sort shaped more or less like a ram's head which is commonest in Ethiopia and India, and a smooth-seeded sort shaped rather like an owl's head. It is this type most favoured in wetter climates, and is most suited to growing in cooler, temperate climates.

Uses

Mixed with oil, salt, garlic and lemon juice, the round-seeded sort are a vital ingredient in houmous. They are sometimes roasted and eaten whole, like peanuts. Wrinkled-seeded, ram's head Chickpeas are an important component of channa dahl, and ground into gram flour they make poppadoms. The glandular hairs which cover the plant exude malic acid, which in some parts of India is expressed and used as vinegar, which can be irritating to the skin.

Chickpeas can be "popped" in the same way as corn.

Cultivation

In cool, wet climates, chickpeas can be grown successfully from a spring sowing. It is reputed to be possible to grow them like broad beans from an autumn sowing, and in mild winter climates they are almost hardy, but they are dependent on a perfectly drained soil to overwinter successfully without rotting off. Autumn sowing should take place in September to give the plants opportunity to establish well before the onset of winter. An August sowing is too early, resulting in plants which are too large and prone to wind damage. The great advantage of autumn sowing in a damp climate, if they can be persuaded to overwinter successfully by cloche or cold frame protection, is that they have plenty of opportunity to ripen the following summer. They can be grown in a greenhouse or polytunnel, but can be quite wasteful of space – they are not high yielding; what they lose in yield they make up for in ease of growing. A rich soil is not necessary, but a sunny position is, and one which is well drained.

Sowing – Spring sowing should take place in mid to late April, as soon as the soil has warmed. In areas experiencing particularly cold springs, using cloche or fleece protection will help germination. Seeds are space sown in drills 40cm apart, 20cm

between each seed, and sown 2cm deep, two seeds to each station. A similar sowing scheme to that used for Dwarf French Beans works well; that is, in double rows 30cm apart, grown in blocks, 50cm between each block. They grow well in deep beds at 30cm stations. They are irresistible to rodents, especially the young seedlings, and will need protecting with netting or similar physical barrier.

Aftercare – Chickpeas do not compete well with weeds and regular hoeing soon after germination is necessary to keep weeds in check. The plants are strong-stemmed and well able to support themselves. Unless drought conditions become extreme, no extra irrigation is necessary.

Harvesting – Encouraging the pods to ripen successfully is the most challenging aspect of growing Chickpeas in a climate where wet autumns are experienced. If they don't look like drying successfully on the plants where they are growing, they can be taken up and hung upside down to dry in a shed or well-ventilated greenhouse. Because the pods are easily damaged by frost when they are green, it is important to anticipate the first frost and take the plants up before they get frozen.

Varieties

The following are owl's head, round-seeded varieties, better suited to growing in shorter, cooler summers than the ram's head sort.

Chickpeas are the subject of an intensive breeding programme by the legendary Carole Deppe, author of 'Breed Your Own Vegetable Varieties' who is selecting for hardiness, and for seeds suitable for popping.

Calia Italian for gold dust, this variety will grow further north than most. Quick maturing (90-100 days), height 50cm.

Kabuli Black Originating in Afghanistan, this variety is most favoured for growing in North America. Solid black seeds, two per pod. Tolerant of cold soils.

Pea Bean

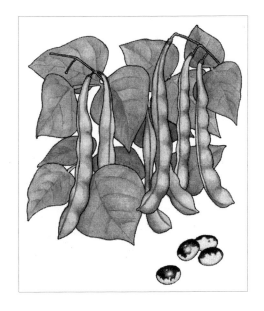

Latin Name – Phaseolus vulgaris
Family – Leguminosae
Type – Half Hardy Annual
Hardiness – Zone 8
Height – Climbing to 2.5m
Rotation – Treat as Legumes

Not a pea, but most certainly a bean, a climbing French type. The pods can be eaten green while they are young, but it excels as a drying bean.

Origin & History

French beans are not French at all, but originate in South America, from Mexico to southern Peru. They have been cultivated for thousands of years, archeological records proving them to have been grown as long ago as 5000BC. They are probably derived from several species, and climbing beans are the same as dwarf beans; the two are the result of different lines of selection from the same basic type.

There's nothing unusual about French beans – in fact they are now one of the most popular beans in temperate areas, despite them being frost-tender, more widely grown than are the hardier broad bean – but Pea Bean is included here to demythologise some of the confusion

which surrounds it. It is in fact a very unusual veg, unusual in that it is so poorly understood.

Pea Bean is an heirloom variety and is actually occasionally encountered in seed catalogues. However, there does seem to exist a great deal of confusion about its origins and identity. It is most definitely a bean, possessing all the characteristics of one: three leaflets to each leaf, twining habit (rather than clinging by tendrils like a pea), purple flowers (which actually some varieties of peas have) and long pods with pointed ends. The seeds are particularly distinctly bicoloured red and white, unlike any pea.

Uses

Pea Bean is one of the best varieties for growing for drying, or as fresh haricot, which are particularly fine as an addition to cassoulet or similar stew. They can also be eaten as a green bean when immature, although Pea Bean is not one of the best varieties for growing specifically for this – pencil-podded French beans are better for eating green.

Cultivation

Pea Bean is grown just like any other climbing bean. It is particularly suited to growing for drying as it is, unlike many other climbing French beans, quick to develop and set its pods in time for them to ripen sufficiently in a short summer. It is probably for this reason that it is such a stalwart heirloom variety in the British Isles. Beans like a well-cultivated soil, and lots of organic matter.

Sowing indoors – Seeds should ideally be raised indoors to be sure of giving them a sporting chance of ripening their beans, particularly if the season turns out to be poor. Sow in late April/early May in individual 9cm pots, or you can use old wooden fruit boxes as what used to be known as 'flats' – line them with newspaper and fill with seed-sowing medium, and sow the seeds at about 3-4cm stations into this, 1cm deep (before the advent of plastic seed trays and cells, flats where a common container for raising

seedlings). They should be planted out quite soon after they emerge if they are raised this way, to minimise disturbance to their roots. They should be planted out at the same spacing as seeds are sown.

Sowing direct – French beans usually fail if they are sown too early into a cold soil. It is better to wait until late May or even into early June, or they can be sown earlier if the soil is warmed first with cloches or fleece and kept covered for a while afterwards, in which case sowing can be from the end of April. Sow seeds 4-5cm deep, space them 20cm apart. They will need a support, and it is usual to build this of bamboo or coppiced hazel beforehand and use the canes to mark each station, and to sow at the base of each support.

Aftercare – Pea Bean is a robust grower and will outcompete most weeds, but the plants are easier to manage if weeds are kept down in the initial stages and so that they don't outcompete for water and nutriment. Regular watering is not important until the beans start to set. Unlike Runner Beans, which require pollination in order to set seeds, and for which it is often recommended that the flowers are occasionally vigorously syringed with water to encourage this, Pea Bean needs no such encouragement.

Harvesting – Green pods can be picked when quite young and used fresh, but they rapidly become stringy if left on the plant for too long, in which case they might as well be left to form beans within, for drying or eating fresh. If bad weather threatens to close in in early autumn before the crop is fully dried, the vines should be pulled and hung somewhere to dry fully, in a warm shed or greenhouse, before the beans are podded and dried for storage in jars.

Varieties

There is another type of Pea Bean: Orka or Ying-Yang bean has bicoloured seeds but they are black and white rather than red and white. Plants are of dwarf habit.

French and Runner Beans

What's the difference between French beans and Runner beans?

They are two different species. They're both of the same genus, Phaseolus: Ph. vulgaris is the French bean, and it is an annual; Ph. coccineus is the Runner bean, a perennial. Normally both are grown as annuals in our gardens, but in sub-tropical areas Runner beans persist for many years. It is possible to grow Runner beans from year to year by lifting the rootstocks after the tops have been frosted off and storing them in the same way as Dahlia tubers – Runner beans form a sort of spindly tuber similar to Dahlias. For many years after their introduction, Runner beans where grown solely as an ornamental. All parts but the pods and beans are poisonous.

Soya Bean

Latin Name – Glycine max
Family – Leguminosae
Type – Half Hardy Annual
Hardiness – Zone 8
Height – 50cm
Rotation – Treat as Legumes

Soya Beans are one of the world's most important crops. But they
need not be restricted to hot climates, they'll grow well elsewhere.

Origin & History

Soya has been in cultivation for so long
that its parentage is unclear. It has been
cultivated in China since the earliest
dynasties, and it is probable that it is a
hybrid between several Glycine species: G.
soja, and G. ussuriensis, a twining species.
Years of selection has removed the plant's
tendency to climb, for the size of its pods
and the inability for the seed pods to
shatter and therefore lose their seeds when
they are ripe. From China it spread to
south east Asia in ancient times, only
reaching Europe by the 18th century, quite
a long time after Engelbert Kaempfer's
discovery, and to the US by the 19th. Only
from the beginning of the 20th century
has it become an important crop in the
United States. It is seldom grown as a field
crop in Europe, where summers are rarely
wet and humid enough. But by growing
modern varieties developed in northern
USA, it is now possible to do so.

Uses

Soya has come to be associated with
processed foods, for which it has a history
of being used. In Japan, various
fermentations are used to produce bean
curd or tofu, soya cheese and milk, all
made from soya flour. Soya sauce is made
from fermenting the whole beans, as is
tempeh, a sort of bean cake. Since its
introduction to the West, it has become

one of the world's most important sources of protein and oil, for the by-product of milling as an animal feed cake, and for various industrial processes, including paint, soap, printing ink and linoleum. The seeds can be sprouted and are excellent eaten fresh, raw, as are the beans which are a popular pub snack, eaten in Japan with beer in the same way peanuts are eaten in the West. Or they can be cooked up like any other bean, in stocks and stews.

Cultivation

All Soya Beans are sensitive to daylength, and most traditional varieties only crop in response to lengthening days, flowering in early summer and so unable to crop successfully in cool, short summers. Modern varieties have been developed, specifically for growing in northern USA, which grow and crop quickly, within three months, and during the shortening days of late summer. It is these sort that should be attempted in cooler temperate climates, even in Britain, when most summers actually suit them very well. They enjoy lots of water, and demand a rich soil and plenty of organic matter.

Sowing – They should not be sown too early, mostly because the warmth that they need is not easy to provide early in the season, except by artificial means, but also because modern varieties don't actually require a very long season to crop, and then they will only do so when the days are shortening. Sow into individual pots, 9cm pots are an ideal size. I sow two to a pot and, if both germinate, I leave them both to grow. Germination is best above 18°C, and they should be sown into seed-sowing medium. Sow the seeds at the end of May, or even the first week of June. Progress is very rapid and they can be planted out within about 3 or 4 weeks after they emerge. By then the weather will have stabilised and the soil will have warmed. Plant them at 20cm stations.

Aftercare – They like lots of hot weather but they are intolerant of drought, so a thick mulch and regular watering is beneficial. Growing through plastic mulch has a lot of benefits, chiefly to keep the weeds down and retain water, but with black polythene you can greatly increase the local temperature. They grow extremely well in polytunnels.

Harvesting – It is unlikely that the weather is kind enough to allow the seeds to ripen on the plants, but sometimes a warm and dry enough autumn is experienced to allow this. To dry them otherwise, pull the plants up if frost threatens and hang them in a dry shed or greenhouse. The fresh beans can be shelled out when they are mature, and used straight away. There is no value in freezing them, although they can be.

Pests and disease – They experience no specific diseases when they are grown in temperate areas, but I have experienced problems with their attractiveness to rabbits and other rodents. Soya Beans, more than any other crop, seem to be preyed on by them. Netting is essential to protect the crop.

Varieties

There are many varieties of Soya, but few which are suited to growing in cold temperate climates.

Black Jet has beautiful matt-black seeds, suitable for drying even in marginal climates due to its quick development and maturity.

Butterbeans is a yellow-seeded variety, for eating fresh.

Envy has bright green seeds, good for eating fresh. It is the variety most suited to British conditions.

Frostbeater is hardier than most, and good for short seasons.

Fiskeby V (that is a 5 not a V) was greeted with a fanfare when it was introduced to gardeners in the UK in the 70s, and is worth seeking out. Very dwarf and quick maturing.

Engelbert Kaempfer

Born in Germany, Kaempfer was formally educated as a physician and linguist in his native country before going to live and work in Sweden. In 1663 he joined the Swedish embassy in Persia, where he took an active interest in the native plants. He joined the Dutch East India Company in 1686 as a ship's physician, working between Indian ports, to Java and Japan; he lived for two years in Nagasaki. It was before then when he was living on the small island of Deshima that he discovered Soya: the crop was a secret carefully guarded by the Japanese. It was while working as the Physician to the Governor of the East India Company that, by bribing the guards and picking plants along the route, he was able to gather the first botanical specimens of this previously-elusive plant. It was many years before it could be properly introduced to Europe.

Kaempfer returned to Europe in 1693 where he gained his doctorate in medicine from the University of Leiden, and then moved back to his home town Lemgo where he served as physician at the court of the Count of Lippe until his death in 1713. Kaempfer chronicled his exploits in the Orient which were published by Sir Hans Sloane as 'A History of Japan' in 1727, and his drawings many years later by Sir Joseph Banks, in 1791. He is honoured by having a plant genus named after him: the beautiful Kaempferia, a ginger relative.

Sunflower

Latin Name – Helianthus annuus
Family – Compositae
Type – Half Hardy Annual
Hardiness – Zone 7
Height – 2m+
Rotation – Treat as Brassicas

Not that unusual but as a garden crop they can be fun and productive
to grow.

Origin & History

Sunflowers were originally domesticated by
the native North Americans, derived from
the large seeded form of Helianthus
annuus, var. macrocarpa, a species
stretching in the wild from southern
Canada to northern Mexico. As with so
many edible plants, it was as an ornamental
that it was first grown in Europe after its
introduction into Spain in 1510. Only by
the 18th century did it start to become
widely grown as a crop. Although
Sunflowers as a crop is now consciously
associated with France, most of the world's
sunflower oil and seed cake is grown in
Russia and the United States, and Eastern
Europe.

Uses

In commerce, Sunflowers are grown for
their oil, and for the cake which is the
result of the expressing process, used as a
high protein animal feed. As a garden crop,
the seeds are excellent roasted in their
shells and used as a snack, or added to
salads to add distinct texture and flavour,
and nutritious, too. The immature flower
heads can be eaten like Globe Artichokes,
picked when swollen but before they open.
Lightly boiled, they have a flavour like
artichokes with a distinct floral aroma.

Cultivation

Sunflowers are quite hardy to late frosts
and can be sown direct into the ground

after the end of April in cold temperate areas. This is fine if they are to be grown as ornamentals, but if you want a successful seed crop they fare much better for being raised early under glass. This is especially so in British gardens, where the season is often very short.

Sow the seeds, two to a 9cm pot in seed sowing medium in March or early April. Give gentle warmth and they will germinate quickly. If both seeds germinate, thin to the strongest of the two. They grow quickly and should be given lots of light if they are not to become too leggy before planting out – if they do get too drawn, they tend to flop and bend and the stems will develop with a very ugly (and sometimes impractical) curve in them.

Planting out can be from the beginning of May. They may be put out earlier if you wish but I find they don't get away to a particularly rapid start if they are introduced to a cold soil. If your plants have got a little bendy and seem a bit weak, give them a short stake in the form of a flower stick or twig. Sunflower stems thicken considerably as they develop and you will find that there is no need to stake the plants once they have got off to a good start. Space the plants 45cm apart each way. They respond well to a rich, deeply dug soil. Although their name suggests that they need to be grown in full sun; they will in fact tolerate a fair amount of shade.

Aftercare is simply a matter of keeping the weeds down, and watering them during dry weather. If you're really after record-breaking height or flowerhead size, then an occasional liquid feed will help. It's lots of water and warmth, though, which is the real key to success with Sunflowers.

Harvest the seedheads when the seeds within are quite ripe. They can be left on the plants well into the autumn but if they are left too long, birds may start feeding on them and they can go mouldy if the weather starts to get very damp. Snip the flowerheads off and put them into a warm dry place. The greenhouse is a good place for drying the heads, or the garden shed. The seeds are rubbed out of the dried heads and can be stored in bags or jars.

Varieties

Only those varieties which produce large flowerheads are any good for growing for seed. Ornamental varieties which produce multiple flowerheads are the best type to grow if you want to eat them fresh, whole.

Buying seed sold for pet food is a good bet, and a very cheap option – you'll certainly get a lot of plants.

Russian Giant is a variety normally sold for growing for record attempts, but as its name suggests it yields well. Seeds are stripy.

Rostov is a Russian variety with plain black seeds, medium height (1.5m) but with very heavy heads.

Tarahumara is a variety originally grown by Mennonite farmers but has been adopted by the Tarahumara tribe of North America. White seeded, high yielding and grown specifically for its particularly good quality seeds.

For eating fresh, Henry Wilde is a Victorian variety, very tall growing (2.5m) producing a multitude of individual heads. Extremely robust and strong stemmed.

Multiple-stemmed varieties are becoming very popular, and new varieties with this habit come onto the market constantly.

F1

Be wary of sunflower varieties which are F1. They are bred for cut flower use and are specifically bred so that the flowers produce no pollen. The advantage for them as cut flowers is that they last longer, but it means that they set no seed. I grew an F1 variety once and was surprised to see that seeds were set. However, I found that they were all hollow and quite barren. So avoid them if you want seeds. They are fine for eating their edible flower buds though.

Yard Long Bean, Asparagus Bean

Latin Name – Vigna unguicularis subsp. sesquipedalis
Family – Leguminosae
Type – Tender Annual
Hardiness – Zone 11
Height – Climbing to 2m+
Rotation – Treat as Legumes

Also known as Asparagus Bean, this warm–weather bean produces pods of great length, up to nearly a metre long.

Origin & History

Yard Long Beans are derived from Cow Peas or Blackeyed Beans, from West Africa and India but now a popular and widely distributed crop in warmer parts of the world. Cow Peas are thought to have first been cultivated in Ethiopia from 4000 to 3000BC. The Blackeyed Bean, derived from Cow Pea, found its way to North America via the Mediterranean, where it was grown since Roman times, and to South America from West Africa via the slave trade. Like many crops which have been in cultivation since antiquity, wherever they have been distributed they have become so highly selected that they are barely recognisable from their wild ancestry.

In China, North America and West Africa the original species, Vigna unguicularis, was selected for the size of its seeds and is the Cow Pea or Crowder; this is V. u. subsp. unguicularis.

In India it is grown primarily as a fodder crop. Dwarf plants have been selected, with short, well-filled pods; this is V. u. subsp. cylindrica.

The Yard Long Bean, Subsp. sesquipedalis, is mainly cultivated in southwest Asia and has been selected for its vigorous climbing habit and the length of its immature pods.

It is this last sort which is best suited for growing in cooler, temperate regions as a long period of warmth is not needed for the pods yield fully-formed beans.

Uses

The immature pods are picked and eaten like Runner or French Beans, and are quite stringless. Raw, the pods have a sweet, crisp texture and a flavour like mushrooms.

Cultivation

Yard Long Beans really require the protection of a greenhouse or polytunnel for them to crop successfully, and even then there is a chance, if the summer is poor, that they will not crop heavily. But if they can be coaxed into production with a little extra heat and some persuasion they are very high yielding and rewarding, and quite delicious. In a hot summer, extraordinary yields are possible and it is very exciting to watch the pods extend: they seem to almost grow by the hour. The plants are strongly vining and are not easily contained in a small greenhouse – they require at least 2m of headroom. They succeed well in hot, continental summers and grow well in most of North America and southern Europe.

Sowing – Sow seeds under glass, in April, in warmth. Sow two seeds per 9cm pot and thin to the strongest if both seedlings emerge. Use seed-sowing medium. Germination is best at 22°C or above.

Aftercare – Growth is rapid and the young plants should be planted out into greenhouse border soil as soon as they have filled their pots. Plant them 30cm apart.

They can be potted on into large tubs but they require a good deal more frequent watering and feeding if grown in containers. Soil should be deeply prepared and plenty of organic matter incorporated. They require frequent watering and a substantial support of bamboo canes, wires or netting. Yard Long Beans enjoy high humidity and high temperatures and if at all possible they enjoy being left to "cook" a little in warm weather by ventilating a bit late in the day, to encourage really rapid growth. Most Yard Long Bean varieties are short day plants and will not start to flower and set pods until the days start to shorten after mid summer. If prolonged cold weather is experienced, it is important that the humidity around the plants is reduced to reduce the incidence of botrytis, to which they are very susceptible if weakened by cold.

Harvesting – Getting the beans to make the full yard long may be a bit pushing it if the growing season turns out to be a bit lack-lustre, but they can be picked when really quite small, from about 25cm in length. They are too big if the beans inside can be seen bulging through and the pods are likely to be stringy at this stage.

Varieties

Most Yard Long Bean varieties originate in tropical or subtropical climates and have been selected for tolerance to drought, which is a bigger threat than cold is to growing them in temperate areas. Some varieties, especially those originating in Japan, show promise for growing in marginal areas.

The variety Black-Seeded matures in 70 days, this ought to succeed well where summers are short.

Charlotte is a variety hardy to drought and heat (which may not be such a great advantage to most Northern gardeners) producing long pods, 60cm long.

Dwarf is unusual in that it does not climb. Extra Long Red-Seeded has pods that can grow to a full yard, but are best picked when shorter.

Red Seeds is a leading variety where Yard Long Beans are commonly grown. Liana has vigorous vines to 3m+ with pods a metre long.

Orient Wonder is a variety developed in Japan shows promise for growing in other parts of the world. It sets better in cooler weather than others. The seeds are slow to form, so pods can be picked when older.

Purple is a Purple-podded variety, with purple leaves. Uniquely amongst all beans, the colour is retained after cooking.

Sabah Snake – The longest of all Yard Long Bean varieties, with white seeds and wrinkled skin, like a snake. An heirloom variety from Malaysia.

Asparagus Beans, Asparagus Peas

There are many vegetables which take their name because of their similarity in flavour and use to asparagus. Similarly, an awful lot of leafy vegetables take their name from spinach because of their similarity (just like many small mammals and reptiles, when eaten, are described as tasting "like chicken"). Asparagus Pea is not so confusing as there appears to only be one species with that common name. More confusing, though, is that there are two Asparagus Beans: Psophocarpus tetragonolobus often comes under this name but is also called the Winged Bean or even the Magic Bean because all the parts of the plant can not only be eaten, but are very high in protein. It is distinctly tropical, originating in tropical Asia. It is incapable of flowering in daylengths not associated with tropics. So, even if enough heat could be provided for it (and it needs a lot) it is not capable of cropping outside its native region.

Grains

There is more to life than bread — and wheat. These grains represent alternatives to the grains we know, and some are broad leaved.

Buckwheat is easily grown as a garden crop (indeed it is better suited, since it is difficult to machine harvest it) and makes an excellent green manure.

Quinoa and Amaranth are ancient crops of South America, all but forgotten outside of their country of origin but which have great potential to be grown elsewhere.

Job's Tears is an ornamental grain from India, like a miniature sweetcorn.

Amaranth

Latin Name – Amaranthus spp.
Family – Amaranthaceae
Type – Half Hardy Annual
Hardiness – Zone 5
Height – 3.5m
Rotation – Treat as Brassicas

An ancient grain, Amaranth was a staple of the Aztecs. Highly
nutritious, the grain is high in protein and gluten-free. The leaves can
also be eaten.

Origin & History

Archeological findings in Mexico reveal
that Amaranth was grown as long ago as
6000BC by the Aztecs. It was one of their
most important food crops. It was so
important to Aztec society that it became
entrenched with religious ceremony
which, to the eyes of the Conquistadors,
was associated with the idolatry, resulting
in those who ate it being persecuted, and
its cultivation prohibited. Amaranth (or, as
the Aztecs called it, tzoalle) never quite
recovered. It remains a marginal crop to
this day. It is better known as an
ornamental, and indeed it makes a
particularly striking crop.

There are several species of Amaranth:

A. hypochondriacus has almost died out as
a crop in Mexico, despite it being the most
productive for grain. It is now grown
mostly in southern India. It grows up to
3.5m in height and is multi-hued: the
tassels are from green to red to golden, and
colours in between. Some ornamental
varieties have been selected for their
colours, usually to give a colour theme.
A. cruentus is smaller, at 1.8m, but is still
imposing. Red forms are grown as a die
plant in India.

A. gangeticus known as bayam, is grown
and used mostly in Asia, especially India. It
is grown primarily for its leaf and
cultivated differently from the types grown
for grain.

A. caudatus is more familiar as the ornamental, Love-Lies-Bleeding, in its green and red forms. It is being successfully grown experimentally as a crop in New Zealand, for its grain. Known as kiwicha by the Incas, it was grown at altitude and is therefore better adapted to a temperate climate.

Uses

Amaranth grains are extremely tiny but are produced in huge quantities – around 100,000 seeds per plant. Unlike Quinoa, they contain no bitter saponins, and therefore require no processing before consumption. They are highly nutritious and can be used anywhere where wheat is used. However, they contain more protein than wheat and indeed any other cereal, balanced with carbohydrates and amino acids in proportions which many nutritionists consider to be near-perfect.

The seeds can be heated and popped like popcorn, or ground into flour and made into tamales and tortillas in Mexico, and for chapattis in India. Because it lacks gluten, it is unsuccessful on its own for making breads and cakes, but combines well with wheat flour. Amaranth pancakes are particularly fine, like blini. The leaves can be eaten fresh like spinach.

Cultivation

Amaranths don't grow anything like as big in cultivation in most coastal temperate

regions as they do in their native South America, but they can make imposing specimens nevertheless. They do not exhibit any reactions to daylength as do many other crops which have been displaced from the tropics, so will always yield a satisfactory crop of grain despite an indifferent summer, even from plants which have not reached the proportions of their Mexican forebears. Indeed I have harvested a decent quantity of grain from plants which have barely made 40cm high. If it is really big specimens you are after, raise plants early indoors and grow them in a rich soil in full sun, and give them plenty of water and organic matter. The sort of conditions that Sweetcorn, Pumpkins and Squashes enjoy suits them very well. For cool temperate regions, A. caudatus is the most successful.

Sowing under glass – Plants are best raised in cells as they resent disturbance to their roots. Sow onto the surface of seed-sowing medium and barely cover the seeds. A temperature of around 20°C suits them, resulting in extremely rapid germination, about 3-4 days. Sown in mid April they should not require any artificial heat. The seeds are so small that they cannot practically be sown individually, so the seedlings need to be thinned when they are large enough, to leave the most robust individual in each cell.

Sowing outdoors – You can grow good specimens of Amaranth sown direct, especially in a continental temperate climate. Wait until after the last frost and sow into drills 50cm apart. Thin the seedlings after emergence and when they are large enough. The spacing of Amaranth depends rather on the size of the plants you are aiming for, and a spacing of 1m is not unreasonable if you're aiming for (and have the hot summer climate for) real giants.

Module-grown plants should be planted out after the last frost, or initially under the protection of cloches if you are attempting to achieve larger plants in a marginal climate. Space them 50cm each way.

Aftercare – Keep the young plants hoed, and water the crop during the driest weather, although Amaranth are very drought tolerant.

Harvesting – Leaves can be taken when needed, from plants which are large enough to stand losing a few. The grain is ready when the crop has ripened, and needs to be threshed like Quinoa to express the seeds. Store the grain as dry as possible, in paper sacks or bags, or in jars.

Varieties

Amaranth is very variable when grown, and it is quite natural for a variety to show a lot of colour variation between individuals within one seed strain: plants which are red, golden, pink, green and orange from one packet of seeds is quite natural, and highly decorative. There has

been a lot of experimental work with Amaranth in recent years, resulting in varieties with so far nothing more than a number designation. Don't be put off: these varieties are particularly well suited to growing in temperate areas.

A422 is a very uniform variety, in habit and in colour. Seed spikes are yellow. Grows little more than 1m. Seeds boast 16.5% protein, the highest of any grain.
A452 is a multicoloured variety, around 2m high, variously gold, red, purple and green leaves, seeds and veining.
A454 is another multi-hued type, similar to A422 but taller.
Bolivia has red seed heads with purplish-black seeds.
Burgundy has dark purple leaves, and red seed heads.
Golden is the earliest maturing strain, best suited to short summers. Yellow seed heads.
Elephant's Trunk is well-known as an ornamental variety, this heirloom from Germany is also very productive. Arching deep-red to purple seed heads resemble an elephant's trunk.
With the Multicolour variety most are multi-coloured, but this one is particularly so. Red, green and yellow leaves with flowerheads similarly various.
Popping is the perfect variety for popping, like popcorn.

Buckwheat

Latin Name – Fagopyrum esculentum
Family – Polygonaceae
Type – Hardy Annual
Hardiness – Zone 5
Height – 50cm
Rotation – Treat as Legumes

A very useful grain, traditional in Eastern Europe and a vital
ingredient of Russian pancakes, blini. Very easy to grow, it makes a
good green manure, too.

Origin & History

Buckwheat originates in Siberia and has
migrated through Asia, via the Mongols in
the 13th century, to become an important
crop in central Asia, Russia and Eastern
Europe where it forms a part of local
cuisine. It is tolerant of poor soils and a
very short growing season, and drought,
and it became an important staple in areas
where other grains do not thrive. Although
the grain is nutritious and the crop is easy
to grow, the grain matures at different
stages (unlike other grains which mature all
at the same time) on plants which are still
quite green and which need to be dried
before threshing. It is not a crop which
lends itself to mechanical harvesting and

has fallen out of favour since farms became
mechanised. Only in some parts of
Scandinavia, Russia, Eastern Europe and
Northern Italy is it still grown on a
commercial scale.

Another species, Fagopyrum tartaricum, is
hand cultivated in the Himalayas and Tibet.
It is particularly well adapted to conditions
at altitude, and shallow, acid soils.

Uses

It is grown principally for its grain which,
ground into flour, is used as an ingredient
in the yeast-based pancakes blini in Russia
and Poland, and for making polenta in Italy
in place of maize. The grain can be boiled
in water or stock to make the nutty

flavoured kasha, another Eastern European speciality.

Cultivation

Buckwheat is very easy to grow, and is in fact more usually grown as a green manure. Although it is tolerant of harsh conditions and a poor soil, it grows better if it is well provided for. It likes a position in full sun.

Sowing – The seed can be broadcast where it is to grow, and raked in. Or it can be sown into drills 20cm apart, and barely covered. Sow in spring, as soon as the ground is dry enough to walk on. Try to sow the seed thinly, to avoid the necessity of thinning later – the seeds are quite large and easy to place.

Aftercare – Hoe off weed seedlings soon after emergence and keep the crop clean of weeds if possible, although a heavy weed infestation is tolerated. Buckwheat is very tolerant of drought, and indeed if a late summer dry spell is experienced this can encourage the seeds to ripen.

Harvesting – To maximise the useful yield, the seeds can be taken off the plants in the field, leaving them to develop more ripe seed before the end of the season. It can be an onerous task, but if the plants are regularly patrolled and the ripe seeds shaken off into a paper potato sack or a clean dry bucket, then the amount of grain harvested can be doubled. Otherwise leave the plants to keep growing until the end of the season, and then take them up and hang them somewhere dry when harsh weather looks like closing in. Thresh the seeds off the plants when they have completely dried.

Varieties

Buckwheat has defied improvement by modern breeding methods. However, one variety, Medawaska, has been developed by North American natives and French Canadians, and shows considerable improvements on the basic type, especially for growing on the American continent.

Job's Tears

Latin Name – Coix lacryma-jobi
Family – Graminae
Type – Half Hardy Perennial
Hardiness – Zone 11
Height – 1.2m
Rotation – Treat as Onion family

A grain crop from India, it is grown elsewhere as an ornamental but shows potential as a crop where it can be grown in quantity.

Origin & History

From southeast Asia, this grain crop is ground into flour or used in brewing. It is utilised in myriad ways by the Japanese who use a particular selection of Job's Tears called Ma-Yuen. This is a soft-shelled sort which is more easily threshed than the standard type. Ma-Yuen was a famous Chinese general who is attributed with introducing the variety from Vietnam two millennia ago.

Uses

Hulled grains are boiled like rice, parched (that is, roasted in the manner of corn, rather like making popcorn) or milled into flour. The grain can also be made into porridge, and used in pastries and desserts. In India it is used for brewing a beer called zhu.

In Japan, the variety called Ma-Yuen is grown specifically for a commercial product utilising an aqueous extract added to milk or whey to produce an acidic beverage. It is also used to brew beer, using the malt syrup derived from it called mizuame.

Cultivation

Job's Tears is quite adaptable to growing in temperate regions, and will yield a reasonable crop of grain in even the worst of summers. Like any grain, a lot of plants need to be grown to obtain a useful quantity of grains. Given that it needs to be raised under glass and planted out, it is most realistic to grow this plant as a novelty (and a very ornamental one at that) rather than aim for a viable crop. It grows very well in a polytunnel.

Sowing – Seeds need to be raised in gentle heat early in the year, to give the plants a sporting chance – they need quite a long season. Sow into 9cm pots individually, 2cm deep into seed sowing medium. Gentle warmth is best as too high temperatures can lead to rather spindly growth: around 16-18°C is fine. I recommend sowing in April, or into early May, but not later. With very early sowings it is difficult to give them the light and warmth they require, but if you do have the facilities to provide this, an early sowing has the advantage of prolonging the growing season.

Aftercare – Plants do not mind becoming root-bound (unlike other grain crops, for instance sweetcorn) but it is better to plant them out soon after they have filled their pots with roots to avoid a check in growth. Plant in a sunny position in late May/June, after the last frost and when the soil has warmed. The soil can be warmed beforehand with cloches or a coldframe, or perhaps a plastic mulch, but I have not found this to be necessary unless they are being planted into a particularly exposed site. Space them 30cm in the row, 50cm between rows. Or in a block, at 40cm

stations, which is an arrangement more befitting a grain (again, like sweetcorn). Weeds need to be kept down by regular hoeing. Job's Tears like lots of water, but will tolerate drought: in other words, better growth is attained by liberal watering, but they will withstand periods of drought.

Harvesting – The seeds go through an interesting colour change, from green to buff through a sort of metallic grey to finally glossy black when they are ripe, at which stage they fall off. You can intercept them before they fall by browsing through the plants as the grains start to change colour, and picking off those which are ripening.

Job's Tears is not hardy, but shows some resilience. Although the first autumn frosts will burn off the tips of the foliage, most of the basal shoots remain intact. I have successfully overwintered plants in a cold greenhouse where they have looked decidedly worse for wear by the end of the winter, but quickly regenerate in the spring.

Varieties

There are no known varieties of Job's Tears, except for Ma-Yuen, which has been in cultivation in isolation for so long it could almost be considered a subspecies. It is certainly worth seeking out.

Latin names: sheer poetry

There's a certain poetry about some Latin names and Job's Tears' Latin name is no exception. Coix is from the Greek koix, meaning grain (proving that Latin names are not strictly Latin at all, but a collection of Latin and Greek, and a few other languages, too, for good measure), whereas lacryma-jobi part translates, quite literally, as "the tears of Job". My favourite Latin name is that of the common annual weed Shepherd's Purse, Capsella bursa-pastoris, literally "the purse of a shepherd". If only all Latin names where so poetic and literal they would be more readily learned and understood, and maybe they would be used more often.

Quinoa

Latin Name – Chenopodium quinoa
Family – Chenopodiaceae
Type – Hardy Annual
Hardiness – Zone 5
Height – 2m
Rotation – Treat as Brassicas

This ancient grain from the Andes deserves to be widely grown for its versatile and prolific crops of seed.

Origin & History

Quinoa (pronounced keen-wa or keen-oh-wa) is a fast-maturing annual originating in the high Andes where it was grown as a grain crop by the Incas at the time of the Spanish conquest. It has been grown in South America for possibly 3000 to 5000 years. Alexander von Humboldt, when travelling through Colombia in the early 19th century, described Quinoa's importance to the area as "wine was to the Greeks, wheat to the Romans, cotton to the Arabs". It was once grown the whole length of South America, from southern Chile to Colombia, but is now restricted to Bolivia and Peru. Humboldt saw great potential in Quinoa to alleviate starvation world-wide, but since his introducing it, it has been slow to gain world-wide acceptance and remains the preserve of the health food or gourmet shop, or considered where it is mostly grown to be the food of peasants or "campesinos".

The wild ancestry of Quinoa is obscure, and it is possibly an amalgamation of several wild varieties. It shows great variability.

Uses

Quinoa grains contain a particularly highly balanced form of protein, and lots of it: about twice that found in other grains like wheat. The grains are used in the same way as other grains – ground into flour to make tortillas, bread, cakes and pasta; made into porridge, added to stews and even made into beer. The leaves are also good to eat, they taste like spinach.

The grain contains high levels of bitter-tasting saponins which must be removed before eating. They are water-soluble and can be removed by repeated rinsings with cold water before cooking. If boiled, this is not necessary as all the saponins will come out in the boiling water, and only one rinsing is required.

Cultivation

Quinoa shows a lot of promise grown outside its native range and, because it originates at high altitudes, well outside of the tropics. To grow Quinoa for grain in temperate areas, though, daylength-independent varieties should be grown. If leaves are all you want, any variety will succeed well. Quinoa has been grown as far north as the north of Scotland where it is often grown as a fodder crop for pheasants – it rarely produces good grain but produces good yields of leafy growth. It is not fussy about soil, but a rich deep one is most likely to give the best yields. A position in full sun is essential.

Sowing – Seed should be sown direct, quite late in the spring when the soil has thoroughly warmed from early May is ideal. Later sowings are not so successful for grain production. Later sowings germinate and progress quite dramatically in a warm soil in early summer. Sow in

rows 40cm apart, thinly, and barely cover the seeds. Seed can also be broadcast but broadcasting does rather complicate weeding and thinning later (especially if lots of Fat Hen seedlings emerge at the time, which are all but identical to Quinoa and can be difficult to discriminate). Seedlings can be raised under glass in modules if that is preferred, sown in April and planted out in May to a spacing of 30-40cm. Spacing of the plants does rather depend on how big they are likely to grow: larger varieties may need up to 60cm between them, and vice versa.

Aftercare – Quinoa is well able to look after itself, requiring no extra watering except for in the worst drought conditions. Emerging weeds, though, will smother the young plants and should be hoed off at the early stages, soon after the quinoa seedlings have emerged.

Harvesting – The seeds are ready when they turn a rich golden colour, like that of ripe wheat. They stay attached to the plant and need to be threshed before use. A close eye needs to be kept on the weather near harvest time; in a damp, maritime climate the seeds are apt to rot if they are left too long in the field in wet weather and the plants need to be brought in and dried upside down in a shed or greenhouse if they look like they are under threat.

To thresh, spread the seedheads out on a sheet or tarpaulin (or perhaps a groundsheet from a tent, which is what I use) and either stamp up and down on them or flail the seedheads with lengths of wood. Small quantities can be extracted by putting the seed heads in a potato sack and jumping up and down on it.

To winnow, toss the seeds into the air outside on a windy day: the heavier seeds fall back down more or less where they started, and the lighter chaff (the debris) gets blown away. It takes a bit of skill and practice to get the hang of this. It is important that the grain remains absolutely dry in storage as it germinates very readily.

Varieties

Quinoa has been the subject of extensive trialling, particularly in the late 1980s in the US and Europe (including the United Kingdom), resulting in the establishment of growing in temperate areas at low altitudes. There around a hundred known varieties, but only those considered feasible in cool, short summers are listed here. Dave takes 90–100 days to maturity. Named rather prosaically after Dave Cussack, who was instrumental in introducing Quinoa to Western agriculture.

Faro takes 100–130 days and is an adaptable variety from southern Chile, originating at sea level. Despite its long maturity time, it is the variety best suited to growing in the UK.

Isluga is yellow and takes 90–110 days. The seed heads are yellow or pink and very attractive. Quite tall but a reliable cropper in maritime districts.

Temuco takes 100–110 days. It contains less saponins than other varieties and grows to 1.5m plus

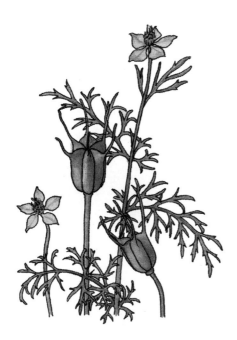

Flavours

Many edible plants do not really represent a meal in themselves, but add variety to what we eat. What may not be familiar to us are in other parts of the world are commonplace as additions to their cooking — epazote is added to beans in South America, and kalonji in north Africa and the Middle East.

The growing of saffron was once a thriving industry in Britain and the bulbs are not difficult to cultivate in a northern climate. The elusive sweet leaf gets a mention here in the hope that it might again become available.

Tender lemon grass, familiar in Thai cooking, can be grown as an annual, and caper, a favourite for pizza topping, makes an easy to grow, and very ornamental, pot plant.

Caper

Latin Name – Capparis spinosa
Family – Capparidaceae
Type – Half Hardy Shrub
Hardiness – Zone 10
Height – 30cm
Rotation – Treat as Permanent bed

It is the flower buds of the Caper plant which are pickled. This Mediterranean shrub is easily grown and ornamental, and can be overwintered in a cold greenhouse.

Origin & History

Capers grow wild from the southern Mediterranean, across the Middle East to India and the Gobi Desert. They are well adapted to hot, dry conditions usually in rock crevasses or in walls, in full sun, amongst building rubble and wasteground. They have been in use for thousands of years, but most Capers are gathered from plants growing in the wild since they are so ubiquitous where they thrive – the cascading branches of Caper bushes are a distinct feature of the Mediterranean landscape. The finest quality buds, are produced in southern France where they are grown commercially, and on a smaller scale in Italy.

Uses

The unopened flower buds are wilted and pickled as a condiment; sometimes the immature seed pods are also pickled (Caper berries). Useful in French dishes such as steak tartare and rémoulade, and as a favourite topping of pizzas.

Cultivation

In cold temperate regions, or in warmer regions where the rainfall is high, Capers are best grown in containers. They are highly ornamental and slow growing, so are well suited to method – being so tolerant of drought, they are very forgiving of infrequent watering and will withstand impoverished conditions. They do require

**GROWING
UNUSUAL VEGETABLES**

bright light to really succeed, and in wetter climates may perform better grown continually under glass, although they can be stood outside in the summer during warm spells. Where the climate is warm and dry enough, they can be grown outside. A regime similar to that for growing Citrus fruits suits them well, although they do not require to be as frequently watered during the summer. Propagation is from seed, or from cuttings.

Sow seed in spring. The seeds need constant warmth for germination and are best raised under glass, ideally in a propagating frame to provide heat at night, or on a sunny windowsill. They should be sown shallowly, just under the surface of seed sowing compost in a half-pot or seed tray. It is a good idea, although not a requirement, to add some grit to the sowing medium to improve drainage. In any case, care has to be taken that the pot is not allowed to remain sodden for too long between waterings. At a constant 18°C or above, and in light, the first seedlings will start to emerge after four weeks. Germination is very erratic, taking anything up to six months or even a year.

Aftercare – The seedlings are slow to develop and can be left in the sowing container until a useful population of seedlings has appeared. When they're of a handleable size they should be pricked out into small pots, into a gritty growing medium, one without too much nutriment. A soil-based growing medium is ideal (for instance John Innes Potting No. 2) as it is not too strong and plants will last in it for many years without it losing its structure. From seed, Capers will flower from their second year onwards. After the second year the plants can be potted on annually. In a favourable climate, young plants should be planted out in full sun and sited where their cascading branches can be appreciated; over a terrace or low wall, perhaps.

Cuttings can be struck in late summer using semi-ripe wood. They are easy to strike in humid conditions away from direct sun. Once rooted, fresh air and more light can be admitted to acclimatise them, and they should be potted on individually. It is important that the growing medium used to root them in does not contain chemical nutrients or rooting will be inhibited.

Harvesting – The flower buds are picked before they open, allowed to wilt for a day then pickled in vinegar after salting overnight. If the flowers are left, you will be rewarded with blossoms of extraordinary beauty, white with long pink stamens in profusion.

Overwintering does not have to be under heated glass if you are sure to dry the plants down thoroughly before the onset of really cold weather. If they are left too wet at their roots over winter, the risk of loss is greater. They may shrivel through drought over winter but will revive when rewatered during mild weather and with the onset of spring. To be really sure of bringing them through the cold, bring your plants indoors during the coldest weather. In the spring, a light pruning to remove dead wood will keep the plants bushy and more manageable.

Varieties

There are no specific varieties, but the spineless subspecies, Capparis spinosa var. inermis, is preferred and can be bought as a seed strain.

Epazote, Mexican Tea

Latin Name – Chenopodium ambrosoides
Family – Chenopodiaceae
Type – Half Hardy Annual
Hardiness – Zone 5
Height – 1m
Rotation – Treat as Brassicas

An indispensable ingredient for Mexican dishes, particularly in association with beans not least for its flavour but also its deflating properties.

Origin & History

A similar plant to Quinoa, Epazote is grown alongside beans in its native Mexico, which it compliments in many ways. The plant has a strong aroma which is reputed to repel insect pests; that same pungency is a pleasant flavour and a few sprigs of Epazote added to the pot in bean-based dishes adds a distinct flavour as well as (and this is also reputedly) deflating the beans – that is, reducing the possibility of flatulence.

Uses

A tea can be made from the leaves, hence the alternate name Mexican or Spanish tea. Otherwise, it is used as a cooking herb.

Cultivation

Mexican tea is very easy to grow, and although classed as a half-hardy annual, it is quite persistent in mild winter areas and will sometimes self-seed.

Sowing – Seed can be sown direct, late in the spring when the soil has warmed sufficiently to give rapid and even germination. Epazote does not need a long season, despite its tropical origins, since only a couple of small plants are needed to yield a useful amount. But it is a handsome plant, and to grow good-sized specimens seedlings should be raised indoors. Sow into cells or modules – the seed is too small to be sown individually, and the seedlings should be thinned soon after germination to leave one in each cell. Use a seed-sowing medium and cover the seeds very thinly. They germinate best at around 20°C, which is easily achieved with a later sowing, in late April or early May.

Aftercare – Plant out at 30cm each way, keep well watered and free of weeds. They can be grown in containers, in which case keep the plants well fed and of course well-watered.

Harvesting – Take the shoots when needed. The tips of the new growth are the best bits, and browsing them encourages side-shoots to be formed which makes the plant bushy; it otherwise has a rather untidy, willowy habit.

Varieties

There are no known varieties.

Huauzontli

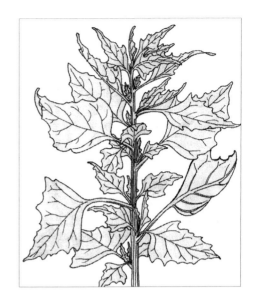

Latin Name – Chenopodium nuttaliae
Family – Chenopodiaceae
Type – Hardy Annual
Hardiness – Zone 5
Height – 1.5m
Rotation – Treat as Brassicas

From South America, this tall annual was bred to grow amongst corn stalks. Resistant to heat and drought it is a good standby crop in a difficult season.

Origin & History

It is very likely that Huauzontli originates from the same species as Quinoa, but because it has been grown mainly in Mexico, at low altitudes in hot, dry conditions, it is better adapted to a lowland, arid environment. Like Quinoa, it is likely to be a conglomeration of several species. Mexicans grow it between corn stalks, and the stems of Huauzontli are tall and the plant habit is narrow as an adaptation to that environment.

It has so far not been taken up for experimentation as a possible international food crop to quite the extent that Quinoa has in recent years. Grown mainly as a leaf crop, it also yields useful quantities of grain. It is distinctive for its spectacular colour change when it ripens, variously yellow, pink, magenta and red.

Uses

The immature flowering stems are particular good deep fried in batter. Leaves are eaten in the manner of spinach, and require very little cooking time: wilting for around 30 seconds is all they require in order to retain their flavour and texture, fried with onion in butter.

Cultivation

Huauzontli is very adaptable to a cool, wet climate, despite originating from a climate which is predominantly hot and dry. It can be sown direct into open ground in late spring, but for really spectacular plants they should be given a good head start by sowing indoors. It is quite hardy and can be sown direct early in the season, but if the seedlings are hampered by a cold, wet soil, they may be overcome by weeds and/or fungal rots. Huauzontli enjoys a well cultivated soil with lots of organic matter.

Sowing under glass – Sow seeds individually into modules. They should not be sown into a pot and later pricked out as the young seedlings are very brittle and few of them survive the move. A seed-sowing medium is recommended, and the seeds should be barely covered. A mid April sowing is quite early enough to get good specimens. With tiny seeds such as these, space sowing is difficult and it is more practical to sow several seeds to each cell, and then remove all but the strongest seedling in each about a week after germination. There is no need to give extra heat to encourage germination – the warmth of the sun during the day is all they need.

Sowing direct – Sow into very shallow drills, 60cm apart, and barely cover the seeds. The seedlings need thinning when they are of a handleable size, to a final spacing of 40cm – plants grown from direct sowings do not make the same eventual size as those raised under glass.

Aftercare – Plant the seedlings out in May, when their roots have filled their cells. They should not be allowed to remain too long in their cells or they may become stunted. Space each plant 50cm apart, equidistantly. They look particularly fine grown in a block, especially when they start to turn colour. No extra care is needed, apart from keeping weeds down; they withstand quite heavy weed infestations by growing above them. Although they grow tall (be sure to site them so that they don't shade neighbouring crops) they do not generally need staking except for the most exposed of sites, where they tend to grow much shorter anyway.

Harvesting – Take the leaves whenever they are needed, a few from each plant. Thinnings can be used whole. When the flowers start to form, the developing shoot can be broken out in the manner of broccoli spears. More will be encouraged to develop to take its place.

Varieties

Chia Roja Traditionally grown by the Tarascan of Mexico. It is grown entirely for its seeds, which are red and ground into flour to make tamales.

Fat Hens – Quinoa and Huauzontli are members of the Goosefoot genus, Chenopodium (lit. goose's foot). Other members are also edible, including the common weed Fat Hen, popular with livestock (hence the common name) and of course Good King Henry. But amongst the other species world-wide worth trialling are:

Chenopodium giganteum is Tree Spinach or Purple Goosefoot. The variety Magentaspreen is distinctive for the brilliant magenta colouration down the centre of each leaf. It can grow up to 2m tall.

Chenpodium murale is Australian Spinach, Sowbane. Not actually from Australia. Very like Fat Hen in appearance, but leafier. Produces useful seeds which can be popped like popcorn.

Chenopodium pallidicaule or Cañihua is another one from Mexico, the small seeds can be ground into a flour of a nutty flavour, eaten with sugar and milk as a breakfast cereal.

Apart from eating the grain, these can all be cooked like spinach.

Kalonji, Fennel Flower

Latin Name – Nigella sativa
Family – Ranunculaceae
Type – Hardy Annual
Hardiness – Zone 6
Height – 30cm
Rotation – Treat as Onion family

This Love-in-a-Mist is grown for its flavoursome seeds, used in Indian and Asian cookery, and in savoury and sweet cakes and biscuits.

Origin & History

From South West Asia, Kalonji is not as widely grown, nor is it as well known for its flavoursome seeds, in the West as it is in the East, although it is gaining in popularity in recent years. It is related to the popular annual Love-in-a-Mist.

Uses

In Indian and Southern Asian cookery at the time of writing it is becoming a very vogue flavouring, gaining popularity for use in fusion cooking. It is particularly championed by, ironically, Nigella Lawson. The black seeds are useful in naan breads and curries, cakes and biscuits in the place of poppy seeds. They are also added to pickles and chutneys. They are said to have anti-flatulent properties.

Cultivation

Kalonji can be sown and grown in the same way as any ornamental hardy annual, and is worthy of a place in the ornamental garden, or amongst herbs. It does not require a rich soil and will tolerate some shade. All Nigellas are easily raised from seed, and will self-sow.

Sow direct from early to mid-spring - they will grow well from a later sowing but may not have sufficient opportunity to ripen their pods in cool summer areas. The seeds can be broadcast and raked in, or sown in rows in shallow drills, approx. 0.5cm deep, 15cm apart.

Aftercare – The seedlings are quite spindly and are initially not very quick to develop so it is important that they do not become swamped by weeds at this crucial stage. Nigella responds to thinning by producing larger seed pods so if you wish to grow pods of a useful size, thin the plants to 15cm apart; they will also grow sturdier if thinned. However, they'll withstand a complete weed infestation and will still produce a few useful pods, but they may be difficult to harvest.

Harvesting – The plants die down, turning strawy, when the pods are ripe. Pick off the pods and crush them to express the seeds, and winnow away the debris. Seeds are best harvested in warm, dry weather. If the weather closes in and becomes too wet, plants can be taken up and dried, upside-down, in a dry shed or greenhouse.

Varieties

There are no known varieties. The species is described as having flowers which are basically white with a hint of blue. Plants I have grown from health food shop-bought seed, though, produced only green flowers.

Autumn Sowing

In areas where mild winters are normally experienced, most of Southern Britain is suitable, it is possible to sow Kalonji in late summer to overwinter. The soil needs to be well-drained, or at least choose a soil which is not excessively waterlogged through the winter. Sow as above in September. Small seedlings will result which will grow little into the autumn and hardly at all through the winter. However, early in spring they will make rapid growth and mature much earlier than plants sown in the spring. This way it is possible to obtain plump, ripe pods in the middle of summer when they stand a much better chance of drying fully.

Lemon Grass

Latin Name – Cymbopogon citratus
Family – Graminae
Type – Half Hardy Perennial
Hardiness – Zone 9
Height – 1.5m
Rotation – Treat as Permanent bed

A common perennial grass in the tropics, it is easily grown in temperate regions. An invaluable ingredient in Thai cooking.

Origin & History

Lemon Grass originates in South East Asia, but has become naturalised in most parts of the tropics; it is a successful coloniser.

Uses

For lemon flavouring and fragrance in mostly savoury dishes, but without lemon's attendant acidity. It is the fattened, sheathed leaf bases which are used, crushed and then sliced lengthwise. The flavour is quite potent and will taint other food unless properly sealed for storage.

Cultivation

Lemon Grass succeeds well in all sub-tropical and tropical regions, but it can be persuaded to produce a worthwhile crop when grown in cold temperate regions. It does particularly well in a glasshouse or polytunnel, even without artificial heat, as long as it is given a long season. Plants can be raised from seed or by division.

Sow seed in spring, early spring if enough heat can be provided, but in later spring it is possible to successfully germinate seed without the need for extra heat input. However, a later sowing will shorten the the growing season. Sow the seeds onto the surface of seed-sowing medium and

**GROWING
UNUSUAL VEGETABLES**

keep well watered. Light is needed for germination, preferably diffuse light. Germination is rapid if a constant temperature of 20°C is maintained.

Aftercare – After germination, give the seedlings as much light as possible and keep regularly watered but not sodden. They respond well to lots of nutriment, so prick them out as soon as they are large enough to handle into individual pots, about 9cm to start with, and into a rich growing medium. Like most grasses, though, they are very tolerant of root disturbance and can be left to grow quite large and then transplanted without suffering much harm, only a short check in growth. As each pot size is filled with roots, plants should be potted on. By late May or early June, it should be warm enough at night to plant them into a polytunnel or greenhouse, or even to risk a few outside in areas with long hot summers, or they can be grown on in large tubs. They are surprisingly tolerant of low night temperatures, but are sensitive to frost.

Harvesting is usually very late in the year, well into autumn if they are being grown in cold temperate regions. Useful stems are usually only produced by the end of September. Tear out the fattest stems when needed, leaving most of the rest of the shoots intact to continue to grow.

Overwintering is just about possible in unheated glass in mild winter areas. In some years it is possible to harvest Lemon Grass as late as December without any artificial heat, but they're usually fairly ravaged by the end of the winter. I have overwintered a few individuals which showed signs of regrowing after spending a winter in a polytunnel, but they failed to make vigorous and useful growth the next year – the plants I raised fresh from seed fared far better overall. Unless you can keep your plants in heat then it is better to start again the next year from seed.

Division: If you're growing Lemon Grass in a favourable climate, it is easy to split clumps to get more plants. Simply dig one up and split it, replanting each portion into improved soil.

Varieties

There are no varieties of Lemon Grass.

There are a lot of plants with the scent and/or flavour of lemons, and from a diverse range of plant families: Lemon Grass, of course, which is a type of grass; then there's Lemon Balm, which is related to Mint and Dead Nettle; Lemon Verbena is for sure a type of Verbena. But even more surprising is to find it in plants as disparate from the rest of the herd as ferns. South American fern Elaphoglossum citriodora has, when lightly brushed, one of the strongest lemon scents of all plants, a smell enhanced by the wet and humid conditions of its rainforest habitat.

Papalo Quelite

Latin Name – Porophyllum ruderale
Family – Compositae
Type – Half Hardy Annual
Hardiness – Zone 8
Height – 1m
Rotation – Treat as Solanaceous

A herb from South America with flavour very similar to coriander.
Easy to grow, it is an excellent coriander substitute, attractive enough
for the flower border.

Origin & History

Papalo is native to the southern United States, Texas down through Mexico to northern South America. The name is derived from the Mexican Papalotl, Nahuatl for "butterfly". It has been used for many centuries as a flavouring and it is likely that it was used long before coriander was introduced from the East to give traditional dishes the same flavour, and where today coriander tends to get used in its place.

Uses

The leaves have a flavour very similar to coriander or cilantro, and can be used in its place. Like coriander, it does not stand being overcooked and the chopped leaves should be thrown into the cooking pot at the last minute. It goes well with grilled meats, in salads, or as an ingredient in tacos and guacamole.

Cultivation

Papalo Quelite is easily grown. It should be treated like any other half-hardy annual, raised under glass or on the windowsill in spring and planted out when all danger of frost has passed. It is undemanding of a rich soil but does enjoy a position in full sun, especially if you want to bring out the colours of the foliage: they have a greenish-blue tinge when healthy, taking on red hues as autumn approaches and the plant runs to seed.

Sowing – Sow the seeds onto the surface of seed-sowing medium in a 15cm dwarf pot. The seeds are tiny and often have a feather attached, making sowing a little tricky, but they can be manoeuvred into place with the point of a label or a pencil point to space them. Barely cover the seeds and germinate at a minimum of 16°C. If you want your plants to flower, sow them in mid to late April to allow them a long growing season, but they can be sown later than this if it's only the leaves you require. Plants can also be raised in modules or cell trays.

Aftercare – Prick the seedlings out into 9cm pots when they are large enough and grow on with plenty of light and air. They are planted out after the last frost at a final spacing of 30cm. They are not naturally branching and it is a good idea to take out the growing tips when they are about 20cm high to prevent them producing a single, rather unstable, stem.

Harvesting – Keep the plants regularly weeded. Water during dry weather. If plants run to flower they can be left for seed.

Varieties

There are no known varieties.

Rock Samphire

Latin Name – Crithmum maritimum
Family – Umbelliferae
Type – Hardy Perennial
Hardiness – Zone 7
Height – 60cm
Rotation – Treat as Umbelliferous

A coastal plant, it was once widely grown for its lemon-flavoured leaves. Enjoys conditions in poor, well-drained soils.

Origin & History

Rock Samphire grows the length of the European Atlantic coast in sand, shingle and on rocky cliffs, and is naturalised in drystone walls. It is very well adapted to coastal conditions and proves difficult to establish inland, and over the centuries many attempts have been made to do so. The 'Gardener's Assistant' of 1925 admits that the cultivated product is not quite as good as plants gathered from the wild (which is forbidden in the United Kingdom) but offers detailed cultivation notes, including watering the plants on occasion with sea salt or with barilla, an alkaline and sodium-rich ash derived from incinerated kelp.

Uses

The leaves and shoots can be pickled and used like Capers, or added fresh to salads.

Cultivation

Rock Samphire is unusual amongst coastal plants in that it has a positive requirement for salt for its successful cultivation. Unlike, for instance, Beetroot or Asparagus which are also originate from the coast but which do not require salt, Rock Samphire does. It also needs to be grown in very well drained conditions, and to be partially shaded for part of the day. Not an easy plant to grow, but it will thrive once established. If you have a dry stone wall then that is an ideal environment,

**GROWING
UNUSUAL VEGETABLES**

otherwise it will grow in a perfectly drained soil. Drainage can be further assisted by creating a steeply-raised bed.

Sowing – Sow seeds in spring, from April, direct where they are to grow. The seeds are quite large and can be poked into the cracks in a wall, if that is where it is to be grown, or in shallow drills spaced 25cm apart.

Aftercare – Weed competition is not great in the sort of conditions Rock Samphire enjoys, but the young seedlings will need to be kept free of them to give them a sporting chance. Weeds are not such a problem in a dry-stone wall.

Harvesting – Take the leaves and shoots when required, from established plants – it may be a year before they are large enough. Rock Samphire is actually quite tender. It is usually protected from frosts in its coastal habitat, and in a hard winter plants can be lost. They can be protected with a layer of leaves or wrapped with bracken, or protected with cloches.

Varieties

There are no known varieties.

Saffron Crocus

Latin Name – Crocus sativus
Family – Iridaceae
Type – Hardy Bulb
Hardiness – Zone 6
Height – 12 cm
Rotation – Treat as Permanent bed

One of the rarest and most expensive of spices, Saffron is the stamen of an Autumn-flowering crocus. Not to be confused with the other Autumn Crocus (Colchicum), though, which is poisonous.

Origin & History

Saffron is assumed to be native of the Near East – the name saffron is closely interpreted in all European languages from the Arabic asafar, meaning yellow – but its true origins are unknown. It is perhaps derived from the wild Crocus pallasi, although the modern cultivated crocus bears little resemblance to that species: Saffron is a sterile triploid (see below) which produces no seed.

It has been cultivated in the Mediterranean since ancient times, having been introduced there by the Phoenicians to their colonies in Marseille and North Africa. The Arabs brought it to Spain in the 9th century, where most of the world's saffron is now produced. It was formerly cultivated in most parts of Europe, including Britain where it was introduced during the reign of Edward III. Saffron Waldon in Essex became the centre of cultivation of Saffron in Britain, where it was grown until the beginning of the 20th century.

The decline in Saffron is surely due to the intense labour required to gather even the smallest quantity; this also accounts for its high price. Estimates vary, but around 500,000 stigmas are required to make 1kg of Saffron. Saffron will always be expensive, given that it has to be hand picked during its brief two week flowering period. Cheap Saffron can never be the real thing: sometimes Turmeric (Curcuma longa), or Safflower (Carthamus tinctorius) is passed off as Saffron, but neither has the flavour nor the colour of the genuine article. To be sure of buying unadulterated Saffron, only buy the whole stamens. They should be red, with a strong scent and pungent flavour; dropped in water, they should swell and release a red dye which dilutes to yellow. But to be really sure you should grow your own.

Uses

Saffron imparts a strong yellow colour to whatever dishes it is added to, and the essential oils it contains add a particular flavour to seafood dishes. It is favoured for rice dishes paella and risotto. Saffron buns and cakes are traditional in Cornwall; Saffron was originally introduced there when it was traded with the Spanish for tin.

Although the Saffron stigmas contain a concentrated yellow dye, it is water soluble and therefore not suitable for dying fabrics, the Saffron coloured robes of Buddhist monks are dyed with Turmeric or Safflower.

Cultivation

Saffron crocus is very easy to grow, but rather more difficult to encourage to flower. If you bear in mind that it succeeds best in the Mediterranean then you'll stand a good chance of success if you can emulate those conditions. Because they grow through the winter to the middle of the following spring they need to be protected against severe weather if they are to produce sizable corms; these large corms will in turn yield flowers. For the best guarantee of success they should be grown in deep pots in an unheated greenhouse or cold frame. They will succeed outside as long as they are provided with good drainage. In both instances, bulbs should be planted in early autumn, September to early October, to flower in October / November.

Planting Outdoors – The bulbs should be planted into a raised bed into which, particularly if the soil is very heavy, some grit has been incorporated. Saffron is a heavy feeder, so it's also good to incorporate a little organic matter, but not so much that it is too retentive. Plant the bulbs spaced 7cm apart and importantly, they should be planted deeply about 15cm. Deep planting actually encourages them to flower. In late summer the soil can often be quite dry, so a good soaking after planting will get them rooting. Flowering sometimes coincides with a deterioration in the weather in cold temperate regions, so you may need to cover the plants with cloches as they come into flower to preserve the quality of the Saffron. Covering also keeps off excessive winter rains which can encourage root rots. They will make some growth through the winter, but little until the days start to lengthen after the winter solstice. When growth becomes more rapid with lengthening days, give them a feed with some high potassium fertiliser (comfrey liquid, for instance) to plump the bulbs up. By mid April they will have completely died down. If you think they are becoming a bit overcrowded, they can be lifted and replanted while dormant, but otherwise they can be left where they are for at least four years undisturbed. Dividing them, though, does encourage flowering.

Under glass they are cultivated in nearly the same way as those outdoors. The corms are planted 7 to a 15 cm wide pot, into a rich potting medium such as John Innes No. 3. I do not recommend a soilless potting mix as it can become stagnant, leading to rots. The pot should be filled half full, the bulbs spaced on this surface, then filled all the way up so that they end up planted quite deeply. Water them thoroughly after planting, and from then on ensure that they are kept moist through the winter. You can be more liberal with watering as the days lengthen after mid winter, and they can be fed. Once they are dormant, turn the corms out of their pots and clean them off, put them into storage somewhere cool and dry until you are ready to replant into fresh potting medium in late summer.

Grown outside or in, the corms divide after flowering. Usually there will be a large corm surrounded by one to four smaller corms. I usually grade these bulbs for replanting, keeping the flowering-sized ones separate from the smaller ones which I use for propagating, planting them at a different end of the bed, or together in pots separate from the larger ones.

Harvesting Saffron is time consuming but, if you've only a few plants, very satisfying. It is important to pick the right part of the flower for the Saffron: the upright anthers are yellow and should not be used; the stigmas are long and red, and floppy. They are fused together at the base. Pluck them out with tweezers. They are quite moist when fresh and should be dried, for a day or two in a warm room, before storage.

IMPORTANT NOTE: It is absolutely vital that the correct Autumn crocus is grown for Saffron. While some other Autumn flowering Crocus species will yield a passable saffron substitute (Crocus pallasi & cancellatus, for instance) it is essential that no part of species which are also commonly called Autumn Crocus, specifically anyColchicum species, is used as they are HIGHLY POISONOUS. To distinguish them, true saffron has three anthers, while Colchicum has six.

Varieties

There are no specific varieties of Saffron. It does not produce seed so there is, alas, no scope for selection. Sometimes an individual will flower in the spring: this is an occasional occurrence and does not indicate a spring-flowering mutation and the same individual may not necessarily flower in the spring again the next year.

Triploids

The site for genetic information for all organisms is the chromosomes. Normally these are paired: humans, for instance, have 23 pairs, while a waterlily has over a hundred; waterlilies need more genetic information than we do so that they can adapt their growth to their ever changing environment – a change in water depth, for instance – while humans do not. Organisms with their chromosomes in pairs are termed diploid. But sometimes a plant is produced which has chromosomes arranged in threes. These are termed triploid. While a triploid may possess all the characteristics of a normal, diploid, plant it differs in that the plant grows very much larger than a diploid, often twice the size, and it is not able to produce fertile seed. Saffron Crocus has at one time in its history become triploid. It would have first come to the attention of whoever discovered the first triploid plant because it would have been much bigger and more prominent, and also, therefore, more productive. It is perhaps no coincidence that many of our crops are triploid – potatoes, for instance – since they are so much more productive than their diploid forebears.

Shiso, Perilla

Latin Name – Perilla frutescens var. crispa
Family – Labiatae
Type – Half Hardy Annual
Hardiness – Zone 8
Height – 1m
Rotation – Treat as Brassicas

Often grown as an ornamental, the fragrant leaves of Perilla are a treat added to salads. Very popular in Japan as a cooked green.

Origin & History

Native to south east Asia and China, Shiso is mostly used as a garnish in Japan in the same way that parsley is used in the West. It has slight medicinal properties and is thought to rid fish of parasites. In China it has long been grown for the oil expressed from its seeds. In the West, it is better known as an ornamental, beloved of the Victorians in Britain who used it as a centrepiece for tropical bedding schemes.

Uses

Perilla has a strong, very pleasant aroma which works particularly well with fish, as a cooked green. Mixed in a salad, only a small quantity of leaves is required for its distinctive flavour and aroma not to be too overpowering.

Cultivation

Shiso is half-hardy, and for success should be raised under glass and planted out when all danger of frost has passed. It can be grown from direct-sown seed later in the year, but plants will be smaller, although they ought to yield a decent crop of leaves before the plants get frosted off. They appreciate a slightly acid soil, full sun and plenty of organic matter.

Sowing – Sow the seeds from mid April, thinly into half pots of seed-sowing medium. 15cm pots yield a convenient number of seedlings, more than enough for a small garden. Seeds should be lightly covered and will germinate at 16°C or above, within two weeks. They can be direct sown in June, in drills 30cm apart, 1cm deep, and the resulting seedlings should be thinned to about 20cm apart.

Aftercare – Prick the seedlings out as soon as they are large enough, individually into 9cm pots. Give them plenty of light and air to prevent them going leggy. They like to be grown on quickly and can be planted out as soon as the last frost has passed. They may need a little protection at first from high winds, but they are robust and need no support once they are established. Plants are big and bushy, and should be spaced 40cm apart, equidistantly. Some weed control may be required at first, but they soon smother out their neighbours. It is sometimes recommended that the growing tips are pinched out to encourage them to branch, but I do not find this to be necessary.

Harvesting – Take leaves off when required, a few from each plant and near the growing tip to ensure the tenderest, tastiest leaves.

Varieties

All Perilla varieties grown for ornament are just as good for growing for eating.
Green is the plain green sort, generally grown just for eating only.
Red is the purple-leaved selection, in all respects the same in leaf shape and size and plant habit, but purple all over.
De Nankin is a variegated form. Basically red-leaved and -stemmed, it has green streaks through its leaves.

Stevia, Sweet Leaf

Latin Name – Stevia rebaudiana
Family – Compositae
Type – Half Hardy Perennial
Hardiness – Zone 9
Height – 75cm
Rotation – Treat as Umbelliferous

The leaves of the Sweet-herb of Paraguay contain a sugar substitute, far sweeter than sucrose. Easily grown, but rarely obtainable this is a robust, productive plant.

Origin & History

The leaves of Stevia contain stevioside, estimated to be 300 times sweeter than sugar. As a substitute for sucrose, it has found favour as a sweetener in drinks and many food products in Japan and Brazil, but it is embargoed for this purpose in the West (see below). In its native Paraguay it was used by the Guarani indians long before colonisation by the Spaniards in the 16th century. They used it for for sweetening drinks and bitter medicines, and called it caa-hee (Honey Leaf). The early European settlers, the Gauchos, put it into their Mate tea for the "relief of physical and emotional fatigue". In the 1970s the Japanese took to using Stevia as a

sugar substitute following health concerns over the artificial sweetener aspartame. Its use in the US was banned in the late 1980s due to health concerns – it became illegal to use Stevia products and stevioside, and illegal to own a plant. Since 1994, following protestations by the American Herbal Products Association, it is now possible to use Stevia as a dietary supplement under the Dietary Supplement Health & Education Act.

Its sale and use have been prohibited in the United Kingdom since 1998 following an edict issued by the Foods Standards Agency.

**GROWING
UNUSUAL VEGETABLES**

Uses

Where its use is approved, the leaves of Stevia are sometimes mixed with those of herbs in herbal tea mixtures to add sweetness. As a dietary supplement, it helps in the treatment of diabetes, hypoglycaemia and candidiasis. The extract stevioside is used as a non-caloric table top sweetener, in confectionery, soft drinks, in toothpaste and in baking.

Cultivation

Stevia is a perennial in sub-tropical areas, or where it is given winter protection in a greenhouse or conservatory. I have successfully overwintered plants for two years running in an unheated greenhouse in the United Kingdom. It will die down completely over winter but quickly regrows. In most cold temperate regions it is easily treated as an annual, grown from seed; grown as a perennial, it can be propagated from cuttings.

Sowing – You can expect the viability of Sweet Leaf to be poor; in practical terms, this means that you can only expect roughly half the seeds you sow to germinate. Black and tan coloured seeds are produced by Stevia: tan seeds are not viable and should be discarded, or sow thickly to account for these. The seeds are very small and are best raised in pots or flats. Light has been found to improve germination, so leave the seeds uncovered but be sure not to let the surface dry out.

They germinate best at around 24°C. Prick the seedlings out into individual 9cm pots as soon as they are large enough to handle, and ensure that the sown pot is not unduly disturbed – germination can be erratic and further seedlings may emerge. They grow away quickly with plentiful light and warmth and should be potted on as soon as they have filled their container with roots. Stevia is very responsive to pot size: if they are grown in small pots, they will stay small but show no signs of wanting to exceed their bounds, whereas if they are continually potted on they very quickly grow large.

Aftercare – At high latitudes, Sweet Leaf is best grown under glass or in a polytunnel. I pot mine on until they are finally growing in a large tub, but they can be planted into the border soil to allow the roots to grow unfettered. Outdoors, they enjoy a deeply cultivated soil with added organic matter. They are unfussy about pH, but if the soil is too alkaline they are inclined to yellowing. A sheltered position is needed to prevent the delicate leaves shredding. The stems are brittle, too, and break away easily at the base so it is wise to provide a stout stake for each basal shoot. They demand a lot of water but do not enjoy a waterlogged soil, so good drainage combined with frequent watering is necessary – mulching with a thick layer of organic matter helps retain moisture and feeds the plants.

Harvesting – Pick the leaves as you need them, cut whole shoots to two thirds their length and remove the leaves for drying. The shoots should be taken before they flower, which they are inclined to do with shortening days in late summer and autumn. It does no harm to let them flower. Only if two or more plants grown from seed are grown together, however, will viable seed be produced: they do not self-pollinate.

Growing from cuttings – Stevia is a very variable, and if you encounter a particularly good individual it can be propagated from shoot cuttings. When overwintered plants come into growth in the spring, detach the stronger shoots and root them in humid conditions in a frame or round the edge of a pot with a plastic bag over it; they root

easily. Some literature recommends overwintering Sweet Leaf under lights, timed to give 14–16 hours light a day. However I find that, as with a lot of sub-tropical plants, they enjoy a complete rest through the winter. When growth recommences in the spring, it does so with great vigour. Plants which are not allowed a winter rest soon tire, and are useless after three years.

Varieties

There are over two hundred different strains of Stevia but no named varieties. It is very variable from seed so it is better, if you can obtain a particularly good form, that the plants are grown from cuttings. Strains from China have shown particular promise for growing in a cool climate.

Seeds

How can I get hold of Sweet Leaf? I see the dried leaves for sale in health foods shops, but not the seeds. Why is this?

Stevia seeds and plants of Stevia are, at the time of writing, quite difficult to obtain. In the US, the Food & Drug Administration (FDA) have specifically prohibited its use as a sweetener or as a food additive. It can be drunk as a tea, or eaten as a diet supplement, but American consumers cannot use it as a sweetener. For a long time its importation was banned but this was lifted in 1995 following lobbying by the American Herbal Products Association who called for its exemption under the Dietary Supplement Health & Education Act of 1994 for use as a dietary supplement. It continues, though, to be banned for use as a food additive. In the United Kingdom, Stevia is under investigation for its suitability as an edible plant or plant product. Pending testing, sale of seeds and Stevia products has been prohibited. Seeds were for a while available but have recently and suddenly been withdrawn.

Wasabi, Japanese Horseradish

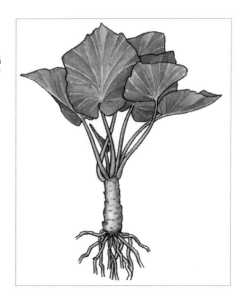

Latin Name – Wasabia japonica
Family – Cruciferae
Type – Hardy Perennial
Hardiness – Zone 8
Height – 40cm
Rotation – Treat as Permanent bed

Wasabi has a lot in common with watercress and enjoys the same conditions. It is used as a condiment; the flavour is indispensable to most Japanese cooking.

Origin & History

Wasabi grows only in Japan, growing wild in coastal habitats and near flowing water. It is seldom cultivated outside Japan, but where it is cultivated it is grown in special Wasabi beds in the same way that Watercress is grown in the West, in artificial pools fed by spring water.

Uses

The thick rhizome is macerated into a paste and then sold in tubes or dried down to make the Wasabi condiment. For maximum flavour, the rhizome is best used fresh.

Cultivation

Japanese Horseradish is grown in the same way as Watercress except that it must be grown in semi-shade, under the shade of trees, for instance, or under shade cloth. It is insistent on fresh water, clear and free from pollutants. It can be grown from seed, but is easier to grow from sections of rhizome. The best sort of set-up for growing it on a small scale is either to grow it by the side of a stream, or in a pit or trench arrangement such as that detailed for Watercress. It is not as hardy as Watercress, and some sort of winter protection, such as a covering of bracken or fleece, is necessary for it to overwinter successfully. Wasabi is fairly slow growing,

taking 15-24 months to produce a usable
length of rhizome.

Varieties

There are no known varieties.

Horseradish

The horseradish familiar as an accompaniment to beef is Armoracia rusticana,
a native of Russia and the Ukraine but widely naturalised throughout
northern Europe, usually as a garden escape, found growing in hedgerows and
roadsides. It is a very persistent plant producing a long, forked taproot which
is the part used for making the sauce, combined with oil, vinegar, and cream.
Relics can occasionally seen where it was once grown on a large scale –
colonies still persist to this day in fields where it was grown, most notably in a
field just outside of Glastonbury in Somerset which is now pasture, but where
the horseradish continues to thrive ungrazed.

Glossary

annual	Any plant completing its life cycle within the space of one year.	**Brassica**	Relatives of cabbage, Brussels sprouts, broccoli, kohl rabi, cauliflower etc.
apomixis	Plants which do not require pollination to set seed. Dandelions, for instance, and lettuce are also apomictic, some varieties taking it to such an extreme that the flowers never open.	**broadcast**	A sowing technique whereby seeds are scattered and raked in rather than sown in drills.
		bulbils	Tiny bulbs usually produced on the end of an inflorescense or in the axils of the leaves, providing a ready means of propagation. Babbington Leek, Rocambole and Chinese Yam produce bulbils.
axil	The junction between a leaf and a stem from where flowers or shoots emerge.		
biennial	A plant growing in one calendar year and flowering, fruiting (and then dying) the next. Strictly speaking, some biennials are actually annuals: they germinate and grow the previous autumn, flowering and setting seed the next spring, all in the space of less than twelve months (eg. Cornsalad).	**catch-crop**	A quick-maturing crop which is used to occupy land usefully between main crops. Radish makes a good catch-crop; so does rocket.
		cells	A modern alternative to seed trays, cell trays provide a self-contained rooting environment for seedlings, eliminating root disturbance. Also known as modules.
blanching	The process by which a plant is tenderised to improve its eating qualities, by one of two methods: 1. In the field, by excluding light by earthing up or covering the plants while they are actively growing. 2. In the kitchen, by immersing the vegetable in boiling water for a short time.	**chard**	A tight edible "bud" of leaves produced by blanching in the field, by excluding light. The chard of Chicory is called a chicon; Salsify can be blanched in late winter to produce chards.
		comfrey liquid	A rich organic sauce made from the fermentation of the leaves of Russian Comfrey (Symphytum x uplandicum).
bolting	When a plant runs to seed.		

One of the most potent, and economical, liquid feeds available to the organic gardener.

Compositae Belonging to the group of plants which includes Sunflowers, Daisies, Marigolds. Distinctive for their flowers which look like single flowers but are composed of two distinct types of flowers: sterile ray florets are on the outside, usually with a long petal to attract insects in, and disk florets which are petal-less and are fertile.

cotyledon The first leaves produced by a seedling.

covergent evolution Where two organisms show strikingly similar characteristics in response to identical environmental conditions, often despite them sharing a common ancestor. Some cacti of the American deserts, for instance, are almost identical in form to some of the succulent Euphorbias of the African desert.

cultivar Another name for variety, but most correctly applied to any variety which has been raised in horticulture rather than in nature.

direct sowing Where seeds are sown directly into the open ground, rather than raised indoors and planted out.

drill A shallow indentation made into soil to receive seeds. Usually made with a hoe or blunt stick.

F1 hybrid Abbrev. First Filial Generation hybrid. A plant-breeding term referring to the result of the first generation cross between two dissimilar parents to produce offspring which are especially uniform and vigorous. Seed saved and sown from these offspring will usually be very variable and therefore worthless; sometimes they are sterile.

freely draining And yet retentive.

genus In botanical classification, a genus is the equivalent to a surname, except it goes at the front of the plant's Latin name, not the end.

green manure Also known as a cover crop, green manures are quick-growing plants with an extensive root system which, in principle, captures nutrients which are otherwise washed away from a fallow soil. They are ploughed or dug in before the crop is sown or planted, to increase the organic component of the soil and return the nutrients.

growing medium The correct word for compost of the sort used for raising seeds or growing potted plants in. It seems pedantic, but it does make it distinct from compost of the sort made from vegetative waste — garden compost — used as a soil improver. It is not recommended that unadulterated garden compost is used as a growing medium.

half-hardy Frost tender. Half-hardy plants will withstand cold, but not

	freezing.
heart	1. The juicy, tenderest, most succulent centre of a leafy crop. 2. The ideal state for a soil to be in; soil nirvana. If a soil is well managed, it is said to be in good heart.
heirloom	A plant variety, rarely of commerce, passed down from generation to generation, or within a small community of gardeners.
improved soil	Soil which has been well cultivated, and usually into which organic matter has been incorporated.
isotherm	A contour on a weather map delimiting temperature zones.
landrace	A primitive variety of plant which has not been subject to the same vigorous selection processes as varieties raised by plant breeders, therefore tending to be very variable.
lodge	When a plant grows too tall too quickly, or too weakly, and falls over or is blown over.
modules	Also known as cells.
monoculture	Where a single crop is grown over a very large area.
mucilaginous	Possessing mucilage; that is, slimy. Some salad leaves or spinach substitutes are this (eg. Salad Mallow, Basella) but in a good way. Mucilaginous is a far more enticing term than slimy, hence its use.
nutrient	An elementary component of plant nutrition eg. Nitrogen, Molybdenum.
nutriment	A good old-fashioned word that ought to be revived, now

	overshadowed by the more scientific term nutrient. Nutrient specifically refers to the chemical composition of that which is nutritious; nutriment is a generic term for the stuff of plant-life itself: fertiliser, manure, moisture — all the good things a plant needs.
palmate	Referring to leaf shape: like the palm of a hand, with digits radiating from it.
parthenocarpic	Forming fruits without the need for pollination. Cucumbers, for instance, are this; they set fruits containing no seeds. Dandelions are parthenocarpic, but they also demonstrate apomixis (q.v.)
perennial	A plant persisting for three years or more.
potting on	Where a potted plant is potted into successively larger pots as it develops.
pricking out	The transfer of seedlings from their seed bed or pot in which they germinated to a new site or into larger containers.
repotting	Where a potted plant is placed into a fresh pot with fresh growing medium but usually, unlike with potting on, into a container of nearly the same size as the one it came out of. Much of the old growing medium is usually teased out and discarded in the process.
root-bound	A potted plant becomes root-bound when it has been left in the same container for too long. Its roots tend to bind

around themselves and plants which are left in this state tend not to establish successfully when planted out. Frequent repotting prevents this.

set
A section of tuber, or a piece of rhizome or corm used for propagating.

slip
A short shoot produced by a tuber which is treated like a cutting as a ready means of propagation. Sweet potatoes are propagated from slips.

specific epiphet
Latin names consist of two parts. For instance for potato, Solanum tuberosum, the first bit is the genus eg. Solanum, and the second bit is the species, or, more correctly, the specific epiphet eg. tuberosum.

spp.
An abbreviation for species, in the plural. Amaranthus spp., for instance, means that there are several species of Amaranthus which are grown as a crop.

staple
A main food crop. One of the biggest staple crops in the world today is wheat.

tender
Plants intolerant of sustained low temperatures.

thong
A root cutting with a bud attached. Sea Kale is propagated by thongs.

turion
A type of tuber produced by many aquatic plant species. Wapato produces turions, as does Water Chestnuts. They're usually formed at the end of a long rhizome, and end in a pointed shoot.

type species
The original species from which subspecies, cultivars and varieties are derived. For instance, Brussels Sprouts' Latin name is Brassica oleracea var. gemmifera: its type species is therefore Brassica oleracea.

Umbelliferous
Belonging to the group of herbaceous plants which includes Carrots, Celery and Parsnips, and hedgerow plants like Cow Parsley and Queen Ann's Lace. Distinctive for their umbrella-like flower heads.

variety
A variant from a species, one which consistently shows characteristics quite distinct from the type. If the variation has shown up in horticulture then it is more correctly termed a cultivar.

vernalisation
The pre-treatment of seeds by subjecting them to alternate warm and cold periods to break dormancy.

volunteer
A plant which appears somewhere where it shouldn't. Not a weed, as such, but an unwelcome offspring from a cultivated plant. Beetberry, for instance, will give lots of volunteers, as will Salad Mallow unless they are pulled before they set seed.

Suppliers

BEANS AND HERBS

The Herbary, 161 Chapel Street, Horningsham, Warminster,

Wiltshire BA12 7LU UK

telephone 01985 844442

Website   www.beansandherbs.co.uk

CHILTERN SEEDS

Bortree Stile, Ulverston, Cumbria LA12 7PB

telephone 01229 581137

Website   www.chilternseeds.co.uk

e-mail   info@chilternseeds.co.uk

Mind-blowing range of unusual plants, including many weird and wonderful

vegetable seeds.

DOBIES

Samuel Dobie & Son Ltd., Long Road, Paignton, Devon TQ4 7SX

telephone 01803 696444

website   www.dobies.co.uk

e-mail   info@dobies.co.uk

Comprehensive catalogue with the occasional unusual veg listed. Used to

supply Stevia.

D T BROWN

Bury Road, Newmarket, Suffolk CB8 7PQ

telephone 0845 3710532

website   www.dtbrownseeds.co.uk

e-mail   info@dtbrownseeds.co.uk

A large range of ornamentals and vegetables, including many unusuals.

MARSHALLS

FREEPOST PE787, Wisbech, Cambridgeshire PE13 2XG

telephone 01945 583407 (24 hours)

website   www.marshall-seeds.co.uk

e-mail   semarshall@btinternet.com

Vegetable seed specialist with an adventurous range: Chinese artichokes, kangkong, sweet potatoes all included amongst their other varieties.

MR FOTHERGILL'S SEEDS

Kentford, Suffolk CB8 7QB

telephone 01638 552512

website   www.mr-fothergills.co.uk

e-mail   info@mr-fothergills.co.uk

Three catalogues in one: ornamentals, vegetables and specialist plants.

ORGANIC GARDENING CATALOGUE

Chase Organics, Riverdene Business Park, Molesey Road, Hersham KT12 4RG

telephone 01932 248541

website   www.organiccatalog.com

e-mail   chaseorg@aol.com

Stockists of a wide range of seeds and sundries selected especially for the organic gardener. Agents for French suppliers Ferme de St Marthe.

POYNTZFIELD HERB NURSERY

Black Isle, by Dingwall, Ross & Cromarty IV7 8LX

telephone 01381 610352

website   www.poyntzfieldherbs.co.uk

e-mail   info@poyntzfieldherbs.co.uk

Specialists in Scottish herbs and edible plants, and exotic edibles: mashua, oca, Chinese artichokes, sea kale thongs.

REAL SEED CATALOGUE

Brithdir Mawr Farm, Newport near Fishguard, Pembrokeshire SA42 0QJ

telephone 01239 821107 (Tues & Thurs)

website   www.realseeds.co.uk

e-mail   info@realseeds.co.uk

Excellent small scale seed company run in a sustainable, sensitive way. Stocks some unusual vegetable seeds.

SIMPSONS SEEDS

The Walled Garden Nursery, Horningsham, Warminster, Wilts BA12 7NQ

telephone 01985 845004

website   www.simpsonsseeds.co.uk

e-mail   sales@simpsonsseeds.co.uk

Tomato and chillies specialists but also stockists of tomatillos, ground cherries and Oriental veg.

SUFFOLK HERBS

Monks Farm, Coggeshall Road, Kelvedon, Essex CO5 9PG

telephone 01376 572456

website   www.suffolkherbs.com

e-mail   sales@suffolkherbs.com

Lovely range of rarer vegetables specifically for the small garden. The most comprehensive stockists of organic seed varieties in Europe, their range includes many unusual vegetables.

THOMAS ETTY ESQ.,

Seedsman's Cottage, Puddlebridge, Horton,

Ilminster, Somerset, TA19 9RL

telephone 01460 57934

website   www.thamasetty.co.uk

e-mail   sales@thomasetty.co.uk

Interesting collection of older and unusual vegetables

THOMPSON & MORGAN

Poplar Lane, Ipswich, Suffolk IP8 3BU

telephone 01473 695200

website   www.thompson-morgan.com

Famously huge range of seeds with the odd unusual veg thrown in.

TUCKERS

Edwin Tucker & Sons Ltd., Brewery Meadow, Stonepark, Ashburton, Newton Abbot, Devon TQ13 7DG

telephone 01364 652403

website   www.edwintucker.com-mail

e-mail   tuckerseeds@agriplus.net

Huge range of seeds, including many unusuals. Some organic seed.

Common & Alternative Names

If you've heard of a plant but cannot find it in the main section, you might be able to find it listed here. Please note that the common names used for the vegetables in the Encyclopaedia section are not in any way definitive: naming anything by a common name is fraught with difficulties because of the number of alternatives which exist, hence this list.

COMMON NAME	LATIN NAME	PAGE NO.
Abyssinian Cabbage	Brassica carinata	22
Achoccha	Cyclanthera pedata	154
Achoccha – Fat Baby	Cyclanthera brachystachya	154
African Cabbage	Brassica carinata	22
African Horned Cucumber	Cucumis metuliferus	167
Allgood	Chenopodium bonus-henricus	39
Amaranth	Amaranthus spp.	214
American Cress	Barbarea orthoceras	46
American Groundnut	Apios americana	86
American Wormseed	Chenopodium ambrosoides	229
Anu	Tropaeolum tuberosum	118
Ash Pumpkin	Benincasa hispida	189
Asparagus Bean	Vigna unguicularis subsp. sesquipedalis	210
Asparagus Lettuce	Lactuca sativa var. angustana	33
Asparagus Pea	Tetragonolobus purpureus	193
Babbington's Leek	Allium babbingtonii	89
Balsam Pear	Mormordica charantia	156
Basella	Basella alba	24
Bayam	Amaranthus tricolour	26
Beetberry	Chenopodium capitatum	183
Bitter Cucumber	Mormordica charantia	156
Bitter Gourd	Mormordica charantia	156
Bitter Melon	Mormordica charantia	156
Black Cumin	Nigella sativa	234
Black Salsify	Scorzonera hispanica	131
Breadseed Poppy	Papaver somniferum	196
Buckshorn Plantain	Plantago coronopus	28
Buckwheat	Fagopyrum esculentum	217
Bulbous-Rooted Chervil	Chaerophyllum bulbosum	91
Burdock	Arctium lappa	94
Calaloo	Amaranthus tricolour	26

Orache	Atriplex hortensis	59
Padval	Trichosanthes cucumerina var. anguina	181
Papalo Quelite	Porophyllum ruderale	238
Par-Cel	Apium graveolens var. secalinum	48
Patience Dock	Rumex patentia	42
Pea Bean	Phaseolus vulgaris	201
Pepino	Solanum muricatum	176
Perilla	Perilla frutescens var. crispa	246
Petty Rice	Chenopodium quinoa	222
Pink Purslane	Montia sibirica	61
Pissentlit	Taraxacum officinale	37
Potato Bean	Apios americana	86
Purple Ground Cherry	Physalis peruviana	158
Quinoa	Chenopodium quinoa	222
Radish Pods	Raphanus caudatus	179
Radish Pods	Raphanus sativus	179
Rampion	Campanula rapunculus	124
Rampion	Phyteuma orbiculare campanulaceae	124
Rats Tails	Raphanus caudatus	179
Rocambole	Allium sativum var. ophioscordon	126
Rock Samphire	Crithmum maritimum	240
Roman Coriander	Nigella sativa	234
Roquette	Eruca selvatica	83
Safron Crocus	Crocus sativus	242
Salad Mallow	Malva verticillata var. crispa	62
Salsify	Tragapogon porrifolius	129
Scorzonera	Scorzonera hispanica	131
Scurvy Grass	Cochlearia officinalis	64
Sea Beet	Beta vulgaris ssp. maritima	66
Sea Kale	Crambe maritima	68
Serpent Cucumber	Trichosanthes cucumerina var. anguina	181
Serpent Garlic	Allium sativum var. ophioscordon	126
Shiso	Perilla frutescens var. crispa	246
Shungiku	Chrysanthemum coronarium	72
Sidra	Cucurbita ficifolia	161
Skirret	Sium sisarum var. sisarum	133
Snake Bean	Vigna unguicularis subsp. sesquipedalis	210
Snake Gourd	Trichosanthes cucumerina var. anguina	181
Snake Tomato	Trichosanthes cucumerina var. anguina	181
Soya Bean	Glycine max	204
Spanish Tea	Chenopodium ambrosoides	229
Spinach Dock	Rumex patentia	42
Spiny Bitter Gould	Mormordica cochinchinensis	157
Stem Lettuce	Lactuca sativa var. angustana	33
Stevia	Stevia rebaudiana	248
Strawberry Spinach	Chenopodium capitatum	183
Strawberry Tomato	Physalis pubescens	166

Summer Purslane	Portulaca oleracea var. sativa	74
Sunberry	Solanum x burbankii	164
Sunchoke	Helianthus tuberosus	109
Sunflower	Helianthus annuus	207
Sunroot	Helianthus tuberosus	109
Sverbiga	Bunias orientalis	76
Sweet Leaf	Stevia rebaudiana	248
Sweet Potato	Ipomoea batatus	137
Tampala	Amaranthus tricolor	26
Texsel Greens	Brassica carinata	22
Thell	Petroselinum crispum var. tuberosum	106
Tiger Nut	Cyperus esculentus	102
Tomarillo	Cyphomandra crassicaulis	187
Tomatillo	Physalis ixocarpa	185
Tree Onion	Allium cepa var. proliferum	104
Tree Tomato	Cyphomandra crassicaulis	187
Tuberous Nasturtium	Tropaeolum tuberosum	118
Turkish Rocket	Bunias orientalis	76
Turnip-Rooted Chervil	Chaerophyllum bulbosum	91
Turnip-Rooted Parsley	Petroselinum crispum var. tuberosum	106
Upland Cress	Barbarea verna	46
Vegetable Oyster	Tragapogon porrifolius	129
Viper Gourd	Trichosanthes cucumerina var. anguina	181
Walking Onion	Allium cepa var. proliferum	104
Walking Stick Cabbage	Brassica oleracea var. acephala	78
Wapato	Sagittaria latifolia	142
Warrigal Greens	Tetragonia tetragonioides	57
Wasabi	Wasabia japonica	251
Water Caltrop	Trapa bicornis	148
Water Chestnut	Eleocharis dulcis	146
Water Chestnut	Trapa bicornis	148
Water Convolvulus	Ipomoea aquatica	44
Watercress	Nasturtium officinale	80
Wax Gourd	Benincasa hispida	189
White Gourd	Benincasa hispida	189
Wild Spinach	Chenopodium bonus-henricus	39
Wild Tomatillo	Physalis philadelphica	186
Winged Pea	Tetragonolobus purpureus	193
Winter Purslane	Montia (Claytonia) perfoliata	53
Wonderberry	Solanum x burbankii	164
Yacon	Polymnia [Smallanthus] sonchifolia	150
Yam Bean	Pachyrhizus erosus	113
Yard Long Bean	Vigna unguicularis subsp. sesquipedalis	210
Zoalle	Amaranthus spp.	214
Zwolsche Krul	Apium graveolens var. secalinum	48

Latin Names

Also available from eco-logic books

Composting with Worms
by George Pilkington

George Pilkington has been working with worms and preaching their benefits for over 20 years. During that time he has set up a company, Nurturing Nature that has won the coveted Green Apple 'Gold' Award for Best Environmental Practice. He advises councils and other organisations and gives lectures around the country on worm composting. This book is the collection of his many years' experience as an unashamed, worm composting fanatic.

In this book you will find out:
- How worms turn waste into compost • Which worms to use • Which worm bin is most suitable for your needs • The best uses for your worm compost • What to do when good bins turn bad – frequently asked questions

All this, together a worm menu, will set you on your way to converting your waste, easily and efficiently to valuable, soil-enhancing compost.　　ISBN 9781899233137
Britain's bestselling worm composting manual with over 12,000 copies in print.

Back Garden Seed Saving
by Sue Stickland

First published in 2001 and updated in 2008 this is the classic seed saving manual giving easy to follow crop-by-crop guidelines to help you save seed for yourself The latest strains of runner beans may give long stringless pods, but will they crop well on a cold windswept site? Dwarf peas may be the easiest to grow commercially, but you will still find the six-foot types in many gardens - they look attractive, crop for longer and taste 'like peas used to taste'. As such varieties have disappeared from the seed catalogues over the past few decades, dedicated gardeners have kept them in cultivation. In this popular book you will also find out about some of the vegetable varieties no longer found in the seed catalogues, and others that are there now but may not be for much longer. It introduces you to some of the gardeners who grow such varieties, their tales and tips, and their infectious enthusiasm.　　ISBN 9781899233151

"Superb practical book ….. and one that will pay for itself in no time at all" Allotment and Leisure Gardener

Valuable Vegetables
by Mandy Pullen

When the author Mandy Pullen turned that a one and a half acre field into a successful, small scale market garden. She found she could grow not only enough produce to feed herself and her family, but have enough left over to run a thriving vegetable box scheme. This unique book is based on her own practical experience.

In this book you can find out how to:
•   Set up your garden and make it productive • Assemble all the tools, equipment and machinery you will need • Use both simple and complex rotations to keep your soil healthy and productive • Maintain the fertility of your plot without expensive fertilisers
• Save money by saving your own seed and propagating your own plants • Organise what and when to sow and plan for a succession of useful crops • Erect and maintain a polytunnel • Prolong your growing season with protected cropping • Deal with weeds, pests and diseases without using chemicals
• Store your vegetables • Set up and run a successful, small business selling vegetables

All this, together with complete cultivation details for:
• 48 vegetables • 21 herbs • All the major soft fruits   ISBN 9781899233120

"I would certainly recommend it for both beginners and small scale producers looking for sound practical advice"
Organic Way

Asian Vegetables – A Guide to Growing Fruit, Vegetables and Spices from the Indian Subcontinent
by Sally Cunningham

The author Sally Cunningham, has been a professional organic gardener for nearly 30 years. Since moving to Leicester she has been intrigued by the exciting mixture of food cultures of that city. And, what started out as a fascination with the huge variety of fresh produce on sale in the Asian shops and market stalls, has turned into a life's work, researching, cooking and growing these vegetables and fruits. Asian Vegetables brings together a wealth of information on over 40 varieties of fruit, vegetables and spices that can be grown in this country. Each plant comes together with details of what to look for when buying, the different varieties available, their nutritional value, comprehensive cultivation instructions, useful colour photographs and much more. With this unique guide both the experienced gardener and those new to growing will bring variety and a fresh, new dimension to the food on their plates and the plants in their garden.   ISBN 9781899233168

"A unique fascinating book that broadens the kitchen gardener's horizon and genuinely says something new"
Kitchen Garden Magazine

eco-logic books • Mulberry House • 19 Maple Grove • Bath • BA2 3AF • T: 01225 484472
For a complete list or to order visit www.eco-logicbooks.com

Cover Key

Acchoca - Ladies Slipper

Chinese Yam

Jerusalem Artichoke

Strawberry Spinach

Yacon

Oca

Growing Unusual Vegetables

Simon Hickmott

Growing
Unusual
Vegetables

Naranjilla

Snake Gourd

Oca

Burdock, Gobo

Weird and Wonderful Vegetables and How To Grow Them

Simon Hickmott